W. A. McClendon, 1895

RECOLLECTIONS OF WAR TIMES

BY

An Old Veteran

WHILE UNDER
STONEWALL JACKSON
AND
LIEUTENANT GENERAL JAMES LONGSTREET

How I Got In, and How I Got Out

Montgomery, Ala.:
THE PARAGON PRESS
1909

Dedicated to all true Southern men and women
and their posterity

Preface

In my declining years I send forth this book as a narrative of some of the events and incidents of my past life while in the Southern Army. It embraces only a partial history of my life in camp, commencing with July 1861, and ending April 9th, 1865, while serving under "Stonewall" Jackson until December 1862, and under Longstreet until April 9th 1865. It is written almost entirely from memory, and therefore I do not claim to be absolutely correct, as forty years have passed since these things occurred, and 'tis said that memory is treacherous. I have avoided all harsh criticisms only where history upholds it. I have endeavored to avoid a repetition of profanity and slang that was so common in camp. All those who are acquainted with me know that I am uneducated, and that I make no claim to correct english. I am conscious that many mistakes have been made, and I respectfully ask the reader to cover my imperfections with the broad mantle of charity and accept this narrative only as a fireside conversation with an old Veteran.

Respectfully,

W. A. McCLENDON.

WHEN WILL THE CONFEDERATE SOLDIER BE FORGOTTEN?

"When the lion eats grass like an ox
And the gallinipper swallows the whale,
When the terrapin knits woolen socks
And the hare is outrun by the snail.
When serpents walk upright like men
And doodle bugs travel like frogs,
When grasshoppers feed on the hen
And feathers are found on the hogs,
When Thomas cats swim in the air,
And elephants roost upon trees,
When insects in summer are rare
And snuff never makes people sneeze.
When fish creep over dry land
And mules on bycicles ride,
When foxes lay eggs in the sand
And women in dress take no pride.
When Dutchmen no longer drink beer
And girls get to preaching on time,
When billy goats butt from the rear,
And treason is no longer a crime,
When the humming bird brays like a donkey
And limburger smells like cologne,
When plowshares are made out of monkeys
And the hearts of Alabamians are stone."

—By Mr. James Barson in Age Herald, June 9th, 1908.

CHAPTER I

THOUGHTS ON OLD TIMES BY AN OLD VETERAN.

DEAR FRIEND:

An old man like I am sitting alone around a fire on a cold day with no sweet little boys and girls to be romping around musing over the events of the present, and what may be in the future, will naturally let his mind run back to events of the past. I said an old man, that is what the boys sometimes calls their father. "The Old Man," but I am not as old as some would suppose, nor wont be the next time you hear from me. So far I have had what some people call many "ups and downs" and if I am to be the judge the "downs" have predominated, but being possessed naturally with a lively disposition and it being sorter in keeping with my faith, I am inclined to accept everything that happens as an act of providence and complain as little as possible. Well, while musing over the past my mind ran back to Christmas time of 1860. When I go to town, I see very few of the old boys that were young then, that remembers the events of that time, and it is a great pleasure to sit with them and talk of the stirring events of those days when A. B. Moore was Governor of Alabama, when John Bright drove the stage from Eufaula in Barbour county down by Abbeville carrying the passengers and mail to and from Columbia in Henry county, and when the Whigs, and Democrats, buried the "hatchet" as a token of bridging the chasm that had so long existed between them politically and as a unit espousing the cause of the South that was then threatened with an abolition administration. In those days of which I speak the post office at Abbeville would be crowded at each arrival of the mail from Eufaula, Sundays not excepted, as that was the mail that brought the news from the seat of government. I was a youth then, in my teens, but all my relatives were strong Southern people and politically were democrats, and ardent secessionists. I had a peculiar fondness for reading Southern newspapers, and whenever I saw anything that C. C. Clay, W. L. Yancey and J. L. Pugh of Alabama had to say, it would catch my eye. There were democratic leaders from other Southern States that were fiery in their oratory, I will mention a few. Bob Toombs of Georgia, M. L. Bonham of S. C., R. M. T. Hunter of Va., W. T. Wigfall of Texas, and the greatest of all was Jefferson Davis of Miss. All those that I have mentioned with many others were prominent leaders of the democratic party of those days and espoused the cause of the South and as a last resort became ardent secessionists. The oratory of these men in the halls of Congress and on the rostrum fired our Southern heart, and when the call to arms was sounded we donned the grey, and under the "Stars and Bars" with a step to the martial music of Dixie and the "Bonnie Blue Flag" we went to the front to resent an insult offered to the South by her enemies. The people know the result. I am truly loyal now to the "Stars and Stripes." I glory in the United States, and am proud that I am an American. I still cherish a love for the "Stars and Bars," and as they were the colors of my first love, I guess that's the reason, for that love was so great that a spat of four years with the Yankees failed to suppress it. There are a few old timers living that remembers the stirring events of those days spoken of and the great leaders of the South that I have mentioned. The young of the present day only know of them from history and out of the few that I have mentioned not one are living. That grand old man, J. L. Pugh, was the last to cross over. Well, we have now what is called a new South. I claim to belong to the old South, and others of my age had as well claim the same. The new South is clamorous for room, and says: stand back, old South, you have had your day, now it's our time and it may be right, as time changes the people change, or as people change time changes, I don't know which.

CHAPTER II

A REMINISCENCE OF OLD TIMES.

DEAR FRIEND:

In the first chapter I said something about the Whigs and Democrats burying the hatchet. Some one might ask the question, did they bury a genuine hatchet, or was it an assumed name for the thing which bridged the political chasm that then existed between the two parties. Yes, it was a genuine hatchet, and as well as I remember it was bought out of the store of A. C. Gordon & Co., was brought out by Capt. J. W. Stokes, now dead, and after an address by John B. Taylor, suitable for the occasion, Capt. Stokes deposited the hatchet in a hole dug somewhere near the south veranda of the present court house, in the town of Abbeville, Ala. The hole was dug for the purpose of raising a liberty pole and the hatchet was deposited in the bottom under the large end of the pole. I was a small boy then, but I felt as great interest in the "Liberty Pole" as A. C. Gordon, D. W. Roach, J. T. McClendon, W. J. Singletary, or H. E. Owens did, but I had a great deal less to say, but I, with a great many other little boys of the town and country, thought it a big thing to be allowed to pull the ropes when the word was given to raise. These were exciting times in the politics of the country. South Carolina had already passed the memorable ordinance of Secession and the people began to hold mass meetings, and invariably would pass resolutions resolving to stand by South Carolina. The mayors of towns, and municipalities of towns, and cities would hold meetings, make speeches, endorse resolutions, until patriotism would run so high until it would cause "hot times in the old town at night." The little Southern boys and girls became to be Secessionists, and all prided themselves in wearing a badge of "Red, White and Blue." So much so, that red, white and blue ribbon was at a premium. South Carolina withdrew from the Union Dec. 20th, 1860. We boys in camp used to sing:

"We honor, yes, honor bold South Carolina,
Who cast her brave bark alone on the deep," etc.

Florida followed on the 7th of January, 1861; Mississippi on the 9th; Alabama on the 11th; Georgia on the 20th; Louisiana on the 26th, and Texas on the 1st February. Thus in three months after the announcement of Mr. Lincoln's election nearly all the Cotton States had Seceeded from the Union. These are matters of history and I only mention them as events of what was going on here forty-six years ago. Well, what did all this bring about? Boys to the front. At this time of which I speak, there were two first class military companies in this (Henry) County. The "Henry Grays" and "Henry Blues." A. C. Gordon, of Abbeville, was Captain of the Grays, and T. T. Smith, of Columbia, was Captain of the Blues. So soon as Alabama withdrew from the Union, and linked her fortunes with the other Southern States, Captain Gordon and Captain Smith, both typical Southern gentlemen, tendered the services of themselves and their companies to the Governor of Alabama, to defend with their lives the cause of the State, and the South. Their services were accepted and each captain ordered to hold himself ready to move at a moment's notice. These were days full of expectancy for those companies, looking every day for orders to move, and at last the suspense was broken, and orders came for the Grays to move, and on the 11th of May, 1861, many left the old town of Abbeville never to return. I had several school-mates, friends and acquaintances in this company, one particular friend that I never saw again, Warren Owens. I volunteered under Captain Gordon to go too, but I being so young my father objected and I was left to wait until I grew older.

CHAPTER III

A REMINISCENCE OF OLD TIMES.

Dear Friend:

No one knew but myself the anguish I bore, the sadness and loneliness that I felt when I was told that I could not go, that I would have to wait until I grew older. Some of my most intimate friends and associates had gone off with the Grays, and there was no enjoyment here for me. To dispel the gloom I would seek the company of what I thought to be my best girl. On one occasion I was in conversation with her talking about the boys that had gone when she looked at me with a smile, and with a cunning expression of countenance, remarked that her sweetheart was off with the Grays. Oh, my! That was a stunner to this boy for I had fancied myself to be her favorite but I found it was all a delusion and I resolved to go to the war the first chance thinking it might be the means of changing her mind and her affections would be concentrated upon me. In the latter spring, and early summer months the North and South were actively engaged, raising, organizing and concentrating large armies at the most assailable points which was only a precursor of what happened in the future. Fort Sumpter and nearly all the arsenals on the Southern coast that was occupied with United States soldiers had been seized by the Confederates without the loss of life. The first clash of small arms between the Federals and Confederates occurred on the 10th of June, 1861, in the low grounds of Virginia near Fortress Monroe. In this engagement the Confederates were victorious, and in history it is styled the "Battle of Bethel." Hearing of so many victories for the South, and only a few getting killed, I began to think that the war would soon end and that I wouldn't get to smell gunpowder much less burn any. But all this time, and while these little scraps were taking place I was watching for a chance to get off. At last a meeting was called in Abbeville by some one to organize a company. I went. There was a large crowd in town that day, mostly old men and young boys. The old men would be in squads, juggling and caucusing about something, and I was watching closely, trying to catch on as to what was up, but at last some one over at the court house began to yell at the top of his voice, "Fall in! Fall in! form line here!" I fell into line with them. We formed in single rank reaching from the old court house across the square. All being in line I began to look for the captain. He was the man I wanted to see, but I failed to locate him. Mr. Henry Maybin and D. W. Roach seemed to be the leading spirits on that occasion, but I couldn't tell who was the Seignior in command. (Both of these old gentlemen have crossed over and gone, they were truly loyal to the South and made great sacrifices for the "Lost Cause.") After "right facing" and "left facing" and trying to obey every other command that was given on the street, we were marched up into the old court house, when some one (I don't remember who) occupied the judge's stand as chairman, and in a rambling way explained the object of the meeting, saying the object was to elect officers, agree upon the color and material for a uniform, and also to name the company. As well as I remember some one moved to make Mr. Henry Maybin Captain, and a vote was taken and Mr. Maybin was unanimously elected, and by the same process D. W. Roach was elected First Lieutenant. I don't remember who the other officers were, but one thing I do remember, that is, I was not even mentioned for the Fourth Corporal's place, which I thought I was entitled to on account of my military spirit. In voting upon the color, and material for the uniforms, they said it should be of a brown color made with cotton aids, the hats to be black, low crown with broad brims, and should be wool. The company should be called the "Home Guards" and should be for home protection. Dear Friends, that let me out. I wanted a suit of English Grey, trimmed in black with brass buttons and a grey cap, and brown leggins. That was my ideal for a uniform. That was the last meeting of that organization that I attended, don't know whether they ever had another me; they intended to stay at home, and that didn't suit. me; they intended to sta yat home, and that didn't suit. So in a short time after that W. C. Oates, then a lawyer of Abbeville, began raising a company to go to the war. That just suited me, and as I was nearly 17 years my parents reluctantly consented for me to go. So I volunteered in his company, a step I never regretted, and I will tell you in the next chapter how, when, and where I got off.

CHAPTER IV

RECOLLECTIONS OF THE PAST.

DEAR FRIEND:
I will have to defer telling you where I went until some future time. I can only tell you of how and when I got off, and of my first stop. I told you in the preceding chapter that I abandoned the "Home Guards," that was organized for Home Protection, and volunteered under W. C. Oates. This was in the early days of July. Oates had been commissioned Captain and had tendered his services to the Governor, and was busy organizing his company for active service. All over the South the young men were volunteering to go to the war, and it was not a question as to who would go, but who would stay at home to take care of the home folks. As to who would stay at home, was a question for some one else to decide. I was fully determined to go. The more I read the papers, and the more I could hear, only increased my desire to get off. While the South was making these preparations the North was not idle in doing the same thing. She was organizing a powerful army in

and around Washington, preparatory to the invasion of Virginia, and the South was concentrating at or near Manassas, Va., about 25 miles from Washington, ready to meet the invaders whenever they came out from behind their breastworks. At last the Federal army advanced and the Confederates met them on the plains of Manassas on the 21st of July, 1861, and after a hard day's battle, the Confederates completely routed the Federal army. The names of the chief commanders with their subordinates of both sides, the names of the troops engaged, are matters of history, and I only refer to them as an event of this particular time. The complete rout of the Federal army at that time had a tendency to check my ardor, as I was ready to agree with some of our leading statesmen, that with that victory for the South, peace would be declared in thirty days, the war would end, and I would not get to see a "wild Yank." But I believed Oates knew better, for he did not lose his energy in organizing his company. As well as I remember, about the 24th of July, the ladies of Abbeville presented us with a flag. We were drawn up in line in front of the old Academy when M. A. Bell, a lawyer of Abbeville, made the presentation speech for the ladies, when Capt. W. C. Oates in his eloquent and patriotic style accepted it for his company, accepting the flag with promises by himself and company which he and company faithfully kept. Who those ladies were I don't remember. I only remember one, Mrs. Harper, a noble Southern lady of the highest type. She is now deceased. The company was named and is known in history as the "Henry Pioneers," and at this time it was full up to the maximum and running over. It was composed mostly of farmers' boys, a hael, hearty set of young fellows, and in a skirmish with the "Yanks" they found us tough stuff, and hard to drive. On the 25th as well as I remember Captain Oates informed us that he had received orders to march, and that he would leave for Franklin on the 27th. This was glorious news, for I was growing impatient. He gave every man the chance to back out that wanted to, only one stepped out. Capt. Oates had to reject one on account of his age being too young. This youth was a long, lean, lanky fellow; fair skin, blue eyes, light hair, and would have weighed about 115 pounds. When this youth was informed by Capt. Oates that he could not take him tears were seen trickling down his cheeks. He turned his back upon us and went his way weeping. This was no other than our big-hearted, whole-souled "Bob" Reynolds. He went off afterwards and joined the 37th Alabama, and at Atlanta he received a painful wound, but he survived, and is living among us today a fine specimen of humanity, weighing about 250 pounds. Considerable difference of "then and now." On Saturday morning of July 27, 1861, I rose early and began making preparations for my departure. After breakfast everything being ready, I bid my mother and sisters farewell, and hastened to Abbeville with my father. There the citizens had furnished wagons and buggies to carry us, and our camp equipage to Franklin. Kind friends, did you ever have to say good-bye? It was a hard word for me to say. About 10 o'clock I bade my aged father good-bye. I never saw him again. His last words are still remembered, "My son, take care of yourself," and turning to Capt. Oates, said: "Capt. Oates, take care of my boy."

Oates fulfilled his promise, as near as the arduous service would admit. We went on down to Franklin and there pitched our tents, went into camp and there waited for the steamer Jackson, which was to carry us up the river. Several things occurred this evening at Franklin, which I will tell of in the next chapter.

CHAPTER V

RECOLLECTIONS OF THE PAST.

DEAR FRIEND:

Franklin is in Henry County, a small village on the western bank of the Chattahoochee river, and on my way to the war this was my first camp. I will say that just before we arrived, Capt. Oates formed us in line, and marched us to a house where there was a long table spread with everything that would satisfy the hunger of man. This dinner was prepared by our First Lieutenant, C. V. Morris, and other citizens of the community, who were watching and waiting for our approach. A large crowd of people had already assembled, and more were continually arriving, mostly relatives and friends of the boys that were from off the river, coming for the purpose of bidding us farewell. About 5 p. m. Capt. Oates formed us in line, and give the command, "To the rear open order, march!" when the rear rank marched two paces backward. This being done, he commanded, "Front rank about face." Then the people began to pass through, shaking hands with every one, with moistened eyes, and briney cheeks, speaking words of cheer, bidding us God-speed, and good-bye. This was an affecting scene. Aged fathers and mothers, brothers and sisters, and some of the boys' sweethearts were there to say good-bye. (My sweetheart was not there. I had already told her good-bye, and had, to some extent, recovered from the effects.) The parting between the Misses Codys and their brother Barnett, was very sad to me. I could not suppress the tear, seeing the manifestations of love of those beautiful girls toward their brother. It is not my intention to write a biographical sketch of the life of any one, but I will assume the liberty to say that I afterward learned the cause why those girls were so devoted to their brother. On account of his genial, loveable and generous disposition, they could not help but love him, and for those traits of his character he became the idol of the company, and those of us that were living at the time he was killed at Gettysburg, realized that in the death of Barnett, H. Cody we had lost a friend, and the company one of its most useful members. He was in his teens, and had passed through all the grades of the non-commissioned officers, and had been commissioned Second Lieutenant when he was killed. I could say more of this noble hearted boy, but will only say that his old comrades that now live to think of him will meet him at the general "Roll Call" to answer "here."

But to return. After all this scene at parting we broke ranks, pitched our tents, and with great anxiety waited for the steamer "Jackson." This delay did not suit some of us for we were afraid the war would end before we could get there, and we wanted to be "going." Night came on, and while some of the boys were circulating around camp, one got too near the bluff, and over he went, but not into the water. The alarm was given and others rushed up to see, and over went another. This created more excitement and caused another rush, but they became more cautious, and "looked before they leaped." The boys got out all O. K., without getting into the water, or being hurt. 'Twas here at this place that I saw all of our commissioned officers at one time. Wm. C. Oates, Captain; I. T. Culver, First Lieutenant; C. V. Morris, Second Lieutenant, and H. C. Brainard, Third Lieutenant. Two of those are still living, Oates and Morris. The company numbered 121 men beside the commissioned officers, full up. As for our uniforms they were all O. K., being a red flannel shirt with grey pants, and was called out fatigue suit, which I found very much fatiguing at that time of the year. Think of it now, being clothed with thick woolen clothes on a dry, hot, sultry day in July. These things happened 45 years ago, and the thoughts of it today almost produces perspiration, but before I get through with my narrative, I will tell of some hot times, sure enough. We were furnished a nice suit of grey for a dress suit later on. We had all we needed then except guns and ammunition, and something pointed out to us to shoot at. The whistle of the Jackson was heard down the river at about 10 o'clock. Oates hollowed out, "Take down your tents, boys, and be ready," which we did in a hurry. The boat landed and we hurried to get everything on board. When we got everything on board, Capt. Oates formed us in line, and we marched on board ourselves. Even at this time of the night the wharf was lined with spectators to see us off. All being on board, Capt. Oates had a few words with Capt. Fry, (the Captain of the boat) when all at once, boom went the little cannon that lay at the bow of the boat, the bells began to jingle, steam was put on, the wheels began to splash the water, when our noble little band composed of J. E. Harrell, A. A. Kirkland (Old Betsy) and Stewart Merritt, having for their musical instruments a fife, bass and kettle drums, struck up the tune of "Dixie," when the "Rebel Yell" was given in full. Oates' company needed no practice or instructions as to how to give the "Rebel Yell," a yell that became famous, and which so often caused terror and dismay in the ranks of the Yankees, and on several occasions that which we failed to do with our guns, we would accomplish with the rebel yell. I can give it yet, and when I am at our reunions and hear and see things that invites it, I just simply turn loose in old rebel style.

Our trip up the river was a pleasant one and was without an accident or incident worthy of note. We halted a little while at Eufaula Sunday morning. There saw some of Hart's company, the E. C. G.'s who informed us that they were going to follow us on the next steamer up. We landed that evening at 5 p. m. opposite old Ft. Mitchell on the M. &

G. R. R. in Russell County, 10 miles southwest from Columbus, Ga. We were about one and one-half miles from the camp, and we were met at the landing by the "Brundidge Guards" Capt. Lewis commanding, as an escort to camp. We formed in four ranks (Hardee's Tactics), preceded by our escort, we started for camp. Our little flag of "Red, White and Blue" that we had received from the ladies of Abbeville was placed in the hands of M. G. Maybin, our ensign, and as the Southern breeze unfurled its folds, the boys looked upon it with pride and as a reminder of those they had left behind. Our line of march lay through a large plantation owned by James Cantey, who was Colonel of the 15th Alabama Regiment, to which our company was attached. Several companies of this Regiment had already arrived and were in camp. They were from Bullock, Pike, Lee, Barbour, Dale and Russell counties and on our way to camp, many of them had stationed themselves on the wayside to look at us. A great many funny remarks were made by them, such as, there comes the red shirted boys from the piney woods. There comes Oates' tigers, there comes Oates' Zouaves, and many other remarks too numerous to mention. We were too dignified to reply. We were in line and had assumed the positions of soldiers, and with heads erect and with elastic step, we marched on until we arrived at our camping ground, when we broke ranks, and the fun began. This was my second stop.

CHAPTER VI

RECOLLECTIONS OF THE PAST.

DEAR FRIEND:

We broke ranks and the fun began. "Ge-whillikins," I never in all my life saw so many soldiers and tents. The boys that had already gone into camp there gathered around us, and began shaking hands just as though they had known us all our lives, and giving us such a welcome we felt good to be there. We said to them what we pleased, and they replied as they pleased, and no one became offended; all like brothers for one common cause. Here a tie was set up, that "old father time" will never extirpate or destroy. The wagons that had been sent down to the landing on the river after our camp equippage. Soon arrived, and we began to pitch our tents in regular military order on the ground pointed out to us by an officer, whom I afterwards learned to be the Q. M. Night came on and we cooked supper, and after enjoying the usual camp gossip for a reasonable length of time we retired, and passed the night as happy as the "Buzzard bird that sported among the flowers," only to be awakened by the squeaking of the fife and beating of drums. This was at 4 a. m. and for the purpose of getting us up to answer roll call. "This is war at last boys," "we're into it," said some one. This was on the morning of the 29th of July, 1861, and the first time the roll of Oates' company had been called in a regular military form. I answered at its roll call that morning for the first time and answered at its last call near Appomattox court house in Virginia, April, 1865. Ft. Mitchell—this is our first camp, and the name suggests that there is a fort there, but not so. It's nothing but a large old field clear of stumps, surrounded by beautiful shade trees and a fine place for the mobilizing of small bodies of troops. Here the 15th Alabama was organized with 10 full companies, numbering in all about 1200 men. The place is located on the M. & G. R. R. in Russell County, Ala., and is spoken of in the life of Andrew Jackson, the particulars of which is lost to memory and I shall not attempt to explain. I was anxious to see the Colonel, the Lieutenant Colonel and Major, and as soon after breakfast as practical I strolled off through camp, and upon inquiry some one pointed out to me Colonel Canty, Lieutenant Colonel Trentlin, Major Daniels, and several other officers of the Regiment. From my dress they knew that I was one of the new arrivals, "One of Oates' Tigers," and they had a great deal less to say to me than I wanted to say to them. They were disciplined, I was not, and I imagined that they looked upon me as an underling. I thought myself to be as good a soldier as they were, and I looked upon them at that time as being a bigoted set of fools, but I didn't tell them so. I afterward learned that an officer had to be a little austere to keep the privates from pulling off their shoulder straps, in order that good order and military discipline might be maintained, and as a private, at certain times I would be placed in position, where I could exercise authority and it was my delight to enforce orders which were as rigid on a commissioned officer as it was a private. I obeyed orders, and they didn't hurt me. We drilled every day, about in squads, and sometimes the whole company would turn out, then confusion would commence. We would become so tangled up at times that we were the laughing stock for some of the older ones, but we kept on trying and later on the "Red Shirted boys from Henry" became noted for accuracy in company drill, and the manuel of arms. We had dress parade every evening. We soon learned what reveille, and "tattoo" meant. Tattoo was a great deal easier to obey, than reveille. We would sit around our camp fires at night, tell old tales, sing old songs, box, wrestle, run, and jump, turn summersaults, pat and dance, and do everything imaginable for fun and frolic. We had crack singers in our company, crack story tellers, crack jumpers, crack wrestlers, crack runners, crack dancers and crack athletes. I was a crack at none of these things, but prided myself on being the crack shot, and was anxious for a chance. Occasionally we would hear some good news, when all the camp would give the "Rebel Yell." These were events of the first days of August, but we did not remain here many days, before orders came to go somewhere, and sure enough we went. Where? I will tell in the next chapter.

CHAPTER VII

"ON TO RICHMOND."

DEAR FRIEND:
Before leaving our camp at Ft. Mitchell several things occured that I would like to tell. The most notable of these was our taking the oath of allegiance to the Confederate States, and being mustered into service for 3 years or during the war. Of course they gave us an oppertunity to back out if we wanted to, but it was no time for backing then, we were regular in and spoiling for a fight. The captain of each company drew for letters which indicated their position that each was to occupy in the line, Capt. Oates drew the letter "G" and our potition was between K and B, on the left wing of the regiment, a position we occupied all during the war. Our tents were branded with H. P. (Henry Pioneers) to distinguish us from the others. Tom Cargile from Eufaula named each company by its letters. We bore

the Sobriquet under his naming of "Hell Pelters." I know the name of some others but will not repeat here. We were divided off into messes, and each tent marked, my tent being No. 7. There was ten of us in mess No. 7, and only one beside myself is living to-day, and he received a wound at the battle of Chickamauga that made him a permanent cripple for life. Here we drew our arms, bright smooth bore muskets, and bayonets of the latest improvement. We also drew cartridge boxes and cap pouches, but did not get any ammunition. That was a feature of the drawing we did not like. I wanted to try my gun at a spot, and if I had, I would have run the risk of being court marshaled, for it was always against orders to shoot off in camp. We were as proud of our guns as the little boy is now-a-days of a toy pistol, or a little girl is of a doll. We drew knapsacks also, some of the boys would put them on and go dashing through camp as if they were stampeded, the straps flaping on either side seemed to increase their fright, together with speed until they run down, during the melee, some would hollow "Whoa! whoa!" catch him, head him, and not let him tear up his harness! They called it Jeff Davis harness, and it being the first time that they had been rigged up that way they feigned themselves to be a young horse being harnessed up for the first time, we had lots of fun then. Poor boys, they were having their fun then, not realizing what they would have to meet later on, only a few of them are living to-day. While we remained at this camp, we were drilling, and doing camp guard duty, and being instructed in everything that would qualify us for active operations in the field. All this time rations were plentiful, and were all that heart could wish. While all these things were going on we were constantly expecting orders to move, suddenly one day about the 20th of August the officers call was sounded at headquarters, when each company commander attended to receive orders from the Colonel commanding. Capt. Oates attended, and when he returned he niformed us that he had orders to cook 3 days rations, and be ready to move at a moments notice.

Glorious news, and the next thing we wanted to know was, when and where, but every one was at sea on that question, but it was up to us to get ready, and we obeyed. The next day however, the officers call was sounded again, our Capt. attended and when he returned he ordered us to strike tents, pack our cooking utensils as quick as we could, as he had orders to go to Richmond, Va. "Thank God, Hallelujah," was shouted, "On to Richmond."

We are going to the war at last. Our company and company "F," (Brundidge Guards) were marched out to the depot which was near by, and boarded the cars for Columbus, Ga. On crossing the Chattahoochee river we said "farewell to Alabama, we are going in your defense." We changed cars in Columbus for Macon, running all night we landed in Augusta, Ga., the next morning. There the ladies had prepaired a long table, and supplied it with every kind of eatables that heart could wish, and we lined up on each side and helped ourselves.

There we changed for Wilmington, N. C., passing through South Carolina we reached Wilmington at night and after crossing the Cape Fear river on a boat we boarded the cars for Petersburg, Va., there we changed for Richmond. The reception and ovations that W. J. Bryan is now receiving in Europe is nothing to compare with the receptoins and ovations given us at the principle cities along our route to Richmond, in August 1861. To say the least of them, the circumstances at that time under which these receptions were given us cut quite a figure in, "then and now." Our company, Captain Oates commanding, and the company from Pike county preceded the ballance of the regiment to the camp at Richmond. The old white faced wonder Seth Thomas clock that has been counting of our time for 80 years has just struck 10 and I will have to close this chapter.

CHAPTER VIII

AN OLD VETERAN IN CAMP AT RICHMOND.

Dear Friend:

In the last chapter I told you of some things that happened on our way to Richmond but I did not tell all and I propose starting again at Ft. Mitchell, and to begin I will say that I never saw but one steamboat, had never rode on a car but once, and had never seen a town larger than Eufaula was at that time and taking everything into consideration I had never been a "hens scratch," from home (if you know how far that was,) up to that time, but my frolicing disposition and eagerness to get off to the war made me want to ride, and see the sights. While waiting for the cars to get ready at Columbus, some of us bought some watermelons, and we indulged in that luxury to our hearts content. The cars being ready "all aboard," was announced by the conductor, when Captain Oates and the Lieutenants busied themselves to see that all was on, and comfortably seated I occupied a seat with Daniel McLellan, he was a man of mature years, was of Scotch descent, and had a family, was also my neighbor and friend. I sat next to the window and he the aisle. The whistle blew and off for Augusta we went. The cars didn't run past there then as they do now, we run all night and had to change cars when we arrived .

The longest stop was made at Macon, Ga., where we got out and strolled around until train time for Augusta. The place was all lit up by some kind of lights, so everything was bright as day, I remember reading a sign that night on one of the large houses not far from the depot, it read as follows: "The Brown House," a large hotel that now stands near the depot. Two years after that I received a furlough of indulgence and on my return to the Army it was my fortune to spend one night at this hotel where I met my old comrade and friend C. S. Kincey, who was on detail in the Medical department. He too has passed over. But I am digressing, on our way from Macon to Augusta, in the night I was seated as before by my friend McLellan. Late in the night I began to turn sick, my lips began to trimble, my mouth began to run salty water. Oh sick, I became all at once. Oh Daniel, hold my head, I leaned over his lap toward the aisle. Dont throw — on me said Daniel, and I didn't, but what I did on the floor of the car was enough. I had a brother-in-law and two own cousins on that train, and after my older cousin coming to me and giving me a drink of water remarked that he thought I would be more particular next time how I ate watermelons, and I thought so too. This was only a little sea sickness on cars.

Notwithstanding the sickness I was ready for that fine breakfast at Augusta spoken of in the preceeding chapter for I was just right to enjoy such, and I did my duty. But while all these things was going on I could not help thinking of home, papa, mama, sister, and my girl that I was leaving. Sometimes I would get what we call the "blues" and drop into a state of melancholly and almost be ready to sink in despair, but cheer up old boy, you are not near dead yet, there are many things to hear and see yet. I was all O. K. after breakfast.

Boarding the cars, crossing Savannah river, we spead our way through South Carolina into North Carolina, crossing the Cape Fear river on a boat at night, thence to Weldon where we arrived between 2 and 3 o'clock a. m., to remain one hour. While there we were allowed to go out and walk around. Soon the train was ready and we started then without change to Petersburg, Va., where we had to wait sometime before we could continue our journey to Richmond. While waiting I had the pleasure of bathing my face and hands in Pocahontas Spring which was near the depot, and also near the Appomattox river, and while on my way to Richmond to the U. C. V. Reunion in 1896, while stopped I sat in the car and looked out through the window at the same spring and my mind wandered back when I thought of the boys that were there with me 34 years ago, which produced a sadness that I could not then nor can I now explain. The boys and girls of our country know who Pocahontas was, know what she did, how she lived, and how and when she died, so I will not stop to explain. While waiting on the cars to proceed to Richmond, only 22 miles, men, women, boys and girls, all having a cheerful look, cheering us on, and proud to see such a fine looking body of young Alabamians coming to their soil to fight the invaders of their homes. We bid them farewell, and sped our way to Richmond. On arriving and just after crossing the James river we disembarked from the cars and formed line, and was marched down by the river passing the Old Lybby prison and went into camp about one mile from the city, and some of the events of this camp will be told in the next chapter.

CHAPTER IX

THE OLD VETERAN IN CAMP AT RICHMOND.

Dear Friend:

Our camp at this place was on a narrow strip of land about one hundred yards wide situated between the York River R. R. on the south, and a high bluff on the north with a gradual slope from the base of the bluff to the R. R. On our way down to camp we passed the noted Lybby prison, used at that time to confine the "Boys in Blue" that fell into our hands. We called them tame yankees, but we saw others later on that was not so tame.

They peeped at us through the grates in silence as we passed on without uttering a word of decision, though at that time we had no sympathy for them in their unfortunate condition. We were hard hearted then, but we learned later on to be more sympathetic, and render aid in meritorious cases which was reciprocated. Our camp equipage arrived on the same train and our company "G," and the company from Pike "F" that had preceded the regiment, proceeded at once to pitch our tents in regular Military style, and there waited the arrival of the other companies which arrived in due time, pitching their tents on the same plot of ground making it Camp 15th Ala. Our commisary department at this time was complete in every detail, furnishing everything we wanted to eat except, "corn bread and greens." This railroad that bordered our camp on one side was called the Richmond and Yorktown R. R., and was being used then in transporting soldiers to and from, and the frequency of them came to be so noticeable and being a great curiosity, that when we heard one coming either way we would rush down the slope and get as near as possible, in order to see the soldiers. One of our company, a fair, fat, tender, chuffy, good natured boy seemed to take more interest than the others in running to see the cars, and on one occasion he fell striking his knee against a rock, cutting a gash which was the means of stopping his runs a few days, and I doubt not but what that fellow carries a scar, a trophy, the effects of that fall to this day. His anxiety to see every passing train became so great, that he became to be a cunspicuous boy, so much so, that when the whistle of an approaching train was heard the boys would begin to call, Parish, Parish, Parish, and they would call Parish at any time of the night. I really thought that sometimes he would become irritated, but he was naturally possessed of a genial disposition, and would accept, and pass it, as a tease from his comrades and friends, and remain in a good humor. I may have something to say of this fellow later on.

Our camp at this time was all life, even the four oldest men we had in our company seemed to have forgotten their ages, and become to be as lively as any of the boys. There were J. J. Wofford, C. S. Blaylock, Seaborn Jones and John R. Steely, familiarly known as Uncle John Steely. Blaylock and Jones died of disease during the following winter. Wofford and Steely survived the war and died only a few years ago, both reaching their four score, a visit to either of one of those old veterans during their last days by one of their old comrades was appreciated and greatly enjoyed. As soon as the field and staff officers arrived a camp guard was established, and sentinels posted with orders as rigid as though we were in the immediate presence of the enemy. Forty rounds of ammunition was issued to each man, and that created a suspicion that something was soon to happen and when I would be on guard from 2 to 4, a. m., I would draw on my imagination, and imagine that the yankee prisoners had broke out of Lybby prison, and would try to slip up on me as the indian would do. These imaginations had a tendency to keep me awake, and I was one that all during the war never to be caught naping on post. We would drill four hours each day, 2 hours in the a. m., company drill, and 2 hours in the p. m., Batallion drill, our drill ground was north up the hill from our camp and was on a level plateau that afterwards became to be the location of a large hospital called Chimborazo, I saw this place in 1895 and will say more about it some time in the future, but suffice it to say that there had been a great change made in the appearance of the place during the 34 years that had passed. It is sad, for one of my age, to think of those days, and to think of the many bouyant and brilliant young men whose delight it was to romp over those grounds. Where are they today? echo answers, gone, gone, and you too must soon follow, and then what, and where, I knoweth not, but have an abiding faith and hope.

CHAPTER X

THE OLD VETERAN IN CAMP AT RICHMOND.

Dear Friend:

This camp was so full of incidents that it was impossible for the most indolent soldier to take the "blues." The squeaking fifes, the beating of drums, the music of cornet bands, the marching of well dressed, well drilled, and well armed soldiers with gorgeously attired officers on their prancing chargers, dashing hither, and thither, and occasionally the boom of a cannon could be heard in the distance, all had a tendency to drive away "dull care," and almost be the cause of forgetting the loved ones at home. All of these things I greatly enjoyed, for it just suited me, but I learned later on that every sweet has its bitter, for sometimes I would be on camp guard at night from 12 m. to 2 a. m., and would be invested with the countersign, and not allowed to stop walking for two hours, pretty tough I thought but I was in. I would become so lonely that my mind would wander back a thousand miles and imagine the condition and situation of things, and the loved ones at home, I would look at the bright moon and stars on my lonely beat and wonder to myself if any one on earth was thinking of me. In order to overcome this melancholly state of mind, I would begin to repeat poetry that I had memorized, and every speech that I had ever made when I was in school that I had not forgotten, and last but not least, hum on old love songs that would come to mind, but the one that best suited the occasion was an old song that another fellow sung when he was drawing on his imagination just as I was, when he began singing,

"Backward turn backward,
O time in your flight,
Make me a child again,
Just for to-night."

He had rather been a child that night and with his mother. I was sorter that way myself but I kept that to myself. These were conditions that a fellow would naturally get into at times, especially by one so young and had never stayed more than a week away from home folks and his girl. All at once while in this state of mind these delusions would be dispelled by some sentry, calling out at the top of his voice, "Corporal of the guard, post No.—." This had to be repeated by every one on post, which tended to keep us awake, as I had already said, I never was caught napping.

During our stay here I had the misfortune to have a large abscess (bile) on my heel, caused by my shoe which disabled me for a time from duty. I was excused by the doctor, and didn't have to go on drill, a thing that I regretted for I was always fond of drilling, but I would hobble to the drill ground and look on in order to catch what I could from what I could see and hear. (To the boys that are now living that was there.) Do you remember the morning when an alarm was given and the long roll sounded at this camp? I never shall forget it, and the scenes that ensued. Dear friend, I will tell you about it. One hot sultry morning in August, about 4 a. m., the drums began to wh-r-r-r when Captain Oates, the Lieutenants and orderly Seargeant, was out in the street in full dress calling and shouting to the men to wake up, hurry, and fall into ranks, the long roll was beating, get your guns men, "hurry, hurry." Everything in camp at that time was hurly burly. Where is my hat! Where is my shoes! could be heard from every direction. Some of us privates knew what the "long roll" ment, and I with others thought a fight was on hand right then and there. We were in line as soon as any of the other companies and waited for orders from Col. Cantey.

While waiting some of the boys knees would tremble and their teeth would chatter as though they had an ague, and I guess mine did the same thing for I was no braver than some of the rest. We didn't wait long before here come the Adj't on his horse as though he was scared half to death, and seemingly in a very excited manner ordered Captain Oates to take his company up the hill in a hurry to the drill ground where the regiment would be formed, and off he dashed at break neck speed. This was Adj't Knuckolls of Columbus, Ga. This happened when the large abscess was on my heel and Capt. Oates offered to excuse me, but I wanted to see what was up, and hobbled on up the hill and took my place in the company after it had took its place in the regiment. Being formed at early dawn the Col. called "Attention Batallion," when he began drilling the regiment, one manuever after another in fast succession, until the perspiration began to flow freely from the men and officers causing a few to fag out.

My position was in the front rank and very early in the commincement of the drill some one behind stepped on my "bile," and mashed it to pieces, it hurt so bad, and I got so mad I turned and drew my gun in a striking position and uttered language that is unbecoming a gentleman. One of the Lieutenants witnessed the occurrence and ordered me to camp where I ought to have been all the time. I appoligized to the fellow for what I said, and he begged pardon for what he had done in hurting me so bad, it being purely accidental, he accepted my appologies and I did the same for him which settled it and we were as good friends as ever. It was the best thing that could have been done for my heel, for it began to cure up right away, but for the mashing it got , there was no telling how long I would have been disabled from duty. The regiment after drilling until the sun was about two hours high come into camp thirsty and tired, and had to hurry to get breakfast in time for the two hours company drill before noon. These days were very sultry and having to wear woolen uniforms made it very fatigueing when on drill, but the time come later on when they were a pleasure instead of a burden. There were other things that happened at this camp that I wish to tell, but I will defer them for the next chapter, when I will leave this place for Manassas, where there was a prospect for another battle. That's what we wanted to get into, we wanted to try our guns.

We were getting restless, and wanted to ride on the cars again.

CHAPTER XI

AN OLD VETERAN IN CAMP AT RICHMOND.

Dear Friend:

One morning in September 1861, while on camp guard with orders not to let no one pass, or approach my line nearer than six feet without complying with certain instructions, I spied what afterwards proved to be a beautiful little maiden of 16 summers, come tripping down the hill towards my line with something in her hand, she came right on towards me regardless of anything as though she intended to cross my line, and go into the camp. When she came within a certain distance, I ordered her to halt and she did so, and with a lovely smile beaming in her face said, "good morning," I replied in the same manner and asked her what could I do for her, when with a smile she came nearer, extending her hand, asked me if I would accept of this little Bible. I thanked her for her kindness and said yes and asked her name, when she said her name was written in the book, and upon examination I found written therein, "Presented by Miss Laura Brauer." She asked me my name and where I was from, and of course I told her, I told her my orders were strict and that I could not engage in a conversation with her while on guard, all the while I was looking for the officer of the guard, and no doubt she discovered my restlessness, she extended her hand and bade me farewell, returning the same route she came. I gazed after her with deep solicitude until she disapeared over the hill. It has never been my pleasure to meet with that little Southern girl since and if living, she too like myself is growing old. The little Bible I carried in my pocket through several warm engagements. It became so soiled from the effects of perspiration that I was afraid it would come to pieces, and when I came home on furlough in September 1863, I left it with my mother and sisters, one of my sisters prized it very highly and it may be in her possession yet, I could say a great deal more about this little Bible but suffice it to say that its teachings kept me from committing many sins. While in this camp the Measles broke out on one of our boys, and on account of friendship existing between his father and Captain Oates, and in fulfillment of his promise that he would take care of the boys, Capt. Oates lost no time in procuring a place at a private residence and having him conveyed thereto, detailing our 1st Corporal J. F. Melvin, then a young man of mature years and manly qualities to nurse him until he recovered. This was only one of the many kind acts of Capt. Oates to his men whenever an opportunity presented itself until he lost his arm in '64 and had to leave us.

And while on this subject, I take pleasure in giving public expressions to my sense of gratitude for kindness shown in times that tired men's souls, and will ever cherish a recollection of these things that occurred so long ago and feel that I would be no less than an ingrate were I to forget the kindness shown by my old Captain, Wm. C. Oates. In a previous chapter I gave only a passing notice of our drill ground, which the boys that are living will remember as "Chimborazo," and said I would refer to it again. Well, It is not the Chimborazo to-day, that it was when we were there drilling. After we left there it was converted into one vast hospital, and remained so until the close of the war. When I was in Richmond the 21th, 22nd and 23rd of July 1895, at the great reunion of the U. C. V., I cut loose from the immense throng of visiting veterans and alone started to see our old camp and drill grounds. I passed on down beside the James, and near where the old Lybby prison stood, the evening we passed it on our way from the depot to camp in 1861. In passing on down I came to a hill on which stood a monument towering fifty feet skyward, that was raised by the people of Virginia to perpetuate the memory of the private soldiers and sailors of the C. S. A. It was surmounted on top with the image of a private soldier standing at parade rest looking Southward. When I reached its base I ascended to the highest step of its pedestal and sat down in the shade of its shaft, when I pulled off my hat and began to wonder "where I was at." Being alone and no one to talk to, I began to think and look. From this place I had a magnificient view South and East. Looking to the South there lay James river just as it was 30 years ago from that day with her sipling waters winding their way to the sea. I imagined that I could almost see "Drewrys Bluff," a famous fort on the South bank that the yankees tried so often to capture but failed until the evacuation of Richmond. The little borough of Rocketts that lay on the north side of the river had been torn away, and factories and foundries had been erected in the place of the Dutch and Irish shops. The Tredegar Iron Works were still there. Looking to the eastward toward our old drill ground, the hospital had been moved, and the place had been built up with magnificent residences. I went partly through it, viewing the beauty and grandeur of her magnificent shade trees and her broad gravelly streets. I traveled through the northern portion on a street car, on my way down to the battle field of "Seven Pines," and was told that Old Chimborazo had become the residence part of the city. While resting at the monument that I have spoken of, and within a stone's throw of this spot there is a street, where that noble little band of about 25 of true Southern boys, a remnant of Oates' company, marched for the last time on the morning of April 2, 1865. There I was, all alone, with all these sad memories of thirty years ago fleeting through my mind. How different my surroundings then, and now. God bless all true survivors wherever they be. "In that great day, oh! what shall the answer be." I will pass from these reveries and return to the incidents of our camp. The most and last important event was that of striking tents, falling into line, and marching through the city over to the Fredericksburg depot. But before we arrived there we were halted in a broad street and were reviewed by our President, Jefferson Davis, and after passing through, he complimented Col. Cantey for our fine appearance, and said he expected to hear a good account of us later on, which he did. The review being over we marched to the depot, and the whole regiment boarded the train, and after giving the "Rebel Yell" the whistle blew, and we were off in the direction of Manassas.

It was glorious to be there then, but later on, what about it, I intend to tell before I finish.

CHAPTER XII

AN OLD VETERAN IN CAMP.
AT PAGELAND NO. 1.

DEAR FRIEND:

Our trip from Richmond to Manassas was attended with all the pleasure that the hearts of well drilled and well disciplined soldiers could desire.

Passing through many beautiful little towns and villages, the people had gathered to see the passing train, laden with soldiers going to the front. I guess it was a daily occurrence for soldiers to be passing that way on their way to Manassas where Beauregard, and Johnston, was concetrating a large army. to be ready to meet the one of the federal army then organizing in and around Washington commanded by Gen. G. B. McLellan (Little Mc). The patriotic ladies and beautiful Virginia girls would be gathered at each stopping place to welcome us, distributing their fruits and flowers and cheering us on with expressions of delight when informed that we were from Alabama, one of the far away Southern States that had come so far to assist others in driving the enemy from their soil, they were delighted. We were the first Alabama regiment to pass by this route, although there were three other Alabama regiments in camp at Manassas, that went by different routes; they were the 4th, 5th and 6th, and were engaged in the first battle of Manassas July '61. The train ran slow and we were all day making the trip. When we arrived at Manassas we were marched out about a mile into a piece of woods, and went into camp for the night. This was the first night we lay on the ground without tents. We had plenty cooked rations and did not have to cook that night. The next day our tents and camp equipage of every description arrived, and we were marched about five miles to a place called "Pageland" and there went into camp right. I don't know why it was called Pageland, unless a man by the name of Page owned the land, for it was nothing but a large old field with the Warrenton turnpike running through it, and near the battlefield of the 1st Manassas, and was a part of the battlefield of the 2nd Manassas. Talk about soldiers, here I began to see them. Comparatively speaking, I had never seen any before. You could see the tented fields in every direction, hear the command of the officers, hear the music, and could see them drilling in every direction at all times of the day, and soon we began to drill, and did our share. Our officers were becoming to be well drilled and the more they improved, the more the companies and regiment improved. The days were warm and sultry, but the nights were cool. Here the measles struck our regiment and especially our company. Here I parted with several that I never saw again. The water at this camp was not good, and the character of our diet had been changed, which had a tendency to impair the health of the men in several ways, which caused them to be moved to hospitals for better treatment. Many went, that never returned. Fortunately for me, I had had the measles and scarlet fever before the war broke out, and I was proof against those contagious diseases and I remained in good health all the time and increased in flesh. I had become hardened to camp life and only had one case of fever during the war. I had a peculiar horror for the hospital and prison and looked upon either at that time as certain death, but afterwards learned that a good hospital was the proper place for a sick soldier. We were so near the battlefield of the 21st, that we all had an anxiety to see it, so much so that some of the boys would slip the camp guard and run the "block" at the risk of being punished and go over and explore the field, and when they returned the fear of punishment did not restrain them from telling what they saw, and in order that those might see who would not run away and go anyhow, the Colonel permitted each Captain to take his company and spend a day on the battlefield. Captain Oates' time came and he marched us over and turned us loose, with orders to assemble at a certain place at a certain time. This was a picnic for us, what we term now-a-days an outing. We were like birds turned out of a cage. We wandered everywhere looking at the sights. I had for my companion on that day, Charley Raley. Since the war, by some untoward circumstance he changed his name to B. M. Stephens and was Probate Judge of Coffee County. He became to be a wonderful man in many respects, but he is gone. I saw all that he saw and he saw all that I saw. One of the most notable places of our visit was the position of the 7th Georgia regiment in the battle of the 21st. It was in a clump of small pines that was torn with bullets from the ground up as high as fifteen feet. It was a wonder to us how that a man could live in such a place, but we learned afterwards. After looking at this place as long as we wanted to, we passed on in search of other sights of the battlefield which we soon found, and I will tell of them in the next chapter.

CHAPTER XIII

AN OLD VETERAN IN CAMP.
AT PAGELAND NO. 2.

DEAR FRIEND:

Charlie and I hastened on in search of other things, and the next thing of interest was a hill upon which stood the famous "Sherman Battery" defended by the "Boys in Blue," which played such havoc on the advancing "Boys in Grey" in their effort to capture it, and notwithstanding the terrible carnage, caused by the solid shot, shell, grape and canister shot that was poured into the ranks of the advancing Southerners who were determined to do or die, and with that intrepidity and valorous daring, which characterized the "Boys in Grey," those that lived pressed steadily forward until the goal of their ambition was reached. The battery was captured. This scene presented a horrible encounter between the "Boys in Grey" and the "Boys in Blue." (Americans). The numerous carcassas of horses that belonged to the battery was evidence of the terrible slaughter of them all around this place, and in fact on other parts of the field could be seen little mounds of earth, that was answering for a covering for a brave "Boy in Blue" who had lost his life fighting for a cause he thought to be right.

These little mounds were very numerous, and occasionally one, and often two hands could be seen protruding and pointing upward toward the sky, having been exposed so long to a burning sun until the skin and flesh had dried to the bone. These were sad scenes and furnished food for reflection. At that time I was full of malice and hatred for the "Boys in Blue" and was just as anxious to kill him as he was to kill me, yet when I would stop and take the second thought, and gaze upon those little mounds I could truthfully say of the dead "Boy in Blue" that sometime, and somewhere, he had been "somebody's darling." Where it was possible, their remains have been removed and are being properly cared for by this great government of ours. In passing over the field, the line of battle of the contestants could easily be traced by the paper torn from their cartridges while loading and firing upon each other, and the blood stained grass where some one had fell dead or wounded. In our ramble we came to the place where Colonel Fisher of the 6th N. C. fell, and the place where Colonel Bartow of Georgia fell, shot through the heart. History says of him that "there, one of the bravest and most promising spirits of the South was quenched in blood." A little farther on we came to the place where General Bee of South Carolina fell mortally wounded, near what is known to-day in history as the "Henry House." From the appearance and condition of this house, it looked as though, at some stage of the action, it had been a special target for the Yankee gunners. All those places were marked by post being set in the ground with signboards tacked upon them with proper inscriptions on them giving information to the thousands that visited this battlefield, and although it had been three months since the battle, the evidences that a terrible battle had been fought were numerous. The position of the gallant old 4th Alabama was pointed out to us as being the place where Gen. J. E. Johnston seized its colors and offered to lead the attack. On that field that gallant old Alabama regiment won a name for herself that followed her until her star went down at Appomattox, and now in time of peace the memory of her gallantry is still cherished by all the true survivors of Laws' Alabama Brigade (lately Perry's). Pardon the disgression and lets return to the battlefield and see the sights. Well occasionally we could see a solid shot, grape shot, canister shot and leaden minnie balls were numerous on the ground, but the most dangerous thing I saw lying on the ground was the unexploded bomb shells. I let them alone. I didn't disturbe their quietude in the least, for they were dangerous and I let them alone. We picked up as many minnie balls and other curiosities as we wanted and carried them to camp. Others did the same thing, and at the first opportunity we sent them home as relics from the battlefield of Manassas. Our time being out we assembled at the place designated, formed line. Captain Oates marched us back to camp on time, and by the time we arrived we were a tired and wiser set of boys than we were when we started out in the morning. After reaching camp each one had something to talk and write about for the next month, but let me tell you dear friend the horrible, sad and exciting scenes of this battlefield was nothing to compare to what I experienced before the war ended.

CHAPTER XIV

AN OLD VETERAN IN CAMP.
AT PAGELAND NO. 3.

DEAR FRIEND:

After returning from the battlefield to camp, details were made from our company for camp guard and fatigue duty for the next day. The nearer we got to the enemy, the more stringent the orders around the camp. The fatigue duty consisted of policing the camp, looking after its sanitary condition, cutting and hauling wood, and going with the forage and commissary wagons to the depot at Manassas Junction, to assist in loading them with the supplies for man and beast. So many of our company became sick with first one ailment and another, until camp guard and fatigue duty became to be pretty tough on those that remained well, and notwithstanding all these duties, drilling four hours each day had to be done, consequently we did not have a great deal of time to cook, eat and write letters to home folks, and also to our girls that we had left behind. They were not forgotten, and it was a great pleasure that we enjoyed in reading a letter from them and answering. All along since 1 had left home in July I had kept my parents informed as to my health and movements. We received our mail regular and we didn't fail to answer, judging from the amount of letter writing you could see going on. Postage stamps were ten cents each and very scarce. We had not "drawed" yet, and we could resort to the "Franking" privilege, a law that Congress had passed to meet this emergency, for the benefit of the soldiers. We could "Frank" and let her go, the home folks would pay for it, but we would not "Frank" to our girl, we always had a stamp to go on her letters, and while I am on the subject of letter writing, I will mention a little thing that occured between myself and A. A. Kirkland, "Old Betsy", when one day he received a letter I called him by name and asked him the news, when, with that old familiar smile he answered by saying, "what you recon." "I don't know," said I, "what?" He replied that "the cat was wearing the kittens shoes." Another fellow near by broke out in a loud laugh. "Old Betsy" passed on, and I was left entirely in the dark as to his meaning and had no further question for him. I soon learned it was intended for a "sell" and I realized it as such and was more particular with him afterwards. Well, I have already said that the water at this place was bad, and great numbers of the boys were being hauled off to the hospitals. Yes, all the boys that were with us then who are living now well remembers the hospital at Haymarket. This was the name of the field hospital that was established near the camp, and in August 1862 was a part of the battlefield of 2nd Manassas. Several of my company died and was buried there. Some time during the latter part of October we moved camp farther east near "Bull Run" where the water was good, but rather scarce in consequence of so many having to be supplied from the same spring. This camp had no particular name, and the letters and official papers were all headed "Camp 15th Alabama, near 'Bull Run, Va.'" etc. We remained at this camp two or three weeks when we moved again, this time crossing "Bull Run" and "Cub Runs" crossing the former at the famous stone bridge on the Warrenton turnpike that leads to Centerville. We encamped this time in a large old field between Cub Run and Centerville, a little town 20 or 22 miles from Washington, D. C. We were now in the midst of a large army of volunteers from each of the Southern States, commanded by Johnston and Beauregard, who were preparing to meet the federal army that was only 16 or 18 miles away, preparing for their second "On to Richmond." While here at this camp I got my first glimpse at Wheats Battallion from New Orleans. They were all Irish and were dressed in Zuave dress, and were familliarly known as the "Louisiana Tigers," and tigers they were too in human form. I was actually afraid of them, afraid I would meet them some where and that they would do me like they did Tom Lane of my company; knock me down and stamp me half to death. That's the way they did Lane and I stayed shy of their camp. Two of them was courtmarshalled for insubordination and condemned to be shot to death with musketry. The day of execution was set and our regiment with a great many others were marched to the place of execution to witness it, and after certain ceremonies by the priest, for they were Catholics, they stood up, when a squad of Tigers (their comrades) marched out in front and halted, then the officer in command gave the order "Ready, aim, fire" and they fell to the ground lifeless. They belonged to Taylor's Brigade and were brave, desperate fighters, and on account of their bravery, and daring, their organization was destroyed at Cold Harbor on June 27, 1862, and the Louisiana Tigers as an organization was known no more. A few days after the execution of the Tigers, Tom Lane was on camp guard one night, and Sam Learry of Company B., donned himself in a Zauave dress, and crawled unobserved to the line occupied by Tom, for it was he that Sam was hunting, and when Tom came walking along, Sam growled in a low tone, "A resurrected Tiger." Tom stopped, peeping through the darkness, he thought he discovered the form of a man with his legs all streaked and stripped, and hesitating as if he didn't know what to do. Sam perceiving this growled out again, "A resurrected Tiger" putting on the Irish brogue. Tom clearly understood him that time, and without any hesitation made a dash for his tent, calling for corporal of the guard, and when Tom was called on to explain, he said he saw one of them Tigers that had been resurrected for he said so. Sam had run into his qu'ters, and was just having his own fun over it. It was so funny that the officers took no steps toward punishing Tom for leaving his post. Always after that when the boys would see anything streaked or stripped they would hollow out, "Tom Lane, here's your Tiger." This lasted as long as Tom lived. He was a good soldier and was killed at the battle of Chickamauga, 1863.

CHAPTER XV

AN OLD VETERAN IN CAMP AT CENTERVILLE, VA.

DEAR FRIEND:
While in camp at this place during the month of October, the Federal commander had tolerated the advance of the Confederates to Munson's Hill within a few miles of Alexandria, and every attempt to draw him out into a general engagement proved unavailing, although it was daily invited by heavy skirmishing by the opposing forces that occupied the front. Generals Johnston and Beauregard having failed to draw the Federals out from their breastworks drew in their lines to Centerville, which was construed by the Federal commander to be a retreat, which induced him to advance his right wing against a small body of Confederates commanded by General Evans, near Leesburg on the Potomac river 10 or 12 miles northeast of this place. The Federals had their plans laid nicely, and advanced in such heavy force as to almost insure his capture or destruction, but Evans with his Virginians, and Mississippians pounded upon them by detail, and when Evans got through with them, their loss was computed to be not less than five hundred killed and drowned, and eight hundred wounded. Official figures give Evans' loss at 153 killed and wounded. After this lesson the Federals attempted nothing but sending out foraging expeditions which had brushes with our cavalry every day, but all the while the Federal commander (Little Mc.) was busy with the organization of his army, and improving its morals to a state of proficiency. At the same time the raw material of the 1st Manassas and the new arrivals of volunteers from the South were rapidly improving in discipline, and soldierly qualities, getting ready for business next year. Some time during the month of October, if my memory serves me right, we were put into a brigade composed of the 15th Alabama, 16th Mississippi, 21st Georgia, 21st North Carolina, and if I mistake not the 6th North Carolina batallion was with us also. All under the command of Brigadier General Crittendon. I think he was from Kentucky. About this time our camp was moved about four miles east of Centerville, and established on the left of the turnpike leading from Centerville to Washington,

D. C., and was within eight miles of where the great Federal army lay. This camp was called Camp Crittendon, named for the Brigadier. Our duties consisted in drilling, camp guard, and picket duty. The entire regiment would have to go about once a week and remain a day and night. We were nearing the enemy now, and every one had to be on the quivive. Here at this camp, that noble young man Jim Nobles, died. His remains were carried by his comrades just across the turnpike and there laid to rest. His remains were preceded by the muffled drum followed by sorrowing friends. He was solemnly laid to rest with the honors of war. He was detailed from our company to act as color guard and was highly esteemed by his associates. Here we had brigade guard mounting every morning, which was a new feature in guard mounting. This was ordered by General Crittendon. It was at one of these guard mountings, one morning, that I saw him for the first time, and I don't remember seeing him again. He soon retired from this part of the service, and a Brigadier General of Baltimore, I. R. Trimble, became to be our commander until he lost his leg at 2nd Manassas. Up to this time, we had not fired a gun, but were in hearing of cannonading down at the front every day, between Stuart's cavalry and the Federal foraging and scouting parties. Our company was detailed from this place and sent down south of Centerville, to a place called Union Mills on the Manassas and Alexandria Railroad near "Bull Run," for the purpose of guarding an ammunition train. Here we had a jolly good time for about three weeks. Plenty good rations to eat, and nothing to do, only a little guard duty to do. We could fish in the day or night, just as we pleased. Here J. S. Calk, (Uncle Sim), George Newman, Jim Howerton, Dr. Gillespie, Punch Daughty, and others of the Grays paid us a visit. Uncle Sim and George Newman were crack fishermen at home, and from the way they were talking and laughing about fishing we imagined that they had not lost the art here. I obtained a 24 hours' leave of absence from Capt. Oates and went over to Sangster's X-roads to visit my old friends of the Grays that had preceded us in May. After supper, we sat around and talked till a late hour. They belonged to the 6th Alabama and it was very interesting to me to hear them tell of the part they played on the day of the battle July 21st. They did not get into the engagement but did a great deal of maneuvering for positions. I retired for sleep in the tent occupied by John Williams, Dick Trawick, and others, and to my surprise, at about 2 o'clock a. m. Lewis Coleman, a Jew, who was corporal of the guard that night, came to the tent where I was and woke me up, saying that there was a man at the guard line on a horse that wished to see me, and upon investigation I found it to be one of my company that Capt. Oates had sent after me, as he had received orders to move, and he did not want to leave me. I bid all good-bye, and some of them, I never saw again. We moved that day about 9 a. m., and as our regiment had moved from Camp Crittendon where we left it, we had to keep marching until we found them, and at a late hour we found them in camp near Centerville. Here we remained the greater part of November, when cold weather came on us, and some time in December, we crossed "Bull Run" at Mitchell's ford and went into camp near Manassas Junction and commenced making preparations to go into winter quarters. The weather was becoming to be cold, much snow, sleet and rain had fallen, until the roads had become so boggy that it was impossible to move a heavy loaded wagon, and all expectations of a battle were banished for that winter.

CHAPTER XVI

AN OLD VETERAN IN WINTER QUARTERS NEAR MANASSAS, VA. NO. 1.

Dear Friend:

When we moved our camp from near Centerville, crossing "Bull Run" at Mitchell's ford, we went into camp near this place and began at once to make preparations to go into winter quarters. It had rained, sleeted and snowed so much that the ground had become to be a perfect slush, so much so that it had put a quietus on active operations of both armies, and they seemed to content themselves by watching each other during the winter, and to get everything ready for active operations by the time the spring opened. Little spats occurred every day at the extreme front between J. E. B. Stuart's cavalry and the advanced pickets of the enemy. We could hear the cononading, but were too far off to hear the small arms. The canonading in the direction of Washington, and the report of the siege guns down at Dumphreis on the Occoquan (something like 20 miles below Washington), became to be so common that no one would scarcely notice it. Dumphreis was held by Hood's Texas brigade, that later on became so famous in the army of Northern Virginia. While all these things were going on heavy details were being made to cut and haul logs to build huts, details were also made to get boards. Alonzo Watson and myself were detailed from our company for that purpose, and we with about 30 others of our regiment who had been detailed, fell into line, and were marched off, commanded by Lieut. Jeff Pryor, of Company "F." After marching 8 or 10 miles we went into camp in the heaviest timbered oak hammock I ever saw. The next day we were divided into squads, when axes, saws and froes were issued and we began to down the large oaks. I was just seventeen and fat and chubby and I would soon get out of breath, cutting and sawing. The officer was not long in discovering my capacity for such work, and he detailed me to stay in camp to assist the cooks, such as bringing water and wood. This job did not consume all my time, and when off duty I would go hunting for squirrels, and anything else that was large enough to shoot that would do to eat. We had plenty army rations, but we wanted some fresh pork, and the officer intimated that he would kill any hog that tried to bite him, and I was not long in taking the hint for I thought I understood what it meant. The next day I set out to hunt a porker, and at last found one in a field about 50 yards from the fence I was at, and within one hundred yards from its owner. I crouched down in the corner of the fence, and began to make a noise, trying to coax him near enough to get a dead shot at him, but he didn't understand my language, and wouldn't come any nearer. I was soon discovered by the man of the house (a free negro), and he seeing his hog so near me, he began to make a noise, the hog raised his head, listened a moment, when he broke and run to the house. I then realized that I had made a "triumphant failure" in my first effort to steal a hog, and that was my last. I reported to the boys in camp my luck, and they insisted that I should try again, but I wouldn't consent. During our stay at this place there came a heavy snow, and I went coon hunting one day, and was not long in tracking one to a large white oak tree, which had signs about the top that it might be his den. I made this known to Alonzo Watson, and he said we would cut the tree down and catch him. I had my doubts, for I was not used to catching coons without a dog, for I knew they would fight and scratch for all they were worth, but Lonzo was not afraid, and we cut the tree down, and as soon as it hit the ground Lonzo stopped the hole with his cap. I cut a good size hole to the hollow which happened to be opposite the coon's head, and Lonzo seiged him with both hands around the neck and began to choke him. The coon turned up both hind legs and began to scratch and squall. I slapped my hands and hollowed, "hold him!" "hold him!" Lonzy! I never saw such scratched up hands before nor since, but he was good grit in every respect, and by his continuous holding on and choking, and pressing the coon against the log, the coon became still, and we carried him to camp, skinned him, and then I boiled him as good as I could, and then baked him, and after all that was done I gave my share to others. I was not fond of coon then, and I haven't changed yet. We remained down here getting boards about two weeks, the wagons hauling every day until they said enough, when we were ordered back to camp. I enjoyed that outing greatly and was sorry that I could not stay longer. When we reached camp the huts had been put up, the cracks daubed with clay and nearly all covered. My mess had built a house long enough to have a fire-place at each end, and bunks enough to sleep twelve men. Here one of our mess had the itch, and you never saw such scratching and clawing as he done, and if he is living and sees this his mind will revert back to the time and place of his torture when he applied the Polk root fried in bacon-grease as a remedy. Great Scott! this only added fuel to the fire, and many funny remarks were made by himself and others, all of which was enjoyed by all hands. While I am on the incidents of this camp I will say that here I saw for the first time a "booger," but not for the last by any means. One of our mess had been off to a hospital and when he returned one of these "boogers" was found on him and he was immediately quarrentined by placing him by himself on one end of the lowest bunks we had. We were disposed to ridicule him for filthiness, but later on they became bodily companions and were so numerous that they would furnish employment for us when we had nothing else to do. These bodily companions had many nick names.

"Old Betsey" called them "dandruff with leggins," when the hair on our heads would become involved. A war of extermination was incessently waged all the time, which only put a moderate check on their increase until the latter years of the war their power began to wane and when peace was made, we parted company to know them no more.

CHAPTER XVII

AN OLD VETERAN IN WINTER QUARTERS.
NEAR MANASSAS, VA. NO. 2.

DEAR FRIEND:

I will now tell you something of our clothing and money. I had forgotten to mention them as two important events of our camp over near Centerville. Well, it was at this camp during the month of November that we drew our grey dress uniforms that had been promised. Our measure was taken during the month of September while in camp at Richmond, and we had almost despaired of getting them, but they came at last, and the joy of their arrival and delivery was not without its sadness, for several of the boys had died since the measure had been taken and were not present to answer when their names were called, and I don't remember what disposition was made of their uniforms. Some of us youngsters had grown so, until it was some difficulty to be fitted, but by changing around we were fitted out and we felt as proud as a peacock looks to be when in full strut. Some of the older ones did not like the cut of the coat, nor the shape of the cap. The coats were "scissor tailed" and the caps were the kind that fell over in front with a place for letters. Ours had H. P. Co. "G" 15th Alabama Volunteers. After being fitted out in our new uniforms we compared favorably in dress with the 7th Louisiana, and 1st Kentucky regiments. I mention these two, for they were the best dressed regiments I saw during the war. We also drew good woolen overcoats, a Godsend for that particular time, for we were experiencing some of the coldest weather we ever saw. It would rain, sleet and snow, and the cold wind from the snow capped peaks from the "Blue Ridge" mountains that we could see in the distance blew so strong that it was a difficult matter to keep our tents up. We had good wall tents and could keep dry, but our fires were outside and in trying to keep warm one side would burn while the other would freeze, and would have to keep turning around. This was a pretty tough time, but I saw worse before the war ended. Here we drew our first money, two months pay; twenty-two dollars for the privates and a little more for the non-commissioned officers. The bills were on the bank of Charleston, S. C. I don't think that there had been any Confederate money stamped at that time. We had money then to buy writing paper, postage stamps, apples, cakes, candy, ground peas and chestnuts. I mention these things because the camp was flooded with these articles as soon as it was known that the army had been paid off. All during the winter we had our share of picket duty to do by going five or six miles to the front and remaining two or three days. It mattered not how cold it was, we had to go. The Yankees had to be watched and they were just as vigilent in watching us. I very well remember the day the battle of Drainsville was fought, it was on the 20th day of December and we were marching through the little town of Centerville on our way to the picket post, we heard the report of cannon in fast succession and a dull roaring sound resembling the muttering sound of distant thunder, which we took to be the sound of small arms. We raised the "Rebel yell" and quickened our step for about three miles. The excitement, and the rapidity of our march had caused us to be thoroughly warmed up by the time we had reached the place of our destination. We were sure that we were going as reinforcements, and that a craving for a fight was going to be gratified, but we were disappointed. We arrived at the picket post, and instead of going on we were halted, and details were made to go on post to relieve those that had been on two or three days. We soon learned that the battle was but a small affair, and had resulted disastrously for the Federals, as their loss was heavy considering the number engaged. This picket post was on the Little River turnpike at a place called Chantills, where we met the Federals the following September and had a severe engagement with them for about one hour, the particulars I will give later on. Without any incident or accident we served out our time, and in due time we were relieved and returned to winter quarters and there spent the Christmas of 1861, snow balling and doing other things for amusement. While at this camp I was strolling around outside the guard line and I came to two graves that had been made during the winter, each one had a neat head-board and my attention was called to the lettering of each that was placed thereon for identification, and upon examination I found them to be the last resting place of two that I knew at home. One was marken T. S. Harvey, Co. "B," 6th Alabama. He was a citizen of Abbeville at the outbreak of the war and was a member of the Henry Greys (A. C. Gordons Company). The other one was —— Bell of the same Company and regiment. They were buried on the right of the road that leads from Manassas to Centerville, via Mitchells ford on "Bull Run." We remained in these quarters during the winter with nothing to do except to do guard duty, go on picket and drill, when the weather was suitable. There was a good deal of sickness in camp and our ranks had been thinned considerably. Some had become so afflicted that they were discharged for disability to stand the service. Others were granted furloughs home where they could recuperate and return to service, and by this means many were restored to health and returned, and made good soldiers. As for myself, nothing would not take hold of me, and consequently I remained, but after awhile I was overtaken and had to give up, of which I will tell later on. I will give you a little experience that I had with some Irishmen up at Manassas Junction one day. I had a permit to visit the place, and while there I fell in with these Irishmen and they appeared to be a little "drinky" and full of fun. They had bought a dozen or more of stick brooms and were going to carry them to camp and when time come for us to leave they asked me to go down with them on a hand car, all right as I knew it went near my camp. Their camp was on the east side of Bull Run, and it was down grade when we came opposite my camp and the thing was running at the rate of 2:40, and I hollowed out "hold up, hold up." "Hold up nothing, nothing, be Jasus hold on" they said and made no effort to stop. I had to get off; I picked my chance to leap, and when I did about half their brooms followed, though unintentionally. They shooked their fist at me and went on.

CHAPTER XVIII

AN OLD VETERAN IN WINTER QUARTERS.
NEAR MANASSAS NO. 3.

DEAR FRIEND:
While we were quietly passing off the winter at this place there had been several collisions between the Federals and Confederates in other parts of the South with alternate success. These conflicts were between small bodies of troops compared to the army of the Potomac (Northern) and the army of Northern Virginia (Southern). Some of these conflicts however small, resulted very disastrously to the South. While it is not my intention to write a report on these particular engagements as they have already passed into history. I only refer to then as events of the latter part of the winter of '61 and the early winter of '62, and shall leave it with you to search history for information on these things. While these things were going on in the western armies, the Federals in the east were making gigantic preparations to overwhelm Johnston's little Southern army that was in winter quarters around Manassas Junction and Centerville. On March the 1st, 1862, the federal army in and around Washington numbered 193,142, fit for duty with a grand aggregate of 221,987 and Johnston with not exceeding forty thousand, was all that stood between this enormous force and Richmond, the Capital of the Confederacy. Johnston had detached "Stonewall" Jackson with eleven skeleton regiments to amuse the enemy in the Shenandoah Valley, which I will refer to later on. Those figures are from an official source and I only refer to them to show you what we Southern boys had to face. On the 22nd of February, (Washington's birthday), President Lincoln ordered McLellan to advance and overwhelm Johnston, but McLellan was tardy in his movements and urged a different line of operation, that of the lower Rappahannock. He obtained delay and did not advance. In the mean time General Johnston was not an idle spectator as to what was going on and he made every disposition that was necessary to meet the advance, relying only on strategy and the valor of his troops. In the winter months of '62 Johnston had aban-

doned the idea of offensive operations on the line of "Bull Run" and had concluded to fall back behind the Rapphannock, where he would be nearer his base of supplies, and be in better position to defend the Capital and to reinforce the Confederate army down on the peninsular in the event there was a sudden movement against either, and for that reason he had all during the winter been quietly transporting his immense stores from Manassas toward the Rappahannock, removing every cannon that could be spared from the embrasures and mounting in their place painted logs in order to deceive Prof. Lowe when he ascended in his balloon to overlook Johnston's army. So perfectly and quiely had all things been arranged that all stores, baggage, the sick, and material of every kind had been removed before we realized that we were going to abandon our winter quarters and fall back. In fact, we were in complete ignorance of what was going on. Our good wall tents that the citizens gave and the ladies of Abbeville made for us, when we first started out in the war were struck, when we first started to build huts for winter quarters, were carried off somewhere and were seen by us no more. The officers fared no better than the privates for their tents were gone also, and after we were ordered out of our winter quarters we had to "rough it" until the next winter. I have already told you that the weather was so bad that it had put a quietus on active operations by both armies, but when March set in with her balmy spring days, it created a stir around headquarters and we were momentarily expecting something to happen. At last orders came to cook three days rations, pack our knapsacks with everything that we could carry and destroy the surplus, and be ready to march at a moments notice. Before we left Abbeville for the war a goodly number of Oates' Company employed "Ned" (Mr. Clendenin's blacksmith) to make them some large knives. I don't know what to call them, but they were similar to the Spanish matchetta, and I guess that would be a good name for them, only they were American. Many were the vain boastings of some of these men who carried them strapped to their side before they had smelt gun-powder. Some went so far as to say they were going to cut Abe Lincoln's head off, and all such vain assertions as that. These assertions were made when patriotism ran high, but later on such was looked upon as being ridiculous, and the matchetts became to be a nuisance and a burden for the men to carry, and on the day we left camp 14 of them were turned over to me, and I gave them a decent interment just outside the guard line near a little branch. I expect that they have long since been unearthed as they were not buried out of the reach of a plow. I mention the circumstance concerning these knives in order to show how men in their enthusiasm for a thing will advance ideas and make assertions that afterwards seem ridiculous and disgusting. I may have been one of this kind, for I was a regular fire eater and was none too good, with no better sense than to have made similar expressions. Well, dear friend, I have disgressed somewhat but will return, by saying that we cooked rations, packed knapsacks, and did everything else we were ordered to do, and remained quietly waiting orders to do something. At last sometime during the night of the 7th of March orders came to move, we fell quietly into line with the brigade and took up the line of march toward Richmond, reaching and crossing the Rappahannock on the 10th, when we "about faced" and waited for the approach of the enemy who were in pursuit. The march from Manassas to the Rappahannock was made with leisure. There were no barking in the rear by Uucle Sam's dogs to cause a hurry. During the winter our baggage had increased so that it was a difficult matter to decide on what to throw away, consequently our knapsacks were packed to their utmost, and as that was our first march we had a time. The farther we went the heavier our turn, and it was amusing to see the boys down with their knapsacks open deciding what to throw away. I was not an exception to the rule.

CHAPTER XIX

AN OLD VETERAN IN CAMP.

ON THE RAPPAHANNOCK RIVER NO. 1.

DEAR FRIEND:
The next day, the 8th, after we had left our winter quarters, the government at Washington issued pre-emptory ordders to McLellan to advance, and on the 9th the grand army was in motion for the purpose of crushing Johnston's army before he could be reinforced. All Washington was in ex-

pectation, for they knew that the second "On to Richmond" had commenced and the second grand army was about to pass its grand climacteric. Fairfax Court House was reached at night and the grand army went into camp, and at a late hour McLellan had received the wonderful tidings that Johnston had retreated. So complete had been the evacuation that nothing was left in our positions, it was desolate, though frowning in fortified grandeur. Our line of march was paralel with the Orange and Alexandria R. R. I said in the last chapter that the march was made at leisure and there was nothing behind to push, and in consequence of our loads a great deal of straggling was done, but I was present at each roll call. After crossing the river we were drawn up in line to await the approach and attack of the enemy, but McLellan refused to challenge and moved down toward the Seaboard. Johnston was quick to apprehend, accurately divined the movements that McLellan was going to make, when he began to move his troops accordingly. Active operations against Richmond was abandoned on this line, and changed and shifted to that of the Peninsular, between the York and James rivers, where McLellan hoped to capture Richmond by a *Coup de main,* but the vigilant Johnston met him promptly by a rapid transfer of his army from the Rappahannock to the Peninsular, where daily skirmishing and sharpshooting was done until McLellan's final defeat on the Chickahominy the last days of June 1862. As well as I remember, while on the line of the Rappahannock our Brigade (Trimble's), Taylor's Brigade of Louisianians and Early's Brigade of Virginians were formed into a Division and placed under the command of that sterling old war horse R. S. Ewell, who shortly after that became to be Jackson's right bower. When Johnston transferred his army to the Peninsular we were left on the Rappahannock to guard the approaches to Richmond by this route, and be accessible to either reinforce Jackson in the valley or Johnston before Richmond. So with this severence I know nothing of Johnston's movements except what I learned from history. Sometime during the month of January or February Lieut. C. V. Morris obtained a furlough to come home for the purpose of enlisting recruits, and it was while we were here on the Rappahannock that he returned with twenty-five or thirty and perhaps more which made our company the strongest in the regiment. Officers from the other companies had been furloughed for the same purpose, but I don't remember when they returned, nor what number they brought back with them. I only know that our ranks had been so depleted by deaths and discharges during the winter, had been greatly strengthened, and we had a strong regiment to enter upon the spring and summer campaign. The day that Lieut. Morris arrived with recruits the regiment was on the north side of the Rappahannock tearing up the railroad. The enemy advanced in such strong force that our regiment had to retire and recross the river. I was a little sick at the time and was left in camp to guard the Company's baggage until they returned, but Lieut. Morris, hearing the cannonading, and wanting to initiate the recruits, formed them into line, using me as a right guide, marched us down to where the regiment was in line, forming us on the left of the company. We were not in line many minutes before a shell came whizzing over striking the ground about fifty yards in our rear, others following in quick succession, getting lower and lower as they obtained our range. One of our batteries were brought up and placed in our immediate front and a regular artillery duel ensued. Our position being in the rear made it very disagreeable and we felt like going into the ground. One of the recruits became so uneasy that he asked me where Captain Oates was. I told him he was at the head of the company. He knew Captain Oates at home before the war and was anxious to see him, when about that time Oates came down the line shaking hands with the recruits that had just arrived, and when he reached the fellow that had made the enquiries he suggested to Oates that it might be safer if he would move his company somewhere else, "for it looks to me," he said, "that if we stay here some of us would be killed." I don't remember Oates' reply, but the fellow afterwards learned that a soldier was there to do or die. He made a good soldier and was teased about it as long as he remained with us. He took it all good-naturedly and treated it as a joke. He was permanently disabled at the battle of Sharpsburg in September 1863. This was the first shelling that we had been under since we had been in service and was only a foretaste as to what was coming on. No one was hurt, the firing ceased, the enemy retired and we were marched back to camp a little wiser than we were before.

CHAPTER XX

AN OLD VETERAN IN CAMP.
ON THE RAPPAHANNOCK RIVER NO.2.

DEAR FRIEND:
As long as I remained with the regiment on this line we had no certain camping place. We were kept moving up and down the river, guarding the different fords and doing picket and guard duty on the north side, until it was fully ascertained that the enemy had fallen back and took shelter in his fortifications, from whence he came only sending out foraging parties, committing all kinds of depredations upon the peaceful citizens that chose to remain at their homes between us. I said foraging parties, marauding parties would be more appropriate for they plundered and took everything they could lay their hands on from the non-combatants and didn't hesitate to offer every kind of an insult imaginable to the ladies who sympathized with the South, that remained at their homes within their line. They would take every dust of meal, every pound of meat, kill the hogs and cattle, take their poultry and drive off their farming stock, destroy the farming tools and appropriate to their own use all the farm produce that they could carry off, and apply the torch to that which was left, not being satisfied with what they could get outside the houses they would go inside and in the presence of the inmates would smash to pieces their fine pianos and furniture of every description and appropriated the jewelry and other valuables that suited their fancy to their own use. Such conduct as this was not approved by their commanding general and was only indulged in by a party of cut-throats who had no conception of civilized warfare. Occasionally our Mosby and Stuart would get after them and they would ingloriously fly and take shelter behind their fortifications. There had been some changes in my company during the winter that I will mention here. 1st Lieut. I. F. Culver had resigned in November and 2nd Lieut. C. V. Morris was promoted to 1st Lieutenant, 3rd Lieut. H. C. Brainard was promoted to 2nd Lieutenant and J. A. Oates (a brother of the Captain) who had been transferred from the Henry Greys,

was elected 3rd Lieutenant, and I only mention these things as I proceed with my narrative to show you our organization when we entered the Valley campaign under "Stonewall" Jackson. When we were not on duty, we were busily engaged in drilling the recruits, getting them ready for that which was soon to follow. I was taken sick while here and the doctors said I had Pluro-Pneumonia, and that I must go to the hospital. My God! I am gone now, for I looked upon a hospital as being a place for a sick man to go to to die, and when the ambulance arrived to carry me to the depot I thought farewell Co. "G," this ends my war record. Arriving at the depot on the Orange and Alexander R. R. I was placed on the floor of an old dingy, solitary tobacco-house, and there, with other sick men, was left to wait for the arrival of the train to carry us to a hospital somewhere. I remained there all day suffering with a scorching fever; the nurse that attended did all he could to alleviate my suffering. It was here while lying upon my back writhing in pain that I for the first time had thought seriously of my parents and sisters, and wished that I was at home with them. At a late hour the train arrived and I was assisted on board and carried to Richmond, arriving there early in the morning when I was conveyed to Chimborazo hospital that had recently been established on our old drill ground. I was registered, sponged off, given a change of clothing, consigned to a comfortable couch or bunk, examined and prescribed for by Dr. Davis, when all necessary nourishments were furnished, I felt much better. I was so well treated by the doctor and nurses that I improved rapidly and in a few days the pain in my side and fever give way, and I was soon convelescent and allowed to go to the city or elsewhere I desired. This was my first experience in a hospital and being so young and inexperienced and being among so many sick and dying men, that at first it had a tendency to cast me down in gloom and despair, but my rapid improvement revived my feelings and in about three weeks I became strong and reported for duty. There were others belonging to Ewell's Division reporting for duty, but the hospital authorities seemed to be at a loss as to the location of Ewell, as it was ascertained that he had moved from the position we left him on the Rappahannock. We were marched down to Richmond and there housed up in comfortable quarters and kept three days before we could leave. At last an officer took charge of us and we boarded a train for Culpepper Court House, on the O. & A. R. R., where we got off and with a guide was marched over some mountains, down valleys and in about two days we reached our command. This was about the first of May and after marching and countermarching, we struck out down the Luray Valley to reinforce Jackson who was fighting, arriving in the neighborhood of Front Royal on the 22nd.

CHAPTER XXI

AN OLD VETERAN UNDER "STONEWALL" JACKSON IN HIS VALLEY CAMPAIGN NO. 1.

DEAR FRIEND:

Our march down the Luray Valley to reinforce Jackson was so rapid, and was made with so much secrecy that the Federal Commander Banks was greatly surprised when Ewell appeared in his rear at Front Royal on the evening of the 22nd of May. Before we began this march we were ordered to put ourselves in light marching order, by turning over to the Quartermaster all surplus baggage that would be a hindrence to a rapid movement. The young men of my company divested themselves of every thing except a blanket and a change of under garments. I turned in my knapsack with several things that I greatly regretted to part with, which I afterward needed, but I never saw again; others shared the same fate. Some of the older ones of my company held on to their heavy loaded knapsacks and on the march when the warm rays of the sun began to beam upon them, they began to fag, and cast off the heavy bed quilts and woolen coverlets that had been such a source of comfort during the cold fall, winter and early months of spring. There was a great deal of grumbling and complaining among this class of men, but all to no purpose; the surplus had to go, as something was going to happen and they had to be there. Jackson had had two or three spats with the Yankees during the winter, one of which he was overmatched and was considerably worsted, after which he only contented himself in keeping them in doubt as to his movements, until he could be reinforced. The first intimation we had of our near proximity to Jackson was the sound of his cannon over on the Winchester pike. The advance of our division was led by the 1st Maryland Cavalry (C. S. A.), and before they reached Front Royal they encountered the 1st Maryland Cavalry (U. S. A.) and a desultory skirmish was kept up for about one hour, when the Louisiana Tigers came to the front and was deployed as skirmishers and advanced to assist our Cavalry. Now look out boys, something is going to drop! the Tigers are in front and you will hear something directly. They had not advanced far before the firing became to be pretty heavy for the number of troops engaged. The Yankees offered a stubborn resistance in order that our strength might be developed. Our company was in line with the regiment standing in the road while the firing was going on. We were expecting every moment to be ordered to the front. While in this position Courtney's Battery of our brigade came dashing by and soon opened upon the Yankees with shot and shell. The firing increased to such an extent to cause us to believe that reinforcements were being pushed in by both sides, occasionally a wounded Tiger would pass, bloody and powder blackened, muttering something that I could not understand. All of these things created such suspense that it caused a chill to pervade my system to the extent of causing my knees and teeth to knock together as though I had an old fashioned shaking ague. The hair on my head seemed to rise and was sorter like the quills of a fretful porcupine, and I had some trouble in keeping my cap pressed down. I looked around to see if any one else was in my condition, and I soon found it to be a pretty general complaint among the boys. The complaint was not confined exclusively to the privates. Some of the officers were similarly affected. The countenance had undergone a change, the natural expression of the eye had banished and it looked to me as though each fellow was trying to conceal his condition and keep it unobserved by the other fellow. It was funny for me to think about afterward. We boys would talk about it and laugh over it, after the danger had passed. Well, was this a symptom of cowardice? I say no, for later on in the war I saw brave and courageous men similarly affected. I had heard these things discussed by old soldiers, giving different reasons for the cause. My theory is that an anxiety to know and see what is going on in front, accompanied by momentary doubts and fears of the result, drawing on the imagination for the worse, is what brings such feelings on at such exciting times. This was what brought them on me, and if I remained still would last about ten minutes, but would soon wear off if on the move. This was the first time that we had been so near a battle and we were sure that we would get to try our guns before the sun went down. As I have already said our 1st Maryland met the Yankee 1st Maryland. This engagement lasted till near sundown, when our 1st Maryland assisted by some infantry, raised the "Rebel Yell" and charged, putting the Yankees to rout, sweeping through the town of Front Royal, crossing the Shenandoah a running fight began in the direction of Winchester. These regiments from Maryland came from the same section of country and many of them were closely related. The Federal regiment was large and at this, its first fight with its brothers, was annihiliated. A few were killed and wounded and the balance were easily captured. History says that fifteen escaped. After the charge and rout of the Federals, our brigade advanced, passing through the little town of Front Royal, advancing along the pike that led to Winchester. (A word to the survivors.) Do you remember crossing a stream on a bridge just about dusk? Do you remember meeting a "Johnnie" and "Yank" both riding one horse? the Yank in the saddle and the Johnnie seated behind? Do you remember that it was said that they were brothers? Have you forgotten how we guyed the "Yank" and how depressed he looked? Do you remember how slow we marched and how cold we got that night? Do you remember packing up like a bundle of cigars around Capt. Oates to keep warm. Are these false delusions or not? Those are my recollections of events that occurred at the time, though it's possible that I may be mistaken. While these things were taking place here, Jackson was not idle over on the Winchester pike near Kernstown. Desultory firing had been going on over there that evening, but with no decisive results. Jackson sent for Ewell that night to go over to see him, to consult as to the program for the next day. Ewell sent Taylor over with his Louisianians to help Jackson, and at early dawn the small arms began to pop, the result I will tell in the next chapter.

CHAPTER XXII

AN OLD VETERAN UNDER "STONEWALL" JACKSON IN HIS VALLEY CAMPAIGN NO. 2.

DEAR FRIEND:

At early dawn over on the Winchester turnpike as soon as objects could be distiguished, the skirmishers of both armies began to pop away at each other. As the light increased the firing increased, and by the time the sun had ascended to one hour's height, the roaring of musketry and the booming of cannon was evidece to us that a general engagement was on, and if the firing was well directed somebody's children was getting hurt. My command spent the night on the turnpike that leads from Front Royal to Winchester, and were not allowed to have fires lest our position would be betrayed to the enemy. It was cold that night with a heavy dew or frost the next morning, I don't remember which, but we passed the night by "stacking" and huddling together in many ways, keeping warm enough to doze and get a few cat naps. We were all glad when the first streaks of day began to appear, and hearing the firing of Jackson's men, all desire for sleep banished and we were up and ready. About sunrise we received orders to fall into line and move, and moving a short distance we were halted and gave way for Courtney's Battery to pass to the front; they dashed under whip and spur. The cannoneers were in high glee, for they were as anxious as we were to try our guns and they felt perfectly safe when they had the 15th Alabama at their backs for support. They had not gone far before they dashed up a hill to the right and coming into battery, they unlimbered and began to shell the enemy. Courtney had not more than got his guns in position before here come a shell whizzing by. Our brigade was quietly formed in line of battle in the rear of our battery and there remained as its support until the artillery duel ceased. It so happened that the position of my company was exactly in the rear of the battery and in direct line of the fire from the Yankee guns. This was an exceeding uncomfortable position to be in, although we were protected to some extent by the hill but was not secure from the fragments of the bursting shells that was hitting the ground in front and in the rear of us, as though they were searching for a victim, but no one was hurt. We were all anxious for the Yankees to advance and try to capture our battery, but instead of advancing their battery was silenced and they retired. Then came a lull for a time with us, but over on the Winchester pike near Kearnstown Oh, my! the battle was raging. Taylor with his Louisianians had arrived and was thrown into action to assist Jackson's Virginians, while we remained at this place holding our position until the time came for us to play our part, and it came later on. We were in great suspense, hoping to hear something favorable from Jackson. Here another chill seized us, but was of not long duration. Our Brigadier General Trimble became restless and impatient for orders to advance. A profound silence pervaded my whole command. All was expectancy. At last, about nine o'clock A. M. the fire became slacker and began to recede toward Winchester. We could imagine that we could hear the "Rebel Yell" which caused joy in our ranks, our countenances brightened and we were anxious to be ordered forward. As the firing would slack the more intent we would be in trying to catch the sound of the "Rebel Yell." Minutes seemed like hours and by 9:30 our doubts were removed, for we were not mistaken. We could distinctly hear the "Yell" and that was as good news as we wanted. Jackson's Division, with the assistance of Taylor's Brigade, had repulsed the Federal General Banks and his retreat had became a complete rout, so much so that it became to be a panic, and when they came running through the streets of Winchester with the Virginians and Louisianians close on their heels in hot pursuit, the citizens of Winchester received them with shouts of derision. Winchester was Southern to the core. The people never became weary in nursing our sick and wounded. This assertion could be verified by one of our distiguished citizens who had the good fortune to fall into their hands when taken sick on Jackson's retreat up the valley. Banks being in full retreat and Jackson crowding him in the rear, it now became our time to play our part. A hot rider with hat in hand, from the direction of Winchester came dashing up to General Trimble delivering a despatch from General Ewell. General Trimble immediately began to dispatch his aids in every direction with orders to his command to move. The opportune moment had come for us to strike Banks on his right flank and thus complete the destruction of his army. The brigade was put in motion in quick time and sometimes double-quick, and often in a run, the purpose to strike Banks in flank on his retreat to Harper's Ferry, while Jackson would crowd him in his rear. The 15th Alabama led the advance and many fell by the wayside exhausted, but I was young then and had good legs, had put myself in light marching order by divesting myself of all unnecessary baggage, in order that I could be on hand when we had to tackle the Yankees with small arms, and that I might be one of the many boys that later on in the war would be worthy to be called one of Jackson's foot cavalry. This movement of our brigade was not made in time. Banks had anticipated such a move and had abandoned nearly everything he had to Jackson, and contented himself with his own escape and a portion of his demoralized army. Jackson's captures were immense in the way of men, and material of every description, including commissary stores. Our brigade pursued them nearly all day in the direction of Harper's Ferry, but we failed to bring them to a stand and we failed to get to shoot again. Our cavalry led the advance and they picked up a great many stragglers. We pursued them to Harper's Ferry, and could proceed no farther. They had took shelter behind their fortifications on Bolivar Heights, and we fell back to near Winchester where we remained several days camping on the pike that leads from Winchester to Martinsburg, near a place called Bunker Hill. There was no town and was designated by a large spring of pure water with the capacity of furnishing enough for Jackson's whole army. While here we were engaged for a day or two in tearing up the Baltimore and Ohio R. R., rendering it useless for the Yankees only a short time, for while we were engaged in its destruction, no doubt but what they were making preparations to repair it as soon as we should leave. While these things were going on important movements were taking place in our rear. These movements by the Yankees in our rear became matters of importance and hasty preparations had to be made to meet them, which was successfully done, which I will show in the next chapter.

CHAPTER XXIII

AN OLD VETERAN UNDER "STONEWALL" JACKSON IN HIS CAMPAIGN IN THE VALLEY NO. 3.

DEAR FRIEND:

I said in the last chapter that important movements by the enemy in our rear had become matters of importance and hasty preparations had to be made to meet them. No one but Turner Ashley, who commanded our cavalry, knew of the movements of the enemy, and his reports to Jackson were so frequent and intelligent that Jackson made no mistake in divining the purpose of their movements. The prisoners that had been captured in the several engagements had all been sent off to Richmond. The immense quantity of army stores had all been transported to a place of safety, and our commissary wagons had been loaded to their utmost capacity. That which we could not carry was sent off to a place of safety, out of danger of being recaptured. This was a great time with us in the way of rations, for we had everything that was good for soldiers to eat, for Uncle Sam knew how to provide for his soldiers and General Banks was called Jackson's commissary. The supply was so great at this time that later on in the war, when rations became scarce, those of us that were living at this time would have been glad to have got another whack at Bank's commissary train. If you will read the reports of General Banks, the Yankee general, and that of General Jackson, the Confederate general of this affair, you will find a great discrepancy, but Banks had to say something favorable to appease the wrath of his government. All of this fighting, making these captures, tearing up the railroad, camping at Bunker Hill, getting the prisoners and captured stores out of the way, occurred between the 23rd of May and the 1st of June, and when we received orders to march. We took the pike toward Winchester, which was only five miles, passing through we continued the march for six or seven miles out on the Valley turnpike and went into camp. All along this pike was evidences of the rout of the Yankees that occurred on the 24th. There were many things thrown away that was of no value, and all that was worth anything had been picked up by our men and sent away, or appropriated to immediate use. While at this camp, my shoes give out, or nearly so, that put me in a bad fix to march, and what to do I didn't know. I made every effort to get a pair, but all in vain. Captain Oates made every effort to get a pair for me, but the Quartermaster's train was not in reach so he failed. On the morning of the 4th we received orders to be ready to march at a moment's notice. It had been raining and in consequence of so much travel by our cavalry and wagons, the dirt on the rocky pike had become to be as batter which exposed the sharp edges of the rocks so that it was impossible for a bare-footed man to travel far, but Captain Oates, who always looked out for the interest of his men, gave me a permit to march at will, but admonished me not to get so far behind as to be captured. Fight first and run last was my tactics on this march. Before starting on this march I went to the butcher-pen, where several green hides were left on the ground, and placing my foot on one of them I cut a piece large enough to fit my foot, then turning it over (the hair inside) I pulled it over my foot and around my ankle and after making holes with the little blade of my knife I sewed it up with a raw hide string. When I finished I looked at them and thought of what I had heard my father say about the Indians wearing moccasins, and I thought to myself, "By George, I have struck the very thing." They felt too soft and flabby and I wanted some way to tighten them up, and I went back to my company and it was gone. I conceived the idea of tightening my moccasins by holding them near the smoldering coals of fire which had been left, which proved to be a success, and as soon as I got them tight enough I started on my journey. I soon reached the pike and began stepping off at the rate of five miles an hour hoping to catch up, but I had not gone more than a mile before my moccasins became flimsy and I began to distrust them. The further I went the worse they got, until they became so loose that I could scarcely walk at all. I sat down to rest, meditating what to do. I was not long in deciding what to do. I cut the stitches and off they come. There I was bare-footed on a rocky pike, my command fast leaving me on a forced march. The provost guard was approaching in the rear, driving the stragglers ahead of them. Next to follow was the rear-guard of the army, consisting of cavalry which drove everything to the front, but

I had a pass and was in no dread of anything in the rear but the Yankees, which I knew would follow as soon as they found out we were on the retreat. After reflecting on what to do, I decided to put on a pair of socks, which I carried along in a little sack, and then I started out again. By this time my command was two or three hours ahead. I took nigh cuts through the plantations when convenient, and traveled in quick time. I was lightly loaded and made good time. I passed through two or three pretty little villages during the day but had no time to halt. I could only say good-bye as I looked in the faces of those beautiful girls, for sad they were at our departure, well knowing what would come to pass after we left. I did not even ask a name, therefore there is nothing left to memory except their beautiful faces and patriotism. The people of the Shenandoah Valley were noted for their culture and refinement and had furnished the greater number of soldiers that constituted the famous "Stonewall" Brigade. On our retirement the Yankees came, and when I had occasion to march down this valley from Staunton to the Potomac in 1863, many changes had been wrought. Many of the bright-faced little boys and girls had disappeared, for all had yielded their beautiful and happy homes to the ruthless invader and had sought homes among their friends in a more secure place. The boys and girls of that day and time that are now living are grown up men and women, and doubtless hold in memory the dark days of '62-3 and '64 which was even worse in desolation of their homes. The invasion of this valley in 1864 by the Yankee General Phil Sheridan when he came with sword in one hand and torch in the other has but one paralel in the annals of history, that of W. T. Sherman's march through Georgia to the sea. The acts of these generals at this time adorns the pages of history and will be read by future generations and will be looked upon as a blemish on the name of an American soldier. They had to resort to the torch, as well as the sword to subdue us, for they found out pretty soon that they could not do it by a square fight face to face with bullets. Dear friend, I have disgressed so far from my subject that I fear I am drawing on your patience and will defer my narrative of the battles that soon was to follow for the next chapter, and will end this by saying that I overtook my company as they went into camp near "Fisher's Hill" and was there ready to answer to roll call. Up to this time we had not fired a gun at the Yankees and we were getting impatient. These were days full of events, but the 8th eclipsed them all, for on that day at Cross Keys the 15th Alabama had an opportunity of meeting the Pennsylvania Bucktails face to face, the result I will give in the next chapter.

CHAPTER XXIV

AN OLD VETERAN UNDER "STONEWALL" JACKSON IN HIS CAMPAIGN IN THE VALLEY NO. 4.

DEAR FRIEND:

Our camps at night on this march up the valley was passed in quietude. There was nothing to disturb our repose except the strains of marshel music made by the cornet band of the 16th Mississippi, which had a tendency to revive the spirits of the tired and foot-sore soldiers of Jackson's Corps. With each piece of music such as the "Bonnie Blue Flag," "Gentle Annie," "Marsailles Hymn," "Maryland, My Maryland," "Dixie," generally ending with "Home Sweet Home." A deafening "Rebel Yell" would be sent up, the sound as it reverberated down the valley was doubtless heard by the advance of Fremont's army that was appoaching from the west, and rear. We had succeeded in passing the danger of being enveloped by the converging columns of Fremont and Shields. The former approaching from the west on Jackson's right and the latter marching on a paralel on the east side of the south fork of the Shenandoah. Jackson caused a bridge to be burned across this stream where Shields intended to cross for the purpose of forming a junction with Fremont across Jackson's path, but the burning of this bridge caused Shields to move on higher up to the next crossing, which was at Port Republic, a small village on the east side of the stream above mentioned. The place, and what occurred there on the 9th will be referred to later on. We broke camp and started on the march up the valley. The middle of the day became so intensely warm the older ones, and all those that carried heavy loaded knapsacks began to fag, and stragling become to be enormous, but the Yankee "bull dogs" that barked occasionally in the rear had a tendency to infuse new life in us, and a regular hustle was on to keep ahead of the rear guard. I had a pass from Captain Oates, and I felt perfectly independent and had no fear of being captured. About the middle of the evening I sat down on a rock by the side of the road to rest, and while there the stragglers were passing in a hurry. The advance of the Yankees had overtaken our rear guard and a brisk skirmish was going on which put new life in the legs of some of the stragglers and got a "move" on themselves to reach their commands. A great many of them were Irish, and several of them in passing told me to come on or "be Jasus" I would be captured. But I was in no hurry, for I knew we had a strong rear guard of infantry as well as cavalry, and the infantry had not been attacked and I was not uneasy. While I was sitting on the rock resting Daniel McLellan, of my company, came along with a big knapsack on his back, which was full of good clothing. He was very tired of his load and was nearly tired out, I told him to halt and rest awhile with me. He said no, the Yanks would get us if we stayed there long, for they were coming in a hurry and would soon attack our rear guard. I told him I couldn't travel on the pike on account of my sore feet, he opened his knapsack and gave me a bran new pair of home knit socks to put on. After getting rid of the old pair I had on, and scraping all the mud off my feet that I could, with considerable trouble I put them on and started on the march paralel with the pike, for I could not endure the sharp edges of the rocks. Fighting commenced in the rear and I moved in quick time for two or three miles, when I come to a rock fence running at right angles with the pike. Behind those fences on both sides of the pike the stragglers and bare-footed men were halting and forming in line for the purpose of resisting the advance of the Yankees in order that we might rest. While here I happened to take position beside an Irishman belonging to Taylor's Brigade who had an extra pair of shoes strapped to his knapsack. He seeing my condition, hastily pulled them off, and in his Irish brogue said: "Here, take these shoes, put them on and see if you can't keep up." I thanked him for his kindness and put them on; they fit nicely and lasted a long time. There was several officers that couldn't keep up, and they assumed command, and after resting as long as we wanted to, we moved off unmolested. The enemy were being held in check by the rear guard. I overtook my command late that evening just before they reached the beautiful little village of Harrisonburg, and passing through that town we turned to the left in an easterly direction towards Port Republic. After we had passed Harrisonburg some three or four miles, Col. Sir Percy Windham, an English officer who commanded the advance of the enemy, made a dash on our rear, commanded by our own Col. Turner Ashley. The sun was fast sinking from view behind a mountain in the west when this fight took place, and resulted in the capture of Sir Percy and the death of Ashley. We heard the firing distinctly, for it was not more than a half mile in our rear. The 15th Alabama was ordered to halt and rest, and while here Sir Percy came along a prisoner under the guard of two cavalrymen. The blood was trickling down his cheeks, caused by a sabre-cut on his head by one of our cavalrymen in his effort to subdue him. He was so refractory that that was the only means to affect his capture. Sir Percy was of stern stuff and a brave officer. The boys guyed him as he passed along, which so enraged him that he would have stopped right there in the road and engaged in a fisticuff if he could have found a partner. He was the maddest prisoner I saw during the war. While here we received the sad news that Ashley had been killed in the engagement, a thing that we all regretted. As a partisan he had no superior; he was heroic in character and his powers of endurance almost incredible. I don't know who commanded after he fell. After the firing had ceased we moved on some two or three miles and went into camp. There was nothing to disturb us except an occasional exchange of shots by the pickets in the rear. The next morning we moved on in the direction of Port Republic, but we didn't go far before we passed a church called Cross Keys. This had the appearance of being an old county church and nearby was a large cemetery, with many monuments that marked the resting place of the dead. After passing this church we halted and remained all day, expecting an attack every moment, but Fremont was waiting for all his forces to come up and giving Shields time to move up and dispute Jackson's crossing at Port Republic, while he, Fremont, would attack him in the rear. This was the condition of things on the morning of the 8th and was only known by the general officers. Early in the morning the 15th Alabama was formed in line of battle on the left of the turnpike at the end of a piece of woods that surrounded the church. There were no undergrowth between us and the church, the trees were large and we had a good view. Co. "A" being armed with Mississippi rifles were thrown forward beyond the church and cemetery to act as skirmishers. By some cause the regiment was formed facing by the rear rank, our right resting near the pike which was on a ridge with rolling ground on either side. Desultory firing had been going on all the morning and from the way that the Couriers and staff officers were dashing around an attack was momentarily expected. We were not long in suspence, for all at once Co. A was attacked with such overwhelming numbers that they had to fire in retreat. They soon came in sight, passing through the cemetery, frequently taking shelter behind a tomb-stone long enough to fire and load. Well do I remember seeing Ben Ryans of Co. A when he took shelter behind a tombstone and fired back at the Yankees. The odds were so great against Co. A that they came in and took their place in line. It was on this move that Lieut. Berry of that company was captured. When the Yankees reached the opening near the cemetery, they halted for awhile; a deathly stillness prevailed in our ranks while we were waiting for the Yankees to come in reach, for we were anxious to get a shot. While we were waiting Colonel Cantey rode to the right up to the pike, when he saw just over the hill a brigade of Yankess in line of battle marching past our right flank. Had they known our position they could have changed front forward on tenth company and had us completely at their mercy, for an attack from that direction would have caused considerable confusion. The Colonel came back and called us to attention, and give the command to retire by the right of companies, which we did, moving in quick time through a wheatfield. The Yankees seeing this retrograde movement advanced through the cemetery, and began to fire into our rear, which caused us to change our time of march, from a quick to a double quick. Zip! Zip! Zip! came their bullets. Whap! and down went Bill Toney of Co. K, mortally wounded or dead. What! and down went Jim Trawick of Co. G. The ball cutting his hat band through to his head, it only stunned him and he rose to his feet and came on. There might have been others hit but I don't remember now. We broke into a run for a short distance until we crossed a fence. The commanders of companies preserved their distance and when Col. Cantey called out "Form Column by the left of companies into line." A line of battle was easily and quickly formed. About this time Courtney's battery came dashing at a gallop, they soon halted, unlimited and threw a few shots of spherical case which put a stop to the advance of the Yankees at that point. When Courtney fired his first shot, Jim Rhodes of Company "K" shouted aloud, "Now d—n you, I guess you will stop." Our regiment remained in position a short time, as a support to the battery, but we were not to remain in that position long. We were moved off to the right, to meet a column of Yankees that were advancing to turn our flank. We came to a piece of woods, and were marching up to take position behind a fence when the Yankee skirmishers commenced to fire on us. Just before we reached the fence our First Corporal, John T. Melvin, was shot through the instep, and in a few moments afterward, Wm. J. Parish was shot through the hand. These were the first men wounded in Company G. The wound of the former made him a cripple for life, and the wound of the latter should have excused him from further service, but when he got well, he returned and reported for duty, and at the battle of Chickamauga his thigh was broken which permanently disabled him from further service. When we reached the fence above mentioned we were ordered to lie down. There was a large old field in front, and about two hundred yards off there was a line of the "Boys in Blue" advancing to attack us. They advanced with such precision, keeping the step, and their line so well dressed that it was a matter of comment afterwards among our officers, but poor fellows, they did not know what was in store for them behind that fence. There we lay, as a Bengal tiger when he crouches down ready to spring upon his unsuspected prey, each man in deathly silence, with eyes fixed upon the advancing foe, only waiting for the command to fire. Dear friend, these were almost breathless moments, not a word, not a whisper by the men, only a word of caution was whispered by the officers. See them advancing; keep cool, Alabamians; take good aim, and not fire too high. They were allowed to come within seventy-five or one hundred yards, when the command, "Fire!" was given. We hurled such a storm of "Buck and Ball" at them that it came very near annihilating their command, which was afterwards ascertained to be the 6th Pennsylvania Bucktails, commanded by Col. Kane. After the first volley we could not see them any more, in consequence of so much smoke. We fired a few rounds at them through the smoke when it was ascertained that they had disappeared from our front, and we were ordered to cease firing. Other demonstrations were being made on our right, and we moved off by the right flank. We had not gone far before we opened fire on a body of Yankees in the woods on a hill, which put them to flight. All the while heavy firing was going on, on the left, and by 10 o'clock Ewell had Fremont whipped, and was then ready to help Jackson whip Shields at Port Republic. Fremont retreated, and left our division (Ewell's) in possession of the field. That evening we buried the dead, removed the wounded, and collected a large quantity of small arms from off the field. We rested quietly that night and early the next morning we hastened on towards Port Republic, a small village with one or two hundred inhabitants. It was four miles away from us, and we went in quick time. Shields had arrived to dispute the passage of Jackson's corps, his own and Ewell's division, but by strategy at the bridge Jackson made the way passable, and his division crossed and began the attack. Taylor with his Louisianians, had preceded us and arrived in time to render great service to Jackson in the defeat of Shields. As our brigade advanced the booming of canon, and the roar of small arms could be plainly heard, which was evidence that a severe engagement was going on. Our pace was quickened until we cross the bridge and marched out into the open plain where the battle had commenced. We could now tell that the firing was becoming slacker, and receding down the valley, the Southerners yelling, which was evidence of victory. Fremont heard the firing but was too slow to render any aid to Shields. He was greatly surprised when he ascertained that we had left his front. He had made all preparations to meet us in an expected attack by us that morning, but when he found out that we had left his front, he hurried on in the direction of Port Republic, arriving at the burning bridge which was the end of his march. He about faced, and marched back down the valley. By 10 o'clock the firing had ceased and a marvelous victory had been won by Jackson which terminated his campaign in the valley. For a more correct, and thrilling account of this campaign in the valley, ending with this victory I would refer the reader to "Surry of Eagle's Nest." After this victory we went into camp near Weyer's Cave, where we had divine service, and resting until about the 23rd, when we started on the march for Richmond to engage in the great battle of seven days, commencing on the 26th of June, 1862.

CHAPTER XXV

AN OLD VETERAN UNDER "STONEWALL" JACKSON ON HIS WAY TO RICHMOND.

DEAR FRIEND:

After the defeat of Fremont at Cross Keys, and Shields at Port Republic, it became necessary that something should be done to divert the attention of the Yankee General McDowell, who was at Fredericksburg and to keep his forces from uniting with McClellan in front of Richmond, and in order to do this, before we broke camp near Weyer's Cave, we were heavily reinforced by Whiting's division, composed of Hood's Texas brigade, and his own under Col. Law, from Richmond, and Lawton's brigade of Georgians from Savannah. The deception of this reinforcement at this time proved successful, for Fremont and Shields became frightened, and retreated until they reached the strongholds on the Potomac. While here at this camp I visited the Texans and Georgians to see my old acquaintances. I had several in the 1st and 5th Texas, boys of my old settlement, who had emigrated to Texas before the war, one of which I will mention, Nathan Oates, my old teacher, who taught school in my old settlement when I was a small boy. There were several incidents of this camp that has flashed upon my memory that I would like to mention. Some of them I deem out of order and will forbear. Suffice it to say that I was glad to meet my old teacher and he seemed glad to see me. He did not recognize me at first, but when I made myself known to him he said, "Oh, yes, you was my boss ball player at 12 years old. I guess you are about 18 now?" I said, "I would be 18 in August." I think that was our last meeting. He was either killed or sickened and died, I don't remember which. I had a brother that belonged to the 1st Texas, but he had died with pneumonia at "Bell Isle" on the James river, and was buried in Hollywood cemetery at Richmond. On my visit to Richmond in 1896, I felt sad when I was on the high bridge crossing the James. The cars ran slow, and by looking through a window to the left, I had a good view of the island. The thought came, there is where my brother died in the winter of 1861. After seeing all my acquaintances among the Texans, I visited the 38th Georgia. There was a company in that regiment from this (Henry) county called the Irvin Invincibles. I had several acquaintances and some kinfolk in that company. Billie and Lat Whiddon. Billie and John Barnes, all gone now. And by the way, I remember seeing our good old man W. W. Kirkland, who is living today. There were others but I can't remember them now. After visiting the 38th I went over to the 31st Georgia and there I found two of my neighbor boys, Ed and Joe Roach, the former has since been Probate Judge of Geneva County. You may be assured that it was a great source of pleasure to meet with old friends so far from home, all engaged in one common cause. I know the ex-Judge will smile if he ever reads this, and recalls to mind the fun he had with his younger brother Joe, in trying to keep him from thrownig away that large woolen, double wove coverlet, that they were toting, those hot June days, on our march to Richmond, but it was very comfortable at night, and Ed knew it. Joe grumbled because Ed would not help him carry it as much as he thought he ought to, but they worried on until they reached the battlefield, and there they supplied themselves with things more suitable for the occasion. There were others in my company that had friends and relatives among these Texans, and Georgians, and a regular interchange of visits went on as long as we remained in camp. At last orders came when we were least expecting it to cook three days' rations and be ready to move at a moment's notice. This put a stop to the visiting. Where to now? No one knew but the general officers. Time enough had been given for the cooking to be done, when we received orders to fall into line and march. We started off to go somewhere, Ewell's division leading. Lawton's large brigade of six full regiments had been assigned to our division and marched between my brigade (Trimble's) and the Louisianians, who were leading the advance of the division. About 8 o'clock a. m. of the first day we arrived at the foot of the east spur of the Blue Ridge mountains, and began to ascend. I don't remember the name of the gap now. The road was broad, and was likened to a flight of winding stairs. Up, up higher, and higher, at every turn until we reached the top. In crossing this mountain that day, one of the grandest sights that I had ever beheld was presented to my view. When about half way to the top I could look up a mile ahead and see the boys in grey marching four abreast, filing around the rugged clifts that had been made smoothe, and looking backward and downward, there as far as the eye could reach, I could see the balance of Jackson's corps advancing. The long line of troops dressed in gray marching four abreast, stepping in quick time, with their bright muskets and bayonets glittering in the sun, made an everlasting impression upon my mind, the sublimity and grandeur of which I will never forget. Sometimes now in my old age, I am caught in reverie, and almost wish that I was young again, and could once more view just such another scene, but alas! my youthful vigor of that day and time have passed, together with the grandeur of that scene, and I can only draw upon my imagination. We had plenty of music during the day to cheer us up and keep life. We reached the top and as the sun went down on the western side behind us, we went down with a quick step on the eastern side, reaching the level plane about one hour before dark. We continued our march till dark, when we went into camp. Whiting's and Jackson's divisions passing, and going into camp also. Early the next morning we started, Whiting's division leading. The incidents of this day's march is lost to memory. Suffice it to say that our march for the next two days was in a fine country, well supplied with English cherries and all those that were disposed to straggle fared sumptuously in that line. On the evening of the 26th Jackson's corps arrived and took position on the extreme left of Lee's army. It is said that Jackson and Ewell rode into Richmond that night, a distance of 15 miles, and had a conference with President Davis and General Lee and formed their plans for the attack the next day. Gen. A. P. Hill, with his strong division, attacked one of McLellan's strongholds late that evening, and after a sanguinary conflict and suffering considerable loss the Yankees were driven from their stronghold on their right, which put Jackson in good shape for the attack the next morning, the 27th. I heard the firing of this engagement, and privately formed my own conclusions as to what was going to happen the next day, Friday, the 27th. On this march straggling was strictly forbidden. It was said that on this march Jackson issued orders to us that if anybody asked us where we were going, say to them, I don't know. In fact, say I don't know to every question asked. It was said, that on this march, one of the Texans saw a large English cherry tree heavy laden with berries. He broke ranks and started for them and meeting Jackson, the following coloquy ensued: Jackson says, "Where are you going?" The Texan replied, "I don't know." Jackson—"What command do you belong to?" Texan—"I don't know." Jackson—"Haven't you had orders not to straggle?" Texan—"I don't know." Jackson—"What is your name?" Texan—"I don't know." Jackson—"Well, what do you know?" Texan—"I know I want some of them cherries." Jackson started to ride off when the Texan asked, "What do you know?" Jackson replied in a low tone, "I know how to keep a secret."

CHAPTER XXVI

AN OLD VETERAN UNDER "STONEWALL" JACKSON IN THE BATTLES AROUND RICHMOND.

No. 1.

DEAR FRIEND:

Jackson's arrival with his corps from the valley to reinforce Lee, was anxiously looked for, and when notified of his near approach Lee ordered A. P. Hill to make the assault on the evening of the 26th, which I have already mentioned. In anticipation of our arrivals, Hill renewed the attack at early dawn on the morning of the 27th. As the sun rose over the tree tops, the rattle of musketry, the booming of cannon, and the shouts and yells of the Confederates was evidence that hot work was going on, and we were steadily advancing to decide it. A. P. Hill, with his strong division, assisted by Longstreet, and D. H. Hill, with their strong divisions, had attacked so furiously, and the discovery of Jackson by the Federal commander steady bearing down on his extreme right, caused him to hastily abandon his breastworks, leaving his tents standing, and a great deal of his camp equippage and commissary stores, only to seek and assume a position still stronger. This battle is known in history as that of Mechanicsville and Beaver Dam, and was the beginning of the second day's battle around Richmond. Jackson's corps had not yet been engaged, but had passed over and through a part of the battlefield in two hours after the battle had been fought, and there I formed my second impression of the horrors of a battlefield, but I would not let my mind dwell upon these things, and went on as merrily as a lark, rejoicing at our success, and fearing the engagement would soon end for the day and I would not get a chance to shoot. After the retreat of the enemy from this place there was a calm, not much firing going on except by the advanced pickets, and an occasional boom of a cannon. The second position taken by the Yankees is known in history as that of Gaines' Mill, or Cold Harbor, and was wisely selected as being one of great strength, and a brave body of troops could not have been driven from them by direct assault unless by overwhelming numbers. About 11 o'clock when the brilliant rays of the sun were illuminating the field, as far to the right as the eye could see, long lines of the boys in gray, with the beautiful Southern cross fluttering in the breeze and their bright muskets, and bayonets were glittering in the sun, with gorgeously dressed field officers, mounted on their brilliant chargers, could be seen. Upon inquiry by some of the officers they were found to be the troops of Longstreet, and the two Hills (D. H. and A. P.) making preparations to assault the enemy in his last strong position. We had been marching slowly all day, bearing steadily to the left, in order that when we did attack, it would be on the extreme right of the Yankee army. General Lee had made his headquarters at the Hogan's House where he remained awaiting the arrival of Jackson. Our line of march led by this house, and it was about 1 o'clock when Jackson came along, and reigned in his horse and the Generals saluted each other, shook hands and then engaged in a few moments' private conversation when General Lee mounted his horse and rode off, accompanied by his staff to the right. This was our first sight of Gen. R. E. Lee. It was then known that a terrible ordeal awaited us in front, which we were soon to meet. We moved on, crossed a branch, marched up the hill and halted. Here our division formed line of battle, Lawton's brigade of Georgians on our right, and Taylor with his Louisianians on our left. The front of each regiment was covered by a company of skirmishers. Ours was covered by Company "A" commanded by that gallant and soldierly gentleman, Capt. Lock Weems, of Columbus, Ga. At the command, "Forward," they moved in gallant style in search of the enemy. That was the last time I saw Capt. Weems. He was killed that day. At this particular time of which I write, the troops of Longstreet and the two Hills had encountered the enemy in his strong position, and the battle on the right was raging with great fury.

Our company officers seemed to be at their best, repeating the orders of our gallant Lieut. Col. John F. Trentten, who had command of the left wing of the regiment. "Steady 15th Alabama" was often shouted by our Col. Cantey. Thus we moved forward under shot and shell, preceded by our skirmishers who had not yet found the enemy. It was an exciting time with us then. The firing on the right became nearer and nearer, which was a sure indication that we would soon join the issue. We marched through a large field that had been occupied that morning by the enemy as a camp, which they had hastily abandoned, leaving their tents standing, and a great many other valuables that we could have appropriated, but we had no time to stop. The word was, onward! forward! on every tongue. Going up a slant and arriving at the top of the hill we discovered a house down near a branch that we had to cross. The house was directly in front of Company "K" (the company that was on our right.) The Colonel perceiving that we were going to become tangled and confused if we tried to break ranks and run around it, gave the command, "the three left companies obstacle, by the right flank, double quick, march." The commander of Company "K" repeated the order, then our Captain followed and Company "B" on our left followed us. We passed the house when the Colonel commanded "the three left companies into line, by the left flank, double quick, march." While all this was going on the Yankees were shelling us for all we were worth. The shells were bursting over and around us enough to have caused a panic, but we were quickly into line, pressing steadily on until we came to a sluggish stream which we had to cross, and our line became somewhat disorganized.

Where, I, with some others crossed, it was boggy, and I bogged down with one foot nearly to my knee, and in trying to extricate myself my shoe string broke and I pulled my foot out, leaving my shoe in the mud. General Trimble happened to be near sitting on his horse looking at us bogging through that place. He seeing my condition, kindly said, "Soldier, get your shoe." I did so, and knocked the mud and water out of it and put it on. By this time the skirmishers in front were hotly engaged, which was evidence that their main line was near, and that we would soon attack. While I was detained in losing my shoe, my company had gotten fifty or sixty yards ahead, but I with others ran, and soon overtook them and took our place in line, not, however, before we cross a broad road that ran nearly parallel to our line of march. When I reached the road I halted for a moment, and looked up the slant to my left. There I saw the red legged Zouaves of the enemy in line. They fired at us down the road as we passed. I distinctly heard their bullets go hissing by, searching for a victim. I instantly raised my gun, and sent a ball and three buckshot among them, and cross over, pausing long enough to look at Tom Burk of Company "B," who had just been shot down, and was in the last agonies of death. A minnie ball had hit him in the pit of the stomach and with each pulsation his life's blood would gush from the hole. In his delirium he made an unsuccessful attempt to stop the hole with his canteen stopper. He was a noble young man with refined qualities. Peace to his ashes! After the regiment had crossed the branch, and the road, a halt was made to rectify the line and as soon as that was done, we began our advance up a hill that obscured us from the enemy. I had reloaded my gun, and had overtaken, and resumed my position in the front rank of my company, and was ready for what afterwards occurred. Our skirmishers had halted on the top of the hill and were fighting a regular line of battle, just down the slant on the other side. The hill was covered with large oaks with a right smart undergrowth, and our march was slow and cautious. All the while the small arms on the right were as a regular roll. You could not distinguish one gun from another. The bombshells bursting, their fragments flying in every direction, hitting a fellow occasionally, and the solid shot crashing through the boughs above our heads, and the commands of officers all added to the excitement of the occasion. While we were slowly advancing up this hill Sam Dickerson was shot through the heart, and was instantly killed. He was a good soldier and resided near Echo in Dale County, and was the first man killed in Oates' Company. About this time heavy volleys of musketry tore loose on our left which indicated that Taylor's Louisianians had found the enemy, and 'twas said (as I have already stated) that here the Tigers were nearly all killed. Their commander, Maj. Wheat, was killed and they disbanded. We moved on until we reached the top of the hill and I will tell you in the next chapter what then took place.

CHAPTER XXVII

AN OLD VETERAN UNDER "STONEWALL" JACKSON IN THE BATTLES AROUND RICHMOND NO. 2.

DEAR FRIEND:

When we reached the top of the hill referred to in the last chapter my company, with the balance of the left wing of the 15th Alabama opened fire upon the enemy which were down the slant on their knees about fifty yards away. We sent such a shower of "Buck and Ball" at them through the bushes and smoke that it left many of them *hors de combat,* and at the same time we received a shower of minnie balls from them that caused several of my company to fall, while others sttaggered and reeled, and went to the rear wounded. Those of us that was not hurt set up a yell, fell upon our knees and loaded and fired in that position as fast as we could. Our company officers were diligent in their duties, encouraging the men by their examples and ordering us to aim low that we might not overshoot and waste ammunition. There was so much smoke that it was only occasionally that we could see the enemy, but we knew he was there by the hissing of his bullets, and the wounding and killing of a man occasionally. We could very distinctly tell when the Yankess would receive reinforcements by the increase of their bullets and their cheers, but the storm of lead that we were constantly pouring at them prevented them from advancing any nearer than their front lines. The yelling and cheering of the Confederates, the roar of small arms, and thundering sound of artillery was so great that I could only tell when I had fired my gun by being punched (kicked) by the breech against my shoulder or jar by the stock against my right cheek bone. I loaded and fired so fast that the barrel of my gun became so hot that I thought it dangerous to pour powder in it, and laid it down and picked up another that had been dropped by a wounded man and used it until mine cooled off. While I was loading, firing and hollowing hurrah boys, "give it to 'em," I would look to the right occasionally and through the smoke would catch a glimpse of our colors fluttering in the breeze, when I would feel cheerful, seeing them maintain their position. While in this position, loading and firing, some in my rear fired off their gun so near the right side of my head that for a moment I could not realize what had happeded, didn't know but what I was wounded, as there was a stinging sensation on the right side and the back of my neck, so severe that it caused me to rub with my hand. I was considerably stunned for a few moments, and the stinging about my neck was caused by grains of powder which was of such force as to penetrate the skin. A great many of them have been picked out since the war, and while it has been forty-four years since the occurrance several grains are visible under the skin of my neck today. When I recovered from the shock I drew back my gun to strike the fellow that did it, accompanied by an exclamation that I will not repeat here, and with a hasty apology the blow was stayed and we continued to load and fire. We were good friends and bore no malice toward each other. He was a good soldier, served through the war, and has long since crossed the line and I am still living to record the occurrence. As well as I remember it was about 2 P. M. when we opened fire upon the enemy and there we remained firing as fast as we could for two or three hours. It was reported to the officers that we were running short of ammunition and details were made and sent to the rear for a new supply, but after using all we had or could get from the boxes of the dead and wounded, we run short before the details returned. I would not shoot away the last round I had, but kept my gun loaded for a case of emergency. While in this condition waiting, we lay flat upon the ground, the battle still raging on the right and left with great fury. The bursting shells, scattering their deadly fragments, together with the solid shot, crashing through the trees, tearing the limbs off made our position extremely perilous, and it would be necessary sometimes to run out of the way of a falling limb. While in this condition General Ewell rode up in our rear with hat in hand, when he was met by our 1st Lieut. J. A. Oates, who informed the General the cause of our inaction. The General told him to fix bayonets and hold his position until he could send for the Texas Brigade to reinforce us. We had already fixed bayonets, ammunition was the thing most desired at that time. The detail with ammunition arrived soon after General Ewell left, and we commenced in a hurry to refill our cartridge boxes. About the time we got through filling we looked down the hill in our rear, and there came the 4th Texas, half bent as if looking for a turkey. We greeted them with a cheer that they responded. They marched up to our position and halted, rectified their line, fired one volley down the slant through the bushes at the Yankees, when they were ordered to cease firing, reload and fix bayonets. The firing from the Yankee's infantry had become slack, but the ten-gun battery, four or five hundred yards in the rear was shelling us vigorously, which was an indication that they were preparing to advance on us, or was expecting an attack from us. While the Texans were getting ready, our officers anticipating an order for a general charge, began to rectify our line and be ready. There was so much smoke that you could only tell an Alabamian from a Texan by a badge or kind of gun he carried. The Texans were armed with short Enfield rifles with sabre bayonets, and we with smooth bore muskets. All being ready, the command "charge" was given, we raised a yell and dashed down the slant pell mell, (the Texans and right wing of our regiment bearing to the right), yelling all the time, expecting a hand to hand encounter when we reached their line, where last seen, but instead of a hand to hand engagement as we expected, when we reached their line numbers of them lay dead or too badly wounded to be moved. There was the result of a two or three hours engagement with "buck and ball" when well directed. We were out of the smoke then, and we could see them from fifty to one hundred yards in front, scattered and running for dear life. They had lost their organization in their retreat, and we had lost ours in pursuit. We kept up our yelling and firing and swept grandly on. The path of their retreat was marked by the dead and wounded. I don't remember any of my company to have been killed or wounded in this charge. There was no skulking with the officers and men. Forward was the word from every officer and private. It seemed that the boys tried to see who could yell the loudest, run, fire and load the fastest. I will relate an incident of this charge that happened with myself and Calvin Kirkland, of my company. We happened to be together at one time in the charge, both running and yelling, when all at once there was smoke out of a gun from behind a pine tree about 25 yards in front, both of us saw it, and as soon as the gun fired, a Yankee dashed off in a run to escape, we both raised our muskets, and having a fair shot at his back, we both fired at the same time, when down he fell and lay still. Calvin looked at me and asked if I fired. I said yes, did you? He replied yes, and we got him. We passed close by him and paused long enough to see several bullet holes in the back of his blouse. We hurried on, and all at once Calvin stopped, looking at something under a clay-root, it proved to be a Yankee that had crawled under there for protection, but had left his feet exposed. I left Calvin talking to him. It was said that Calvin told him to come out, for he knew he was there by his feet, and it was with some difficulty that he got out; he was scared hal fto death, and Calvin told him to go to the rear, which he did. The sun was not more than one hour high and the canopy of smoke was so thick that the sun was gloomily red in the heavens. The Texans had charged somewhat to the right, and they, with other troops, had about this time encountered the ten-gun battery of the enemy, and was making a desperate effort to capture it. The enemy after a stubborn resistance had been driven that evening from every position taken and this was his last stand, and it was known by our general officers that if they could be driven from that position the victory for that day would be complete. While this heavy fighting was going on over the battery other troops of Jackson's Corps was sweeping down from the left driving everything before them, while my command was driving a disorganized rabble in the center. About sundown the firing slackened, a yell was sent up, and it was known that the battery had been captured. Some of the troops that had been advancing on the left proved to be Alabamians. If I remember right they were of Wilcox's Brigade. They were on top of a hill trying to form line. I and others of my command got mixed up with them. Their field officers were on their horses giving commands, some making speeches and such a yelling and tossing of hats I had never heard or saw before. I actually thought, from the number of dead and wounded that I saw that evening, that the war was ended and that I was glad that I was there living to see the end, but that proved to be only a beginnig with me. In my line of advance I came across a line of knapsacks that had been abandoned by the enemy, and on my return when I reached them, I stopped and opened one in search of a shirt. I found what we soldiers called a "biled" shirt with cuffs and collars which I had no use for, so I laid them aside. I also found a revolver and an opera glass, which I also laid aside but I have always been sorry that I didn't keep the glass, for I needed it the next morning to look at Low's baloon. I passed through a part of our battle ground picking up two well filled Yankee haversacks. I soon found a part of my command where they had gone into camp, and we began to talk of those that had been killed and wounded. I don't remember but two that was instantly killed and four wounded. Two of those that were wounded are still living, J. H. Whatley and C. C. Stone. The killed were Sam Dickerson and George Byrd. There might have been others killed or wounded but I don't remember. I examined my haversacks and found them rich with hard tack and bacon, a sack of ground coffee, with a string of dried apples about two feet long in each sack. I made my supper on hard tack and bacon. Our camp was in hearing of the groans of some of the wounded that had been left lying on the battlefield. I was tired and nearly exhausted. It had been so warm that evening that I had sweated so much that there was hardly a dry thread in my clothes. I had hollowed so much, that when I cooled off my throat become so sore that I could scarcely swallow, but as tired as I was, I with some others took a light and went to some of the wounded that was calling to their comrades for help. The first one I found was a Louisianian with one thigh broken. He was lying on the ground within three feet of a wounded Yankee shot through the bowels. He was delirious, but could call for water and his mother, "O Mother." Poor fellow, I was sorry for him; I gave him water and turned him as well as I could on his blanket and spread his "gum" over him to protect him from the cold dew. I also fixed the Louisianian as comfortably as I could, giving him water also and leaving plenty with them to keep them from perishing for the want of it until they could be removed the next day. I was so tired and worn out that I left them alone in the dark and returned to camp and went to sleep; was up early the next morning ready. Some of the boys were sitting by the fire smoking and telling the events of the day, while others were sound asleep. I claim the honor, if honor it be, of being the first one of Oates' Company to fire a gun in this engagement. The gun referred to in the preceeding chapter that I fired at the red legged Zouaves in the road, was in my opinion the first. Well, my dear friend, these things happened on the 27th of June, 1862, more than forty-four years ago. Who will be here 25 years from now to tell of this days victory for the Sunny South? I have no idea that it will be me.

CHAPTER XXVIII

AN OLD VETERAN UNDER "STONEWALL" JACKSON IN THE BATTLES AROUND RICHMOND
NO. 3.

Dear Friend:
After the hard day's battle o fthe 27th you may be anxious to know what we did on the 28th. Listen: Without the aid of a diary, or record of any kind, it is impossible to tell half of the things that did occur on these memorable days of the war around Richmond, the Capital of the Confederacy, but as I sit alone with my mind concentrated on the events of these bloody days of my past life, I have to write of things as I remember them. Well, as well as I remember I rose early on the morning of 28th rather cold with stiffened joints, caused by heat and exertion of the evening before. I hied away to a spring near by and laid off my old dingy, dirty shirt and with the free use of soap, water and towels, I rid myself of about ten days accumulation of dirt, when I donned my "biled" shirt that I mentioned in the preceeding chapter. It was new, had never been worn, starched and ironed, and was as white as snow, and I had no coat to hide it, as the weather was so warm that I had throwed it away three days ago, and was going into these

battles with my shirt sleeves unencumbered, with nothing but a Yankee gum and a half tent fly, (the old soldiers know what they are), a well filled Yankee haversack, full of good rations, a conteen of water, a good gun and plenty of ammunition; that was all I wanted. My shirt was so white that it was the subject for many remarks, some of which was so suggestive that it would have caused a "milk and cider" sort of fellow to have wanted to get rid of it, but my strong and unfaltering belief in the doctrine of predestination caused me to wear that shirt, though white as snow, without fear, it made no difference. After cleaning up I went back to camp and found some of the boys up, but many still asleep taking their rest. I was up early, for I wanted to get in shape for the fight that I expected that day, so I was greatly improved by my cleaning up, and my ailments were soon forgotten. About sunrise reville was sounded and we attended roll call. There were several absent, but I can't remember who now. Needham Murphy, a brave and noble hearted young man of my company was not able to rise and answer when his name was called, and he lay prostrate upon his blanket spread upon the ground there suffering the tortures of a burning fever which was caused by heat and over-exertion of the evening before. As well as I remember Captain Oates sent for an ambulance and had him carried to the hospital for treatment, and that was the last time any of us saw Need Murphy. We all liked him and was sorry to hear of his death. After roll call we began to make fires and make coffee and stew dried apples that we had found in the Yankee haversacks, with many other good things such as ham, soda and sweet crackers, with cans of condensed milk, presed vegetables to make soup, chocolate and green tea, and a great many other luxuries that I can't remember now. It was a feast with us then, but hush! the booming of cannon far to the right was heard, which was evidence that this was to be another day of carnage. The sun from the Eastern hills began to pour forth her rays of warmth, melting the cold dew that had fell during the night upon the dead and wounded that had been left on the field during the night, although every exertion had been made by our people to care for the wounded and bury the dead of both armies, and after working all night, many wounded remained to be moved and many dead to be buried. The care of the wounded and burying the dead

—6

was not our job, there were men detailed for that purpose, and our job was to be kill and wound some more Yankees or be killed or wounded by them, and as the booming of cannon and the sound of small arms began to increase far to the right, we knew we were not long to be kept waiting. See! yonder comes Colonel Canty on his charger. He commands "fall in." This done we move off left in front. We were carried through a part of our battle-ground where we got a better view of the damage we did the Yankees the evening before. We continued our march with the balance of the brigade, crossing a small branch, then ascending a hill in an open field, the position of the ten-gun battery of the enemy that the Texans, with the aid of other troops, succeeded in capturing the evening before. Here were evidences of a mighty struggle. The guns were still there with their brave defenders lying dead or wounded beside the wheels and under the guns where they were shot down or bayonetted by the Texans and Georgians. The last effort to recapture those guns was made by a brigade of Yankee cavalry, but the unerring aim of the Texans and Georgians was so effective, emptying so many saddles at the first volley that it produced a panic and they fled in confusion across the Chicahominy. I mentioned in the preceeding chapter the capture of this battery and I only refer to it now because our line of march of the next morning brought us over the ground and we became eye witnesses to the evidence of the struggle. While near this place about 8 A. M. a balloon was seen to ascend from the South side of the Chicahominy for the purpose of overlooking our position, when Captain Courtney of our brigade unlimbered two of his three-inch rifle guns and threw a couple of shells at him, they exploding near by, which made him come down faster than the boy did when found by the old man up one of his apple trees. We remained on this historic spot but a short while. It was ascertained that a few of the enemy still remained on the North side of the Chickahominy, and Ewell's Division, accompanied by Stewart's Brigade of cavalry, was sent to attack them, but upon our approach they fled to the South side, burning the bridge behind them. We moved farther to the left and seized the York River R. R. bridge to prevent a retreat in that direction. We formed line of battle, threw out skirmishers, and waited for the advance of the enemy, but he did not come that way. While here in line Colonel Canty rode in front of us as if on review, he observing my white shirt, called me by name and said, "You will be a conspicious object for the Yankees to shoot at today." I made no reply, but thought he would be as conspicious as I was, if he continued to ride that fine horse. The firing that we heard early in the morning had nearly ceased, and from the clouds of dust seen rising on the South side of the Chickahominy was evidence that there was a general commotion among the troops on that side. The abandonment of the road and burining of the bridge was evidence to us that no further attempt would be made to hold that line, and a way out of this trouble was anxiously sought for by the Federal Commander. My memory is not clear on all the movements made by us on that day. I know we were not engaged that day, but was kept moving around pretty much all day marching, etc., and halting near a railroad where the enemy had a depot of supplies. It was dark and drizzling rain, we were halted in the road and received no command but to "rest." When ordered to rest we broke ranks and began a search for a dry place to sit or lie down, but it was mud everywhere. I squatted at the root of a pine, spreading my gum over my head to keep dry, my musket resting across my lap. We had orders not to build fires or make a noise, but some of the men would cuss a little anyhow. We remained in that position all night, and I tell you dear friend I was glad when I saw the streaks of day began to appear in the East. The Yankees had been driven from every position taken, and the scene around this depot was evidence of a hasty retreat, for there were scores of barrels of ground coffee, sugar, rice, syrup, salt, tea, flour and meal and other things. Our haversacks were filled with everything that we needed, and the thing most desired was to move out of that mud. The fighting by some of the troops had commenced, and we expecting to be called on every minute. At last orders came to move and we did in a hurry, but before we reached the battlefield the Yankees had been driven again, and our advanced troops were in hot pursuit. We passed through the field where the dead and wounded Yankees lay thick and our folks were caring for them as fast as they could. I was taken sick and stopped, and when our Regimental Surgeon Dr. Rives came along, I reported to him and he prescribed for me, and he give me an unlimited permit to remain in the rear and come on when I got able to travel. I halted and my company soon passed out of sight in pursuit of the enemy in his retreat down the peninsula. I sat down by a pine, near by was a Yankee that had been wounded that morning, both his thigh bones had been broken and he was also leaning against another pine. He did not complain at all, but kept cursing our troops all the time they were passing. In conversation with him I ascertained that he belonged to the 2nd Vermont, and was the only abolitionist that I conversed with during the war. He was one of the bitterest kind. He was the only wounded Yankee that I saw during the war that refused to accept some favor that I could do. He wouldn't accept a drink of water that I offered; he hated me, and didn't mind to tell me so. He was a bad 'un. He was properly and humanely cared for by our people. I remained at, and around this place till late in the evening, when I started in the direction of the army. Going about four hundred yards I came to a camp of sick soldiers, where they were halting for treatment. I had plenty of medicine, with directions from Dr. Rives and needed no assistance from the doctors at this place. I remained there all night, and will reserve the balance for the next chapter.

CHAPTER XXIX

AN OLD VETERAN UNDER "STONEWALL" JACKSON IN THE BATTLES AROUND RICHMOND
NO. 4.

DEAR FRIEND:

I remained that night (the 29th) with a whole lot of sick soldiers, and the next morning the surgeons were busy examining the sick and loading the ambulances for the hospitals at Richmond. I was billed to go, but asked to be excused, telling the doctor that I was feeling better and would be able to go to my command in a day or two. There were plenty of nurses and doctors to give medicine and wait on the convalescent. During the day heavy cannonading and a low dull sound of small arms could be heard in the direction the army had gone. I could not help but feel uneasy, laboring under great suspense in not knowing how the battle was going, or knowing what command was engaged. I enquired of every one that passed from that direction and at last I received the glad tidings that Jackson's Corps had not been engaged. I was uneasy about my company and was fearful that my continued absence might create a suspicion in the mind of my captain that I was a skulker from duty, but Dr. Rives had reported my condition to my captain and he was somewhat surprised when I returned. About the middle of the P. M. Alf Dozier, of the Henry Grays and his brother Guss, of my company (the Henry Pioneers) came along, both sick and had passes to the rear. Guss, finally relieved me of my suspense when he told me that our company had not been engaged, but had been under fire without casualty. Alf was on his way to the camp of the 6th Alabama, where they had left on the 26th of June to join in the great battle of the 27th. Alf insisted that I should go back with him, and I consented to do so. All three of us reached his camp about sun-down. The tents, or a part of them, were still standing and myself and Guss stayed with Alf in his tent that night. Several of the 6th had been left in camp sick, not able for duty, and one of the Grays that I well remember was Lieut. A. T. Owens, who was left sick or was detailed for some kind of duty, I don't remember which, he knew me and my family at home, and he treated me very courteously. All during the day I was possessed with an uneasiness that I could not account for, and in the P. M. I resolved to strike out for my command. I made known my determination to Alf and Guss, but they insisted that I should remain until the next day and they would then go with me. No amount of persuasion or promises could deter me from my determination, I had resolved to go, and go I would. About 3 P. M. I struck out for my command, Alf and Guss following about a mile out. Heavy cannonading was going on away down the James River. We went up-stairs in a house that stood near the road and opened a window in the East end, and there remained for about one hour listening at the heaviest cannonading that had been heard since the war began in that part of the army. It proved to be the battle of "Malvern Hill," the results of which was not very favorable to the Confederates. It was the last stand that the Federals made on their retreat, until they finally reached cover under their gunboats at Harrison's Landing on the James. After listening as long as I wanted to, I became impatient and bid Alf and

Guss good-bye. I reached my camp that I had left the evening before and remained all night. Early the next morning, feeling first-rate, I prepared and ate my breakfast and started in search of my command. I made good time and was not by myself on this march, for there were others on the same errand that I was, hunting their commands. Late in the P. M. we began to come to troops in camp, and began to inquire for our commands. At last about sun-down I found my company and went forthwith and reported to my commanding officer, Lieut. C. V. Morris, who seemed glad to see me and was somewhat surprised at my speedy recovery. We remained in this camp but a few days when we took up the line of march in the direction of Richmond, passing through some of the battlefields where the Federals had made temporary stands on their retreat, leaving their dead on the field. Many of the dead were unburied and the stench was almost unbearable. The next day we passed through Richmond. The news of our approach, and the line of travel through the city had been made known in advance, and the people had gathered on each side of the street to welcome and cheer us on. The entrance of "Stonewall" Jackson's Corps into the city of Richmond at this time was an event that will never be forgotten by me. The ovation that we received from the old men and women, the beautiful girls and boys made each one feel himself a hero from the Shenandoah Valley under "Stonewall" Jackson. The patriotic heart of George Washington could not have been swelled with more pride when on one occasion they strewed his way with flowers, than did the hearts of Jackson's Corps when we marched through Richmond at this time. We marched through, and out about four miles northward and went into camp, but not to remain idle many days. This was about the middle of July and the balance of the year 1862 was stirring times with this old veteran.

CHAPTER XXX

AN OLD VETERAN UNDER "STONEWALL" JACKSON IN HIS SUMMER CAMPAIGN AGAINST THE FEDERAL GENERAL JOHN POPE
NO. 1.

DEAR FRIEND:

The seven days' battles around Richmond resulted in a complete victory for the Confederates over the Federal army commanded by General McClellan having ended, our corps was marched through Richmond and as I stated in the last chapter we went into camp four or five miles North of Richmond and only rested a few days. It was ascertained by our generals that another large Yankee army was organizing on the Rappahannock River in Culpepper County, for the purpose of advancing against Richmond on the line of the Orange and Alexander R.R. The army under McClellan, which had been defeated before Richmond, was known as the Army of the Potomac, and this new army that was organizing was known as the Army of Virginia, and was commanded by General John Pope, a braggart from the West. His first general order to his army declared war upon the noncombatants that remained in his lines, ordering the arrest of citizens and those refusing to take the oath of allegiance were to be driven from their homes, and if caught again within their lines, they would be treated as spies and be subject to the extreme rigor of military law. This order is amusing to any one who are familiar with all his defeats from Cedar Run on the 9th of August, clear on through several engagements including the last days of August on the plains of Manassas, where his defeat was so disastrous as to cause his retreat and finally his resignation. In some succeeding chapter I will tell of these engagements as I recollect them. But to return. To meet this demonstration that was gathering on the Rappahannock River, Jackson, with his corps about the 20th of July was ordered to proceed to Gordonsville, where he would be in position to check any movement that Pope might make until General Lee could reinforce him from Richmond. We marched to Hanover Junction and there boarded the cars for Gordonsville, when we marched out some five or six miles in the direction of Orange Court House, and went into camp. We privates were perfectly ignorant of the situation of affairs, not knowing what was in store for us a few days later on. We had a fine camp and drill ground, good water, good health and a plenty to eat. Our camp was in the midst of wealthy and patriotic citizens. There were three families near together by the name of Graves. One of them was a widow lady about 50 years old who had two sons in war. She had a great deal of personal property around her premises that needed protection, and she made an application for a guard, and fortunately for myself, I and Mose Maybin was detailed to guard her premises. She lived some three or four miles from camp, and when we reported we asked her for orders, she told us to make ourselves at home, eat our meals with her at her table and keep the foraging class of soldiers away from her bee-gums, chicken-roost and corn-field, which were at that time in roasting-ear, or nearly so. Some of the soldiers had been pulling them and she wanted that stopped. In connection with this guard duty I will relate a singular circumstance that happened; though strange, 'tis true. Every morning after breakfast we made our rounds of her cornfields, returning and going again at ten, returning at twelve. One day while on our second round we met a fellow with a sack of corn just pulled. We arrested him, took his corn away from him, took his name, company, regiment and brigade. After all this he began to inquire what we were up to and what we meant. We told him our orders and that he could go, we would only report him to his captain. He began to beg, making all sorts of promises and Mose and myself become sympathetic, promised him we would not report him if he would tell others what they might expect if they were caught in that corn-field, and for that to be his last offense. He promised faithfully and we didn't report him. His name was Solomon and belonged to the 9th Louisiana Regiment. The strange part of my stry is that we met again after the war, some time in the 70's. While sitting around one of my neighbor's cane mill one night with several of the neighbor boys chatting and chewing cane, a gentleman came out from supper, introducing himself as Mr. Solomon. He took a seat near by, and pretty soon began to talk, telling his old war stories. I became interested in him and asked him what army he belonged to, corps, division, brigade and regiment. He said he belonged to Lee's Army, Jackson's Corps, Ewell's Division, Taylor's Brigade and the 9th Louisiana Regiment, and also his company, but I have forgotten now. I looked at him closely and imagined that there was something about him that I could recognize, and ventured to ask him if he was with the army when it was in camp near Gordonsville just before the battle of Cedar Run. He said yes. "Did you ever see me before," I asked. After looking at me closely he replied that he did not remember. I asked him if he was the Solomon that two soldiers arrested coming out of Mrs. Graves' corn-field with a sack of roasting-ears about the second of August, '62. He looked astonished, laughed and said yes, and went on to tell how kindly he was treated by them two soldiers and said they were Alabamians and belonged to Trimble's Brigade. I then told him that I was one of them boys. He gathered me by the hand and seemed proud to see me. He again looked at me closely and said that "your eyes are familiar, but you had no beard then, I would never have known you again." He inquired of me about the other fellow, Mose Maybin and seemed to regret it when I told him that he was killed at Sharpsburg. Solomon was a traveling sewing machine fixer, and I have never seen him since that night. In a day or two after that I and Mose was called into camp, and regretted very much that we could not remain with Mrs. Graves longer, as we were having such a good time. We moved our camp near Roberson's River, a tributary of the Rapid Ann River, where we done picket duty at Liberty Mills, on said River a few days before we marched to attack Pope, then in camp around Culpepper Court House, about twenty-five miles away.

CHAPTER XXXI

AN OLD VETERAN UNDER "STONEWALL" JACKSON IN HIS SUMMER CAMPAIGN AGAINST THE FEDERAL GENERAL JOHN POPE
NO. 2.

Dear Friend:

We had not been in camp on Roberson's River but a short while before a promiscuous detail was made to go on picket. I being the next man on the roll for such service, was told by my orderly to report to Seargeant (I have forgotten who), who was to command the detail that was to go on picket. There were eight or ten in the squad and we marched off in the direction of the enemy, crossing the bridge just above Liberty Mills. A cavalryman who was our guide informed us that the Yankees was not very far off, their reserve being in camp at a place called "Jack's Shop" some three or four miles in the direction of Orange Court House. After marching about a half mile we turned to the left and ascended a long hill, reaching an abandoned dwelling house from which we had a fine view of the surrounding country, especially up the road in the direction of "Jack's Shop." On reaching the house on the hill our cavalryman charged us to keep a sharp look out and be on the alert, for an advance by the Yankee cavalry was momentarily expected, and that we only had a few cavalry in our front to watch their movements. The next thing to be done was to establish a picket post, and advanced vidette. One man of our squad was detailed and the picket post established down on the side of this road, some two hundred yards from this house, the place of the reserve. It was getting late, the sun was nearly hid. We remained on this duty undisturbed until the next evening. The place selected for our vidette post was an admirable one for our secretion, but in plain view from the house on the hill. The roadbed was some five or six feet below a level, and we had a plain view of about one hundred and fifty yards up the road in the direction of "Jack's Shop," when the road made a curve to the right, which could be plainly seen from the house where the reserve was. It came my time again to go on post from 2 to 4, and as well as I remember about 3 o'clock the carbines in the direction of the enemy began to crack. I thought something was going to happen and I began to feel chilly, being down there so far off from help alone. I kept a close watch up the road, all the while drawing on my imaginations. Presently I saw two of our cavalrymen coming slowly, looking back occasionally. They came slowly on until they arrived opposite where I was concealed in the jam of the fence, they did not see me until I spoke, when they told me to look out, the Yankees were advancing, and they passed on toward the bridge. It was then up to me to look, and I did look too, first up the road and then up the hill where the reserve was. The chill got harder, imaginations become more rapid, how and what was I to do when the Yankees come along there, was what was flitting through my mind. I looked and looked, wondering, I couldn't run, I would be obliged to stand. I did not fear capture when my help at the reserve was so near, unless there were too many for us, and in such an event I thought I would be notified in time. I was in a bad fix then. Look out! Some one said up on the hill; I was watching and not asleep, I was too chilly for that. I fixed myself; I knew that something was going to happen, and something had to be done. There he comes, "a boy in blue" riding slowly, looking cautiously on every side, I was watching and had my mind made up what to do and say. I was ready, kept my eye on him all the time, he came slowly on until within about fifty yards he halted, turning around in his saddle and said in a low voice, "Come on you——cowardly scamp." More behind, thought I. The reserve upon the hill was watching all this, but they kept concealed and said nothing. (I thought to myself, I have the advantage and I am going to keep it.) He started again and came slowly on. I let him pass me a little when I rose quickly with my musket cocked, finger on the trigger, the breach against my shoulder aiming at his right side when I stormed out at him to surrender. He saw at a glance the situation. There was no time to parley and what he had to do had to be done quickly. He had his carbine in his hand with the breach resting on his thigh. He lost no time in throwing it down and dismounting. He then unbuckled his belt that had his sabre, cartridge box and a fine Remington 44 calibre revolver attached. While all this was going on I kept my aim on him, giving him no advantage. I made him hang all those things on his saddle and march off eight or ten steps, which he did. I croseed over the fence, mounted his horse and rode him to camp, keeping the Yankee well in front. Just about the time that I mounted, the other Yankee that was following fired at us, and from the noise of the bullet it went wild in the air. I traveled in a double quick until I arrived at the bridge when I met another detail going to relieve our squad. and I never went back to them. I don't know who took charge of the Yankee, but the quartermaster took charge of the horse, gun and sabre, allowing me to appropriate the revolver to my own use, which I did by selling it to Lieut. H. C. Brainard. That horse stayed with our regiment a good long time. Captain Oates soon became a field officer and the quartermaster furnished him this horse to ride. I don't know how long he kept him, but he could stand the roar of small arms and the bursting of shells without flinching. I ascertained that the captured Yankee belonged to the 1st New Jersey Cavalry commanded by Colonel Joseph Karge, of Bayard's Brigade. Perhaps I may meet him some time. From some cause the Yankees did not advance in force, they only advanced their feelers far enough out where we were and after ascrtaining that fact they fell back in the direction of Orange Court House. Jackson was anxious to attack Pope, but felt too weak with only his and Ewell's Division. He had kept General Lee informed as to his and Pope's strength and his desire to attack and asked General Lee for reinforcements, when Lee sent Gen. A. P. Hill with his division from Richmond. There were daily clashes between our cavalry and that of the Yankees on the Rapid Ann and around Orange Court House, which generally resulted in favor of our cavalry. General Hill having arrived with his division Jackson lost no time in preparing to advance toward Culpepper Court House where Pope was. On the 7th of August, my 18th birthday, we broke camp and began to advance. We made slow progress that day, camping near the Rapid Ann, not being allowed to make fires in order to conceal our advance which the enemy could easily see from his signal station on Clark's Mountain. On the morning of the 8th our advanced cavalry drove in the Yankee pickets, and we began to advance slowly. Our cavalry pursued the enemy's cavalry on the dirt road from Barnett's Ford to Culpepper Court

House, (or near there) and was followed by the Infantry, our division leading. The Yankee cavalry on this day displayed unusual activity and Lawton's Brigade of Georgians were detailed to guard the wagon train. This kept them from participating in the battle of the next day, known as the battle of Cedar Run or Slaughter's Mountain, which I will tell about in the next chapter.

CHAPTER XXXII

AN OLD VETERAN UNDER "STONEWALL" JACKSON IN HIS SUMMER CAMPAIGN AGAINST THE FEDERAL GENERAL, JOHN POPE.

No. 3.

DEAR FRIEND:

The battle of Cedar Run (on Slaughter's Mountain) was fought on the 9th of August. This was an exceedingly warm day, and our progress was slow. Late in the afternoon, arriving in about eight miles of Culpepper Court House, we found the enemy's cavalry strongly posted near Cedar Run, a short distance west and north of Slaughter's Mountain. General Jubal A. Early with his brigade of Virginians, was the leading brigade of our division, followed closely by ours, and the Louisiana brigade. As soon as the enemy were discovered our batteries came to the front, and a few well directed shots caused them to retire. As soon as their cavalry retired they threw forward a long line of infantry skirmishers, followed by heavy reserves. In the meantime Early had thrown forward his skirmishers, and were following with his brigade as a support. While all this was being done each side was bringing new batteries into play, and a regular artillery duel ensued, and at the same time the enemy was extending his right by throwing large bodies of infantry in that direction. The battlefield of Cedar Run was not a level plane, the ground was hilly and undulating, with an occasional clump of cedar on the small hills. There was a wheat field with shocks of wheat standing which gave the Yankee skirmishers some protection for awhile. Our brigade, the 15th Alabama leading, moved off to the right, along and near the base of the mountain, keeping our movements concealed until we could arrive at right angles to the enemy's left. In this movement it was designed by our Brigadier General (Trimble) that after gaining the enemy's left, the 15th Alabama would swoop down on him with such suddenness and terror that would double his left back on his center, and at the same time with a heavy pressure upon his right by the other troops would cause him to sing the old song, "Right about boys, skedaddle." We gained our position and had a splendid view of the battle, and had a golden opportunity of crushing the enemy's left, but could not do so on account of our own shells. General Trimble dispatched his couriers to General Ewell informing him of our condition, but there was no relaxation in the fire of our guns at that time, the battle was raging in the center and on our left. The enemy had succceded in extending his right so far until he had flanked the left of Jackson's old division, and bore down upon them with such a force as to cause confusion in some of his brigades, but A. P. Hill arrived about this time with his division, throwing forward three or four of his brigades against the advancing enemy, which put a check upon their ardor, which caused them to turn and flee for safety. After this repulse of the infantry the last effort to retrieve the fortunes of the day was made by a charge of the Yankee cavalry upon some of our infantry. This charge upon our infantry was met with great firmness, and the slaughter was so terrible as to cause those living to escape the best they could. The battle never commenced in earnest until about 5 o'clock, and from then until sundown it raged with great fury, when about that time the Confederates began to advance and press the rear of the Yankees on their retreat towards Culpepper Court House, where the main body of Pope's army lay. The firing of our own artillery that had hindered our advance no longer existing, our brigade advanced en-echelon of regiments, the front being covered with skirmishers from the 15th Alabama Regiment. It was growing dark, and the enemy discovering our advance threw forward a battery, and opened upon us with canister that wounded three men of our regiment. Had this battery remained in position five minutes longer we would have certainly captured it, for our Brigadier General was on his mettle chaffing under disappointment for not having an opportunity to assault the enemy's left which lay so fair before us, while the battle was raging in plain view in the center and right of the enemy. The battery limbered up and moved off in the darkness, just in time to escape notwithstanding our rapid pursuit. Darkness found us in possession of the ground occupied by the Federal left, where some abandoned ambulances, wagons and ammunition fell into our hands which was removed the next day. The Federal troops that engaged us that day were commanded by the Federal General N. P. Banks, who bore the soubriquet in that day and time as being Jackson's commissary, and it was camp rumor that Jackson was glad of the opportunity of meeting his old valley adversary with his wagons well filled with army supplies, and that it did not take any great amount of parleying between Jackson's and Banks' men before an agreement would be made that Jackson's men should have the rations. It was a general thing, when we tackled Banks we got rations. Here I will leave General Banks with a routed corps to be mentioned later on. With the close of this day the battle of Cedar Run was ended, another victory for "Stonewall" Jackson's corps was added to the pages of history. Jackson was anxious to keep right on in pursuit until he reached Culpepper Court House and our brigade through the darkness led the advance, advancing about one mile it was ascertained by Jackson that McDowell's corps and other troops had arrived as reinforcements to Banks. He ordered a halt and we went into camp in the Yankee camp grounds. The next day the 10th, we took position and remained all day waiting for an attack, while others were removing the wounded, collecting the small arms from the battlefield, and burying the dead. Late that evening we moved somewhat to the rear and went into camp. The next morning the enemy sent in a flag of truce asking for a cessation of hostilities until 2 o'clock, that they might bury their dead that had not been buried by our men. The request was granted, and the time finally extended until 5 o'clock. We remained in our position until near night when we returned to our old camp near Gordonsville, only to remain a few days before starting on that memorable march, which for rapidity, boldness and daring, is without a parallel in the war between the States.

CHAPTER XXXIII

AN OLD VETERAN UNDER "STONEWALL" JACKSON IN HIS SUMMER CAMPAIGN AGAINST THE FEDERAL GENERAL JOHN POPE

No. 4.

Dear Friend:

After the battle of Cedar Run, it was ascertained that the enemy was being largely reinforced, and Jackson withdrew his corps and went into camp near Gordonsville, where he hoped that the Federal General Pope would follow, and attack him in this position. Jackson could have been reinforced by General Lee from Richmond, who was watching the movements of McClellan down on the James. General Lee was not slow in penetrating the design of the enemy for his movements were such as to insure him that they had abandoned their design upon Richmond by the Peninsular route and was breaking camps and transporting their troops around by Alexandria for the purpose of reinforcing Pope at Culpepper Court House. General Lee knew what was going on among them, and he accordingly began to draw off his forces to reinforce Jackson, in order that he might defeat Pope before he could be so heavily reinforced from the army of the Potomac. About the 13th of August General Lee arrived with a sufficiency of forces as to enable them to attack Pope at once, and he and Jackson formed their plans to advance. On the 16th the troops began to move from the vicinity of Gordonsville towards the Rapid Ann River. Our advance was to the north of the Orange and Alexandria R. R. in the direction of Culpepper Court House, where Pope's army lay in great force. General J. E. B. Stuart having arrived from the Peninsular it was planned that he, with his cavalry, should proceed to the rear of General Pope, destroy the railroad bridge across the Rappahannock, and Longstreet and Jackson were to attack his left flank. Orders were issued for this movement to take place on the 18th, but the necessary preparations not being completed by that day its execution was postponed until the 20th. The Federal General, by some means became aware of Lee's designs and hastily retreated across the Rappahannock. In the advance our corps crossed the Rapid Ann at Summerville ford, and moved toward Brandy Station, on the O. & A. R. R., halting for the night near Stephensburg. The day had been hot and sultry, and our march had been rapid, and we were tired when night came on. We were anxious to halt and rest, but we had to march two or three hours after dark, and at last we came to a large old field where each regiment was marched out to the left its full length, when we were halted, stacked arms, and ordered to camp in the rear of our guns, and down we lay on the ground. Each brigade was closed en-masse by regiments and by that means our division occupied a very small space. Lawton's brigade of Georgians were close by in our rear, and it mattered not how tired a fellow was, there was always some soldier ready to start some mischief to have fun, and this camp was not an exception to the rule, for at a late hour when all was still, and asleep, some fellow in the 31st Georgia began to hollow at the top of his voice, Wo! Wo! where are you coming? Wo! Stop that blind horse. Others began to hollow Wo! Wo! exclaiming, head him! head him! Several rose up, asking "What is it?" "What is it?" when some one answered it's a blind horse loose in camp. Stop him! Stop him! The excitement became so great among them Georgians until some would imagine that a blind horse was really going to step on them, and would rise up in such a hurry, often with their blankets over their heads hollowing Wo! Wo! Some of them became so frightened that they knocked down their guns where they were stacked, and others at a distance would hear the guns rattling, would think that the blind horse was stumbling over them. The noise waked me, and I soon discovered that it was over among the Georgians, and I lay still until all the excitement was over, then the laughing began, but they were not all laughing, it was not so funny to some of them. Some were cursing and wanted to find and know the fellow who started it. I saw Ed Roach the next day, and I asked him what was the matter over in his camp last night, and he told me all about it, and we laughed heartily. It rather makes me smile now when I imagine just how it was. Ha! Ha! At early dawn the next morning, we were formed in line awaiting orders to march, but before marching our brigade was closed en-mass by each regiment being formed in close column of division, and our Brigadier sat on his horse in the midst of us, and there addressing us as his "Lads" informed us of the hazardous undertaking that lay before us, and what he expected of us, and what we might expect of him, and the probable results that might follow. We were no longer in doubt, and soon orders came to march, and we started off in the direction of the Rappahannock. On our approach near the river we were greeted by a shell from the enemy who occupied a strong position on the opposite side, which commanded the position on our side, and we began to move up the river as if searching for a crossing that would turn the enemy's right. Our artillery and that of the enemy would keep up a regular duel across the river, while our infantry unobserved kept moving slowly on up. Each position that our corps would take would be occupied by some of Longstreet's troops as soon as vacated by us, and we would proceed further on up the river. All the while the enemy on the other side of the river, would keep pace with our movements, and would shell us at every point exposed to their view. This kind of movement was kept up until the 22nd when it was ascertained that Sigel of the Federal army, had thrown a brigade across Hazel River (one of the tributaries of the Rappahannock) to support a force of cavalry that had been sent over to attack our wagon train. This movement was well known to Jackson, and he ordered General Ewell to detach one of his brigades to meet this force while he moved on up the river with the balance of his force seeking a place to cross. Our brigade was ordered to halt to meet this movement, and in the afternoon reconnoisances were made, and by verbal information their position was fully ascertained, and upon the arrival of General Hood with his brigade as a support, our Brigadier ordered us to attack, which we did which was so sudden and furious, that they fled after the first volley, we pursuing, firing and yelling, until they came to a small stream; in they plunged, crawling up the bank on the other side to be shot in the back and fall backwards in the water. That was fine sport for this boy then. 'Twas here that we killed their Brigadier General Bolin. Those that lived hastily sought protection in Sigel's camp under his guns, and we were not molested by their dashes any further. As well as I remember not a man in my company was hurt, but old Company "G" surely did hurt the Yanks at this place, as our opportunity was so fair. The fight being over we withdrew leaving the position in the hands of General Hood, and we proceeded on up the river in a hurry to overtake our division which was some distance ahead. During the 23rd and 24th there were continual clashes between our batteries and those of the enemy across the river. The river was so swollen by the heavy rains which prevented our crossing at the place first selected, consequently Jackson had to seek another crossing. In pursuance of the plan of operations agreed upon by Lee and Jackson. Jackson was directed to cross above Waterloo, and move around the right of Pope's army so as to strike the O. & A. R. R. in his rear, getting in between him and Washington City. This was a movement attended with great danger, but in that day and time there was nothing too daring for "Stonewall" Jackson with his foot cavalry to undertake to do, especially when directed by the masterful mind of R. E. Lee. Longstreet was to divert his attention, by threatening him in front, and follow us as soon as we were sufficiently advanced. Our corps cutting loose from the balance of army crossed at Hinson's Mill 4 miles above Waterloo, passing through the little village called Orleans, camping for the night near Salem after a long and fatigueing march. The days were hot and sultry but we had divested ourselves of everything that would be a hindrance to a rapid movement and with an abiding faith in our commander, coupled with an unfaultering belief in the justness of our cause, we felt like we were superior to anything we had to meet. This was our first day's march to get in Pope's rear.

CHAPTER XXXIV

AN OLD VETERAN UNDER "STONEWALL" JACKSON IN HIS SUMMER CAMPAIGN AGAINST THE FEDERAL GENERAL JOHN POPE

No. 5.

DEAR FRIEND:

After a hard day's march on the 25th we reached the little village of Salem, about two hours after dark. We passed through the streets as quietly as we could, and went into camp on the left of the road, making as little noise as possible. We stacked our guns and were ordered to rest in the rear and as near to them as possible, with orders to be ready to move at a moment's notice. We spread our gums and blankets and laid down to rest. I had not been resting but a few moments before I heard our Adjutant tell our Orderly to detail one man for picket duty, and report to Lieutenant Brainard, who was detailed to command. I become uneasy at once, fearing that I was the next man in order for that kind of duty, and sure enough the Orderly called my name. I answered and rose up promptly buckled on my cartridge box, folding and throwing my gum across my shoulder, and taking my gun from out the stack, I reported promptly to Lieutenant Brainard. There were ten or twelve others beside myself for that duty. In a few minutes when all had reported we marched off very quietly up a public road conducted by one of Stuart's cavalry officers. When we halted he told Lieutenant Brainard that that was one of the main roads that led to Washington City, and that the enemy's scouts had been seen in that direction that evening, and he need not be surprised if he were attacked before day, and keep his men wide awake, and not be surprised. On hearing that, it had the effect to drive away all desire to sleep. I was jumped up, and had forgotten all about being tired from the long hot day's march, and I was about as watchful as any of the others. Two men were put on post at the time, alternating every two hours. It came my time from two to four, but before I had served out my time, two of our cavalrymen came out to us with orders to Lieutenant Brainard to call in his Videtts, and go to his command, the cavalrymen took our places. We soon reached camp and our command was all hustle and bustle, getting in line making preparations to move. Our squad was disbanded, and each one of us ordered to report to our respective commands. With the first streaks of the dawn of day, orders were received to march, Ewell's division leading the corps, and the Louisiana Brigade, followed closedly by ours, leading the division. After leaving Salem that morning we diverged to the right crossing Bull Run Mountain at Thoroughfare Gap. Our passage was undisputed and we made rapid progress that evening, passing many beautiful homes that had been made desolate by the execution of General Pope's infamous orders that he issued to his army when he took command at Culpepper Court House, the substance of which has already been referred to. This day's march completely turned the right of Pope's army, and he was so stupefied that he was not aware of the fact until the middle of the afternoon, when he hastily about faced and after committing several blunders in the issuance of antagonistic and peremptory orders to some of his corps commanders, he began to try to extricate himself from his perilous position by a retrograde movement toward Washington City. 'Twas late in the afternoon that we passed through the little village of Gainesville, where Jackson was met by General Stuart, who had by another route made a rapid march with some of his cavalry to overtake us. He guarded Jackson's right flank that evening, and with a part of his cavalry guarded our rear that night. The day had been warm, and sultry, the roads dry and dusty, and the mixing of that dry dust with perspiration caused a very unfavorable comment on our appearance by a lady in Maryland a few days after that, which I will refer to later on. It seemed as the sun turned, and was lowering himself toward the western horizon—our pace was quickened, sometimes double quick and sometimes in a run to keep up. About sunset we came to a little creek; there was no bridge nor no way to cross in a hurry but to wade. Our Brigadier sat on his horse near by and in his good kind way spoke words of encouragement, calling us his "lads" and telling us to hurry, "wade right through, my lads," there is an important job for you just ahead. We were now nearing Bristoe Station on the O. & A. R. R. We were now clearly in the rear of Pope and on his line of communication with his capital. Presently we heard the whistle of an approaching train coming from Warrenton Junction down where Pope's headquarters had been that day. The Louisiana Brigade that had been leading that day formed line parallel with the railroad track and gave her a broadside as she passed, while that was going on we were rapidly approaching but arrived too late to fire on the first train. Some of our cavalry had preceded the Louisianians and had charged upon the depot, capturing nearly all the Yankees that were around the place. They also cut the wire which completely severed the communication between General Pope and his Capital. When my brigade arrived the command, "On the right by file into line," was given, and we were ready for the next train. Myself, T. M. Renfroe and others tore up a rail on an embankment that was about four feet high, and just about the time we got it torn up we heard another train coming from below, regardless of anything, not dreaming of what was in waiting for them at the depot. As soon as the engine became opposite the right of the Louisianians the firing began; the whole brigade gave her a broadside in passing. Our regiment was formed on the left of the Louisianians and as soon as she got opposite our right we peppered her side until she reached the place where the rail had been torn up, when the engine leaped headlong from the tracks burying the pilot, and front trucks in the ground clear up to the head of the boiler. The engineer and fireman were killed. Several Yankees were on the train wounded. Some few escaped in the darkness on the other side. Listen! There comes another train. See! There is her headlight, don't fire on her, for she will be compelled to stop. Sure enough she run with full speed into the rear of the train which had just preceded her, and such a piling up of freight boxes I had never seen before and don't want to see again, but it was fun for me then, it was war, and that was what I was so crazy to leave home for. The other trains from below took the hint and didn't venture, but were destroyed the next day to prevent capture. There was a wounded Yankee officer brought off the train and laid on a blanket by a fire, and he was greatly astonished when he learned that it was Jackson's troops on the ground. He wanted to see Jackson and in a short time Jackson came walking along and Capt. Oates pointed him out. The Yankee expressed surprise at his appearance. By the time all this was over it was growing late. Manassas Junction with her immense amount of supplies was only four miles away, and its capture was one of the grand features of the expedition, and our Brigadier volunteered his services for that job. All those that are living, that were on that march that day, will never forget the closing scenes of that night around Bristoc Station. But what about tomorrow? See next chapter.

CHAPTER XXXV

AN OLD VETERAN UNDER "STONEWALL" JACKSON IN HIS SUMMER CAMPAIGN AGAINST THE FEDERAL GENERAL, JOHN POPE.

No. 6.

Dear Friend:

After the capture of Bristoe Station and the wreck of the trains, there was a calm, and General Trimble, who had volunteered to capture Manassas, proceeded up the railroad quietly through the darkness to execute the desire of the Commanding General, taking only two regiments of his brigade, the 21st Georgia and the 21st North Carolina, leaving the 15th Alabama at the station with orders to clear the track of the wrecked cars. The officer in charge de-affairs, on examination reported it to be impossible for us to clear the track of the wreckage with the means at hand, and consequently the project was abandoned, and there was nothing for us to do but to either go on to Manassas or remain there the balance of the night. I was anxious for the latter, for I was almost exhausted, for the want of sleep and rest. In a short while we were ordered out to the rear a short distance, and break ranks and rest, but be ready to move at a moment's notice. We threw ourselves upon the ground, and in a few moments we had passed into dreamland perfectly unconscious, and indifferent as to what was going on at Manassas or what might take place on tomorrow. It was about 12 at night and a little sleep was what I needed. The long day's march of the 25th, the loss of sleep at Salem, and the long hot day's march to Bristoe Station the next day, coupled with the excitement, and fatigue around the station, began to have its effect on my power of endurance, but all this was known only to myself. I was in perfect health, had plenty of rations and ammunition, two commodities that no soldier likes to be without, especially the latter for by its proper use we could get all the rations we wanted. "Uncle Sam" had been very liberal in furnishing these commodities of war, but not without displaying some displeasure, and would offer resistance to such an extent that some of the "Boys in Blue" and some in "Grey" would get bit by the same kind of snake, and after a spirited controversy, the "Boys in Blue" would say, "Take them, your government is poor, ours is rich, and we can get plenty more." There was an immense quantity of these things stored at Manassas that General Jackson wanted, and he had sent General Trimble to capture them. We rested undisturbed until early dawn of the morning of the 27th, when our Orderly came around waking us up, saying get into ranks, we have orders to move. We formed promptly, and were not long kept waiting for orders to move. When orders did come we marched toward Manassas, and we soon learned that General Trimble had captured the place and that he wanted us to go to his assistance at once to aid him in holding the place, should he be attacked by superior numbers which was then threatening him from the direction of Washington City. We were followed by the 12th Georgia, which had the night before been transferred to our brigade. We arrived at Manassas about sunrise. General Trimble met us and put us in position to resist an attack. It was not long before details were made from each company to get bacon and crackers, coffee, sugar, rice and everything else in the way of rations that a soldier needed, for they were there in great abundance. Poor Yanks, we were then feasting on what "Uncle Sam" had intended for them, but that was one of "Stonewall" Jackson's ways. Each man was supplied with just as much as he could carry. Marches had been so continuous, bacon and crackers so plentiful that we had quit cooking, and had broken up the "Mess" plan and had paired off in two's and three's. I had formed a partnership with Barnett Cody and in supplying myself with rations it became necessary that I should have some way to carry my turn. I was not long in devising the means. I procured a good Yankee knapsack and put a 25 pound side of bacon in one side, and Barnett seized on to another knapsack and put in about 20 pounds crackers, besides these we had as much coffee and sugar as we wanted. We didn't take any rice or beans, for we had no time to cook. The other boys, in fact all that wanted to, supplied themselves the same as we did, as there was nothing short in the quantity, and all had an equal showing. There was an immense amount of government stores of every description. Long trains were switched off on the side tracks that contained clothing for Pope's army, all of which went up in smoke upon our evacuation. General Jackson arrived upon the ground shortly after we did, and I saw him when he met General Trimble. He extended his hand and congratulated him for his success. The sun was about one hour high when the Federal General Taylor was discovered with his New Jersey Brigade advancing to recapture Manassas. He was just from Washington, and had disembarked from the cars just across Bull Run, about three miles away. He was perfectly ignorant as to the force he was advancing to attack, and came gallantly on until in range of the artillery in the forts which had been turned and were now manned by our men. They opened upon him with such deadly effect and at the same time he was attacked by some of our infantry, together with some of Stuart's cavalry that they become panic stricken and demoralized, and their retreat became a complete rout and a great many of them were killed or captured. General Taylor himself was mortally wounded, and Jackson said of him in his report of this affair, that this advance was made with great spirit and determination, and under a leader worthy of a better cause. On the arrival of General Hill's division they, too, supplied themselves with all they could carry. General Ewell with three brigades of our division had been left at Bristoe Station to watch and retard the progress of the enemy who were fast approaching in great numbers to "bag Jackson and the whole crowd," for such was one of the boastful orders of General Pope to General Kearney. In the afternoon General Hooker of Pope's army arrived with his division, and lost no time in forming and attacking Ewell's division, but failed to drive him from his position. Ewell held him in check, until Jackson could ration all his men, that were present, and load all of his available wagons, and appropriate to our use everything that we could carry, after all this being done preparations were made to destroy the balance. When all this was accomplished, Jackson ordered Ewell to withdraw with his three brigades and come on to Manassas, which he did while under fire, without being pursued. When they arrived at Manassas, they helped themselves to everything they wanted. We joined the division. Our brigade was sent in pursuit of the fleeing New Jersey men as far as Centerville, when we were recalled, and camped somewhere between Manassas and Centerville. The next morning our division struck out for Centerville passing our old winter quarters abandoned in March, crossing Bull Run at Mitchell's Ford. We halted near Centerville and remained there till in the afternoon. I don't know what route the other two divisions of Jackson's corps were marching. I only remember that when we left this place we took the Warrenton Pike re-crossing Bull Run at the Stone Bridge. I felt all right then, and was at my best; was good rested and had lost my desire for sleep. The sun was lowering behind the Western horizon, and our march had become so spirited that we were not mistaken in guessing that something was going to happen in front, and our presence was necessary. Boom went a cannon, followed in quick succession by others. What did it mean? It was in our front, between us and Longstreet, but where was Longstreet? He was left on the Rappahannock on the 25th and was to follow us as soon as we had advanced far enough to keep out of his way. It was the guns of Longstreet trying to force his passage at Thoroughfare Gap. General Ricketts of the Federal army had been sent there with his division to guard the Gap, but Longstreet outflanked him and came on. The fact was that our march had been such and was made with such rapidity that we were in a perilous position, but this was only known by the general officers. The march had been such as to place Pope's army between us and Longstreet, and we were between Pope and Alexandria only 20 miles away, where McClellan was landing his forces to reinforce Pope. He had already sent him two of his corps which augmented Pope's force to about sixty-five or seventy thousand men, but "Jackson and his whole crowd" were not to be "bagged" by Pope. Jackson's old division commanded by Brigadier Taliaferro, unbeknowing to me, was in the advance, and had met the enemy's advance in the road near a small place called Groveton. Taliaferro left the main pike turning to his right when Jackson, who was watching everything, saw a favorable opportunity to attack and proceeded to do so with Talioferro's division. It was growing dark and our division was hurried forward as reinforcements. Our brigade was immediately deployed and thrown into action, and notwithstanding the darkness of the night it was the most sanguinary engagement for the length of time my company was in during the war.

CHAPTER XXXVI

AN OLD VETERAN UNDER "STONEWALL" JACKSON IN HIS SUMMER CAMPAIGN AGAINST THE FEDERAL GENERAL, JOHN POPE.

No. 7.

DEAR FRIEND:

The fight that occurred that night was very obstinate by the enemy, not lasting more than an hour. The position of the left wing of the 15th Alabama was in a thick clump of bushes, covering a space not exceeding four acres and was very rocky. Our march, in line of battle which was preceeded by a line of skirmishers, led through this clump of rocky woods until we reached an old dilapidated fence that skirted it on the opposite side. Our skirmishers had halted at the fence and were firing on the enemy, which were only a short distance in front. The space in front was clear, but the night was so dark that the "Boys in Blue" could not be seen or located only by the flash of their guns. The command of their officers could be disticly heard. Our officers were giving orders pretty loud, and I guess the Yankees heard them. They must have heard General Trimble for it seemed to me that he could have been herd a mile away when he commanded "Forward, guide center." I have never heard as loud command before nor since. The enemy in our front proved to be the 2nd Wisconsin, Gibbon's Brigade, King's Division. I have seen somewhere that it was styled the Iron Brigade. Although dark, they had our range as well as we had theirs. We could locate each other by the flash of our guns. Their position was out in the open, ours behind the old fence referred to. We were not over fifty yards apart, and our casualties were heavy considering the time engaged, but there was no comparison in losses between our command and that of the Yankees. During the engagement word came from somewhere to cease firing, that we were firing on our own men. This order was repeated to our company by 1st Lieut. C. V. Morris, of our company. I remember distinctly telling him that they were not our men for I could see the brass buttons on their coats by the flash of their guns, and they were certain to be Yankees to be firing on us, and if they were not I had killed some of our best men. Lieutenant Morris made a personal examination for himself when he became convinced and ordered us load and fire, which we did until they ceased firing on us and withdrew. The fire from the Yankees was rapid and heavy. They literally tore the old rotten fence into fragments; a rail was no hindrance to one of their 56 calibre bullets shot from an Austrian rifle. Here, in a very short time, my company lost five good men killed, to-wit: T. M. Barnes (Mats), Jones Hickman, Calvin Kirkland, Lot McMath and Alonzo Watson, and several wounded, some severely. There might have been others killed, but I don't remember, as I am only writing from memory. My position in line at this fence was in the immediate rear of Alonzo Watson. We were both on our knees, he firing through a crack, and I firing over the top of the fence. I stood as high on my knees as possible in order to rest my gun on the top rail, my left elbow was at one time resting on his shoulder when all at once I heard a "thud" and felt a ja rand poor 'Lonzo began to relax and sink, exclaiming in a low tone, "Oh Lordy, I am a dead man." These were his last words, life soon became extinct, but I didn't move but kept loading and firing until the fight was over. We moved our position a little to the rear and rested for the night. Our dead and wounded were all moved during the night, the dead buried and the wounded carried to the hospital in the rear. I well remember the brightness of the sun the next morning as he came up from the East, casting his rays of light over wood and dale, and over the bivouacs of the contending armies. We built small fires and made coffee, and made our breakfast off bacon and crackers, for they were plentiful. There was no breeze to scatter the smoke, and it went straight up through the branches of the small trees. This smoke located our position to the enemy, and presently here come a shell crashing through the bushes. I heard it strike the bushes, and looking in that direction I saw it coming toward us smoking, as if it were about to explode. It had hit the ground before it reached the bushes and had partly spent it's force and was coming slow, and could easily be seen. Others saw it and several yelled "look out," and every one of us fell flat to the ground. As it happened every one of us fell out of its range, and when it struck the ground it exploded, scattering its fragments in every direction above us, and no one was killed, only one man in my company being hurt. Mose Maybin, his legs being slightly bruised, caused by fragments of rocks that were scattered around when the shell exploded, though it did not disable him from duty. There were a half-dozen or more cups of coffee sitting on the little fire, and the shell exploded so near that it scattered the coffee in every direction, and we missed that for breakfast. It damaged my old musket to such an extent that it was unfit for use, a thing that I did not regret, for I had been wanting to get rid of it for some time and was determined to do so if I could get hold of a good rifle, and my captain did not object. On several occasions I had felt that I was overmatched by the Yankees in the way of arms and ammunition, and I was anxious for a change. After the explosion of the shell the fires were all extinguished, and the shelling ceased in that immediate locality, but some desultory cannonading and sharp-shooting was going on to the left of our position. Before leaving this place I obtained permission to go out in front of where we had fought the night before, which was but a short distance. When I reached the Yankees position I saw the effects of our fire upon them. The 2nd Wisconsin was in the immediate front of the 15th Alabama and their line of battle could be easily traced by the dead and wounded that lay upon the ground. They were commanded by Colonel O'Connor, who fell mortally wounded in this engagement. I felt confident that I saw him that night on his horse among his men, I shot at him once, but don't know the effect. As I have already said, they were armed with Austrian rfles, carrying a 56 calibre minnie ball, I now availed myself of the opportunity sought of changing guns, and I picked up the best looking rifle I could find, and supplied myself with a bountiful supply of ammunition to suit. When I returned to my company, Captain Oates made no objection to my gun and was very anxious, and had made repeated efforts to have his company armed with rifles. As the sun rose to two or three hours high the booming of cannon and the cracking of small arms began to increase. Staff officers and couriers were dashing around, which was a pretty sure sign that something was going to happen. We were soon formed and moved by the left flank. General Ewell had been seriously wounded the night before and General Lawton was commanding the division. He formed the division in line of battle on a ridge paralel to an unfinished railroad, which ran through that section. The movements of the enemy had caused Jackson to change his line somewhat, and so as to form it on, and paralel of this old unfinished railroad which was an admirable position for defense. In conforming to this new position our brigade was hurriedly moved to the left, moving along the line of the old railroad. Sometimes we would be protected by being in a cut, and at other places we would be shelled and shot at with small arms like all fury, until we would pass the exposed points. In passing these exposed points is what I term passing the fiery ordeal, in fact, and at one place I hesitated and stopped in a cut, preferring to wait until the fire slackened in front. Sam Gardner, of Co. "I" stopped with me, and we remained together until the regiment passed and the firing had ceased. We consulted together as to which one of us should make the break, for we knew that on our first appearance a shower of balls would be sent at us. I finally consented to make the break first, and we eased along to the starting point unobserved, when I "ducked," with gun in one hand and hat in the other, I ran the gauntlet. It seemed from the volley that a whole company might have fired at me, but they missed their mark and I was soon under cover. I stopped and looked back at Sam and laughed at him and told him to come through; he hesitated, and I finally told him that I could not wait any longer and hurried on to my command which had halted not far away and was formed behind the embankment waiting and expecting an attack, as the skirmishers in front were hotly engaged and the Yanks reported to be advancing in heavy force. About 3:30 P. M. they assaulted A. P. Hill's Division on the extreme left wing with a heavy force, but was repulsed.

CHAPTER XXXVII

AN OLD VETERAN UNDER "STONEWALL" JACKSON IN HIS SUMMER CAMPAIGN AGAINST THE FEDERAL GENERAL JOHN POPE
NO. 8.

Dear Friend:

The heavy assaults that were being made on A. P. Hill's Division, who occupied the left of Jackson's Corps were met by his troops with great courage and obstinacy, and each assault was repulsed with great slaughter. In order that the reader may comprehend and understand the positions of our troops at this time I will say that A. P. Hill was on the left, Ewell in the center and Jackson's old division on the right. Now you have our position. The line of battle was along an unfinished railroad, each division, of course, had its own reserves. It seemed to be the full determination of the enemy to crush Jackson before Longstreet could arrive, but at this time while all those heavy assaults were being made on Jackson, Longstreet's troops that had forced their way through Thoroughfare Gap, the evening before, were in hearing and coming with quick step to succor their overtasked comrades. There were but two brigades of Ewell's Division, our's and Lawton's, that were on the front line at this time, the other two, Early's Virginians and Taylor's Louisianians were in the rear as our reserves, to be put in when necessity demanded. The heavy assaults made upon A. P. Hill having failed, the enemy doubled his forces and attacked our position with great determination and vigor. Our skirmishers in front that had been so hotly engaged all the P. M. finally yielded to overwhelming numbers and come running in, closely followed by a line of battle. They came hurrahing and huzzahing as if they thought that would cause a panic among us, and that we would run. We were true and tried veterans of Jackson's Corp, and no such racket as that could run us away. Our position was a good one for defense, and we were determined not to yield it unless the officers so ordered. Here came their first line, and when in range we give them a volley, they halted and lay down flat upon the ground. On came the second line until they reached the first and they halted. The third line came hurrahing until they reached the others that had preceeded them, and they halted. Our fire was so fast and accurate that they could not be made to advance any nearer and the fire was so fatal that it caused them to become one intermineable mass of humanity, and the efforts of their officers to get them to advance had no effect and they would do nothing but retreat. But they did not lose hope nor cease their effort to break our line. They would form with fresh troops and advance again and attack with great determination to break our line, but we were not to be broken. With all their hurrahing and great display of bravery we were not the boys to be run away from that position. Attacks of this character upon Jackson's line continued 'till dark, each attack being repulsed with great loss to the enemy, but while these attacks were being made upon Jackson late in the P. M., the advance division of Longstreet's Corps, commanded by General Hood, arrived on the right and rear of Jackson, near Gainsville, where they were met by General Stuart, who put them in posession of all the facts regarding the positions, and conditions of things generally, when Hood with his division followed by others, filed to the right to meet a demonstration then being made by the enemy on Jackson's right. Hood was not long in finding the enemy, and with his accustomed vigor proceeded to attack at once. The attack was made by the gallant Texans, assisted by troops just as brave from Southern States. The attack by these troops was of such spirit and determination that the Yankees gave way at every point, and darkness put a stop to this conflict for this day, August 29th. The arrival of Longstreet was being anxiously looked for by us, and it did not arrive a whit too soon, for the heavy and incessant attacks that had been made on us had been so frequent, and with heavy odds against us that I could not help but feel a little uneasy for fear he would break our line somewhere; but after each assault the "Rebel Yell" could be heard which was animating and was always accepted as a signal of victory and tended to restore confidence. The news of Longstreet's arrival was published along the line, and was greeted by the "Rebel Yell," which was heard by the defeated Yankees. I don't remember that my company lost a single man in this whole day's fighting; we were well protected by being behind an old railroad embankment, and there was no part of us exposed except our heads, although my memory may be at fault, some one might have been wounded or killed, and have escaped my memory, not impossible. Night coming on, the battle ceased, we remained in our position, resting on our arms during the night amid the dead and wounded of the enemy who lay in heaps a few paces in front, the wounded most piteously calling for help, but conditions were such that none could be rendered by either side. An awful night it was, never to be forgotten by me, and I do hope, dear reader, that you may never have such an experience as I had that night. Americans against Americans.

CHAPTER XXXVIII

AN OLD VETERAN UNDER "STONEWALL" JACKSON IN HIS SUMMER CAMPAIGN AGAINST THE FEDERAL GENERAL JOHN POPE

NO. 9.

DEAR FRIEND:

The battle on the 29th of August on the plains of Manassas was not a decisive one, but was yet to take place. The Federal general was quick to boast, and unscrupulous in his dispatches; he had already telegraphed General Halleck, the commander-in-chief at Washington, that he had won a great victory, and was master of the situation, when in fact he had not gained a foot of ground, and all his heavy assaults upon our line had been repulsed with heavy loss. After each assault and repulse of the enemy they would be followed by our skirmishers until they would halt to reform. Our skirmishers would engage their skirmishers when they attempted to advance. When the night came on the enemy ceased his attacks and went to making preparations for a renewal of the battle the next day, the 30th. Our skirmishers had followed them so closely that when they halted the commands of their officers could be distinctly heard and understood, which left no doubt of a certainty that they intended to renew the battle at early dawn. They had heavy reserves that had not yet been engaged,

—8

and it was those troops that they were putting in position to assault us at dawn. All these things that were taking place in front were made known to our officers and they made all preparations that was necessary to be in readiness to meet them in the morning. Such as rectifying our line, and having us furnished with a bountiful supply of ammunition. There was not to be anything short about that, every man to his place, and when the enemy came he was to keep cool, load, take good aim and fire. I considered at this time that an inexaustible supply of ammunition was one of the first necessities, and rations the second; for with plenty of ammunition and it accurately expended, I could get rations, when upon the other hand, without ammunition I would have to run and devour what rations I had on a retreat. See? I still held on to my Austrian rifle and replenished my shortage in ammunition out of the cartridge boxes of the dead Yankees that used calibre 56. By 11 o'clock all preparations for the morrow was made, and it was comparatively quiet along the main line, but in front on the picket line a desultory fire between the pickets was kept up all night, firing at the flash of each others guns. There was a sentry kept on watch on the embankment of the railroad for the purpose of giving the alarm should a sudden attack be made on our skirmishers in front, but none occurred. When we received orders to rest, we spread our "gums" or blanket on the ground and laid down, and there in silence I remember to have breathed a silent prayer, rendering thanks to God for his protecting care over me during the day just closed, and asking a continuance of same tomorrow. I was tired and weary and it was some time before I could go to sleep. I was disturbed by the cries of the wounded "Boys in Blue" who lay just over the embankment in front. As I lay "ruminating" over their condition I could not help but have sympathy for them in their unfortunate condition, I drew, in my imagination a picture of my self in their condition, far from home, no one but an enemy to look to for help. They had obeyed the commands of their offcers, and had fought us bravely and had met their fate like men, just as we would have done had we been in their places. As the morning of the 30th broke we were quietly aroused from our slumber and got under arms. Some of the boys made small fires and went to making coffee, and our breakfast was of bacon, crackers and coffee. As the light from the East lifted her mantle over the field it was discovered that the skirmishers were from one to two hundred yards apart, and the firing began in earnest. The cannonading along the whole line commenced, which betokened the approaching contest. Our whole corps maintained its line of the previous day, and Longstreet, also far to the right held his position of the evening before. Another one of Longstreet's Divisions arrived that morning and was held in reserve. About 8 o'clock A. M. our orderly was called on for a detail of one man to go to the front and relieve the skirmishers who had been out since the evening before. It was not my time to go on skirmish, but being armed with a rifle, and the orderly knowing that I preferred that kind of fighting to any other, did not hesitate to detail me, and I did not hesitate to go. There were similar details made from each company, and we were deployed in front of the railroad embankment, and advanced to the positions of our skirmishers. They were hotly engaged and it was a dangerous undertaking to reach them and equally as dangerous for our skirmishers to withdraw. On our arrival at the proper place, I took position behind a tree and began to put in some good shots with my Austrian. It would pop like a small cannon and was a subject of remark by my captain which I will refer to later on. The "Boys in Blue" lay flat upon the ground content with holding their position and keeping us employed. For a good part of the day the action was fought with artillery. Our artillery was admirably posted in our rear, and having obtained an accurate range of their heavy masses of infantry, their fire was the most destructive of any previous engagement during the war. An advance of their infantry was momentarily expected, for they were in plain view in our front, and their movements could be seen which had every appearance that an advance was soon to be made in heavy force. The Federal General Pope had at last succeeded, after many blunders, to organize his forces by putting Heintzleman's Corps on his extreme right, and McDowell's on the left, while the corps of Porter and Sigel with Reno's Division was to occupy the center. About 3 P. M. he had completed his formation and a general advance was sounded. Boys! look out, they are now coming! The bugler in our front sounded, first, attention, then the advance, which they did in rapid style. Their position was in an open field, our's in the woods and behind trees, and I tell you, reader, when they came within easy range we dotted the ground with them, but others were sent to fill their places, until their skirmish line became to be a solid line of battle closely followed at a run by other lines. No amount of killing and wounding we could do would check them. The grand and desperate assault was on, and they seemed determined. We had to retreat; they didn't give us time to fire in retreat, but come on rapidly, firing volleys into the woods and huzzahing all the time. But stop! Somebody is not far away and is hearing all this, waiting and ready to give them a warm reception. When I reached the embankment I just naturally fell over among our men and about faced. "Look out boys, they are coming, lots of 'em." The boys were ready, but by some cause unknown to me they failed to attack all the front of the 15th Alabama, but seemed to have divided, a part obliqueing to the left and a part to the right. That which went to the left could not be seen, but on the right they were in an old field in plain view, and the whole of the 15th Alabama got in some deadly work at a right oblipue. They just simply jammed up against the embankment, opposite the right of the 15th Alabama and one of the Louisiana regiments. They were so thick that it was impossible to miss them. Cicero Kirkland, of my company, who is living today, in his enthusiasm and reckless bravery, mounted on top of our breast-work and poured buck and ball into them as fast as some of the boys could load and hand him a musket. I expected to see him shot down every second. The Louisianians ceased firing and threw cobble stones over the embankment at them. I saw them going over lighting upon the heads of the Yankees just as thick as I ever saw corn go into a pen at an old time "corn shucking." It was more like that than anything that I can compare it to. Doubtless you may not know what an old time "corn shucking" is as the Southern farmers have long since abandoned the practice. Ask an old time darky, he will tell you all about one. But to return, they advanced and attacked our line in closed column of division, (an old soldier knows how thick that made them) and they were in plain view of Colonel, now General, S. D. Lee, who at that time was in command of about twenty-four pieces of artillery which was posted on a cannonading hill in our rear, where he could play upon them from start to finish, or until they would get near enough for the small arms, and it would be dangerous to fire over our heads. What a slaughter! what a slaughter of men that was. At first bomb-shells, sharpnel shells, then grape-shot, and as they came nearer canister was poured at them which mowed them down, but still those that lived would close the ranks and press forward. I don't remember just how many stands of Stars and Stripes I saw in this mass of troops. They would go down often to be raised again by some one else. The pressure was so heavy that I saw the 13th Virginia coming in a run to reinforce this part of the line. When they reached the embankment they never halted, but crossed over right in the midst of the "Boys in Blue." This was a sublime spectacle to gave upon. The Virginians and New Yorkers engaged in a deadly strife contending for the mastery of the situation. I saw Virginia's colors dip several times at the Stars and Stripes. I could plainly see the motto of Virginia, *Sic Semper Tyrannis* that was inscribed upon their flag, and no one knows but myself the feeling it created in me, to see these colors so close together dipping at each other, and the men falling around them. The Virginians were assisted by Louisianians and Alabamians, and it was not long before a general stampede among the Yankees took place, and some few that lived escaped, but the slaughter among them had been great. This attack was made by some of the best troops in Pope's army, Porter's Corps. While these attacks were being made on Jackson, Longstreet's troops on the right were crowding them upon their center, and upon the general giving away of the enemy in front, Jackson ordered his whole line forward, driving the enemy before us. Longstreet about this time, anticipating an order from Gen. Lee for a general advance, threw forward his whole command against the Federal left and center, and swept grandly on, putting the enemy to rout from each stand made by them, causing another stampede in their efforts to cross Bull Run at the memorable Stone Bridge. Longstreet's forces engaged the enemy on a part of the old battle-field of 1st Manassas. Our advance was slow and cautious. We contiuned the advance about one mile, meeting with no resistance. It was dark, the pitiful cries for help from the wounded "Boys in Blue" far to the right could be heard, but there was no time nor opportunity to render assistance. We were halted, stacked arms and lay down in the rear of them to rest for the night, August the 30th, the balance I will tell in the next chapter.

CHAPTER XXXIX

AN OLD VETERAN UNDER "STONEWALL" JACKSON IN HIS SUMMER CAMPAIGN AGAINST THE FEDERAL GENERAL JOHN POPE

NO. 10.

DEAR FRIEND:

In reflecting over the latter clause of the last chapter, my mind wandered back to the scenes of this particular time and place, and there are a few things that I remember that came under my observation that I wish to tell before I pass from the events of the 30th, to that of the 31st, and I will begin by saying that the last attack that the enemy made upon our position was with such numbers and with such a determination to crush us, that the pressure become so great as to cause Jackson to ask Longstreet for reinforcements, but Longstreet in speaking of this affair afterwards said, "That from an eminence near by the masses that were attacking Jackson were in plain view and within easy range of batteries in that position and that it gave him an advantage that he did not expect, and he made haste to use it by ordering up several batteries and began to enfilade their line, which proved to be so destructive that it was evident that the attack upon Jackson could not be continued ten minutes longer, and he made no movements with his troops toward reinforcing Jackson." This may not be *verbatim et literatim*, but is the substance of his report of this affair. The "Boys in Blue" had made heroic efforts to crush us and break our line by increasing their strength to five, yea ten to one, but we "Boys in Gray" were fully determined in the defense of our position, it mattered not what numbers were brought against us. The boys in blue could not stand the resistance they met in the front from the small arms and the enfilade fire from the artillery into their left flank, throwing grape-shot, cannister-shot, solid shot and bursting bomb-shells of every description, dealing death at every step, producing scenes of carnage that was horrible to behold. This was the last attack made on our line on the evening of the 30th, and as I said in the last chapter, a general stampede followed and a few of the living escaped. I mean to say, that this was the conditions of things in our immediate front, for it looked to me from the heaps of dead and wounded that lay on the ground that there were but few that escaped. After this repulse the small arms in our front ceased, but our artillery in the rear played upon the retreating fugitives with deadly effect until they went entirely out of sight and range, when their artillery began to reply, though feebly. In a few minutes after this repulse we heard a great yelling on our left down among the troops of A. P. Hill's Division. All eyes were turned in that direction and was anxious to know the cause. The yelling came nearer and nearer until it struck the left of our division, and at last around the curve of the old R. R. a man on a horse was seen coming in a slow gallop, with head bare and a cap in his hand in acknowledgement of the cheers that were being given, and as he approched some one recognized him and shouted that's "Stonewall" Jackson and we went wild with enthusiasm, throwing our hats in the air and giving the "Rebel Yell" at the top of our voices. He came on top the railroad embankment mounted on "Old Sorrel" in a slow gallop, followed by one courier. He was dressed in an old dusty, dingy, faded gray uniform with the legs of his pants stuffed in the legs of a coarse pair of boots. Three faded stars and a wreath that he wore upon the collar of his coat was the only mark that distinguished his greatness. He did not go far before he halted, and with raised cap in hand, he hollowed out at the top of his voice "Attention." All was ready in a moment, when he in a sharp shrill voice commanded "forward," and at the word we dashed over the embankment and moved on slowly and cautiously. Our advance lay through a piece of woods about one hundred yards wide, when we came to a large open field. The firing on the right over on the Warrenton Turnpike was of the heaviest character. This was Longstreet's forces driving the left wing of the enemy on to his center. They swept the enemy before them from each successive position. It was the most sublime and thrilling scene that my eye had ever beheld. As far to the right as the eye could range the Southern Cross could be seen fluttering in the breeze and the bayonets glittering in the sun when they would emerge from a scope of woods into an open field. We could hear the "Rebel Yell" which was evidence that the

"Boys in Blue" was on the run, and the "Boys in Gray" were in hot pursuit. When Longstreet's troops were giving the finishing strokes on the right our corps in solid line were slowly advancing, the front well covered by skirmishers, for the purpose of attacking them in flank should they attempt to cross Bull Run at Sudley Ford. They had become so demoralized that they had lost their organization and had but one object in view, that was to cross Bull Run before Jackson could overtake them. There was nothing in our front, but as I have said before, away to the right the battle was raging with great fury. Long streaks of smoke was curling over the tree tops, wafting away on the evening breeze and as the sun was setting the last stand made by the enemy near the "Henry House" (of the 1st battle of Manassas fame) was broken and the Yankees fled precipitately leaving their dead and wounded on the field. Our whole front was the brillant spectacle of a victorious army in pursuit of what might be correctly termed a demoralized and panic sticken rabble, but the darkness of the night put an end to the pursuit and by 10 o'clock quiet prevailed all along the line, except now and then a shot from a scout could be heard. On several occasions during this day, (the 30th) there were scenes of close encounter, and a more murderous strife never before occurred on American soil. Taking it all in all, this was a grand day for the Confederates. The timely arrival of Longstreet's forces on the right, relieved us from the pressure of overwhelming numbers, and give us a chance of a more equal contest. The firing having ceased and the advance halted, and as I said in the preceding chapter we stacked our arms and rested in rear of them that night. I was greatly fatigued and slept soundly, with nothing to disturb me except groans of wounded "Boys in Blue" that lay about on the ground. The doctors and litter bearers were busy all night doing what they could for suffering humanity. When we awoke the next morning the 31st, it was ascertained that the enemy had retreated to Centerville, where he was met by the army corps of Sumner and Franklin, said to number nineteen thousand fresh from the army of the Potomac. General Stuart kept General Lee so accurately informed as to the movements, positions and conditions of the enemy that General Lee made no mistake. Centerville is a small village about 20 miles from Washington City, and was well fortified, and it was in these fortifications that Pope with his shattered and demoralized army took refuge, and halted long enough to issue a scanty supply of rations and ammunition to his men and began to reorganize to resist our advance. General Lee was in full possession of Pope's position and condition, that on the morning of the 31st he ordered Jackson to turn his position by crossing Bull Run at Sudley Ford. Before we started on this march, I with others from the regiment, were detailed for fatigue duty, and was ordered to report to some officer, I don't remember who now, and he took us back to our battle ground of the evening before. There we stacked our guns, and each man was furnished with a spade and we were ordered to bury the dead Yankees. I had never buried any one, and didn't know how, but I soon learned. I did as I saw others doing, that was to press their stiffened limbs together, getting them as straight as possible, then rolling them in a blanket and laying them as near due East and West as I possibly could, then spade out a hole about 20 inches deep their full length, then turn him in on his back and throw the earth on him. If he had no blanket, nor nothing else that I could wrap him in, I would put his cap or hat over his face to keep the dirt out. That was a terrible job for me. The weather was so warm, and some of them had been there two days, that it was with some difficulty that some of them could be handled at all, and I tell you, my dear reader, I could hardly endure it, but I had to. Orders them days, were orders and had to be obeyed. I guess there were a hundred or more engaged in that kind of work, while there were others engaged in removing the wounded. It did not take long to bury one, as the ground was soft and mellow, and was easy to spade. I suppose I buried as many as fifteen during the time I was there. That was a job that I was tired and sick of, and was glad when about the middle of the P. M. we received orders to go to our command, and we left a great many unburied. All our wounded had been carried to hospitals and our dead buried. Our command had moved, and we were late finding them. They had crossed Bull Run at Sudley Ford, and had taken a country road that led into the little river turnpike that leads in the direction of Fairfax Court House. When I reached my company, Captain Oates called me to him, and there told me for my gallantry and deportment in the skirmish and battle of yesterday he would promote me to be his 4th Corporal. This compliment was very unexpected, as I was not aware of the fact that I had done anything to merit it, and ventured to ask at what particular time, he remarked, "I was watching you on the skirmish and could distictly hear the rapid report of your Austrian rifle, and knew you were getting in some good work on the Yankees." I thanked him for the compliment and felt proud that my conduct had been such in all these hard engagements as to meet the approval of my commanding officer. Up to that time I had never thought of or sought promotion to any office; I was content to be a private, and as such do my whole duty to my coutnry. By this promotion my position in the ranks was changed. I now had to leave my old place and march at the foot of my company. I was then the "Little Corporal" of the Henry Pioneers. We did no fighting on the 31st and rested quietly during the night.

CHAPTER XL

AN OLD VETERAN UNDER "STONEWALL" JACKSON IN HIS SUMMER CAMPAIGN AGAINST THE FEDERAL GENERAL JOHN POPE
NO. 11.

DEAR FRIEND:

Our rest on the night of the 31st was one of quietude, all "calm and serene." We were away from the battlefield, out of hearing of the groans of the wounded, and being jaded, tired and weary, a good night's rest at this particular time was a great blessing, and I felt greatly refreshed when I rose the next morning and answered to roll call. As well as I remember my company was about sixty strong when we entered upon this campaign about the 20th, and this roll call revealed the fact that from various causes such as death, disabled from wounds and absent sick, we had about twenty-five or thirty to answer. The boys that were there present that morning had passed through three bloody days of turmoil and strife on the plains of Manassas, and there stood as living monuments of God's unbounded mercy, ready, at the command of Lee and Jackson to make another battlefield as horrible as any of the others of the last four days. The officers high in authority didn't seem to be in any great hurry, and we were given plenty of time to make coffee and eat breakfast. We had been no trouble to our commissary since the morning of the 27th, as our supply that we had provided ourselves with over at Manassas had not been exhausted, and besides that, we had had access to the well-filled haversacks of the dead boys in blue, so that there was nothing short in the ration department at that time. As the sun began to rise over the tree tops and pour his warm rays over the fields, the occasional boom of a cannon, and the familiar sound of the pickets rifle could be heard far to the right in the direction of Centerville. After a lapse of time we fell into line and began to march along the Little River turnpike that led in the direction of Fairfax Court House, a little town between Centerville and Washington City. Our march was slow, with frequent stops, lasting sometimes as long as an hour, as if to give time to our generals to locate the true positions of the enemy. We moved on in this way until we had fairly turned Pope's position at Centerville, and was just about to get in his rear again when he took the alarm and began to move his troops to prevent it. Our march was so slow that it was late in the P. M. of the 1st of September that we reached Ox Hill, better known to the 1t5h Alabama as Chantilly. The place was nothing more than where the road from Centerville intersected the Little River turnpike, where we had picketed during the winter of '61, and early winter of '62. On reaching this place we were halted in the road and were commanded to front," facing to our right in the direction of Centerville, when all at once the skirmishers that had been marching on a paralel with us all day was attacked. A. P. Hill's Division was in our rear, and when the firing commenced, he ordered three of his brigades forward to support the pickets. Our brigade, being the rear brigade of Ewell's Division, which preceeded Hill that day, was ordered forward also. We had not gone far before we met our skirmishers in retreat, closely pursued by the Yankees. In a short while the firing on the right by Hill's troops became extremely heavy for the numbers engaged. We were in a thick body of woods, so thick that we could only see a few yards in front, but the hissing bullets from the enemy as they came rapping the bushes and trees, and occasionally hitting a man, was evidence to us that they were not far away. We halted and delivered several rounds in that direction. During this engagement, a cold and drenching thunder shower swept over the field, striking us squarely in the face. The noise of the falling rain to some extent drowned the noise of battle. The commands of our officers could not be heard in some time, but notwithstanding the heavy down-pour of rain, we kept on firing until dark put an end to the conflict. The enemy ceased firing and we did the same. We were ordered to about face, and retire, which we did, going nearly back to the turnpike and camping for the night. I will here relate a strange incident that occurred while we were falling back from our advanced position to where we halted and went into camp. From the circumstance, it seemed that sometime during the evening, the enemy had been in possession of that part of the woods that we had advanced in, and in maneuvering around, one of them had dropped his watch, and in our falling back Daniel McLellan of my company hitched his foot in the chain and picked it up. It was a fine gold watch and chain and he sold it to Lieut. H. C. Brainard of our company for the sum of $130 in C. S. A. currency. Lieutenant Brainard afterwards sent it home as a present to his sister Laura, who after the war married Capt H. C. Reynolds. They are now both deceased, but have living children with us today, one of which is the owner of this same watch. Strange, but true. This battle was of no decisive result, to either side. The fact is that General Pope was so badly beaten that he was anxious to gain a little victory, however small, in order to cover his false dispatches that he had been sending to Washington from the field, and in order to do so he ordered his fighting "Joe Hooker," McDowell, Reno and Kearney's Divisions of Heintzleman's Corps to attack us, which they did, resulting to them the loss of two of their generals, Kearney and Stephens, the former a West Pointer and having the reputation of being one of their best division commanders. The attack that he made upon us at this time was with the hope that he might gain a little victory and thereby have something to support his ludicrous claim of having the victory, for such a claim had been made by him, after he had been driven from off the Rappahannock, on an on over the plains of Manassas, and with his demoralized army had sheltered himself behind the entrenchments at Centerville. The attack developed our position, and he realized at once his position and condition, and he telegraphed General Halleck at Washington that he thought it best under the circumstances that his army should withdraw to the entrenchments around Washington, and set to work to re-organize and re-arrange it, and that by doing so some disaster might be avoided, for he had no idea of the demoralization that existed among officers of high rank in the Army of the Potomac, arising form a personal feeling in relation to the change of commanders. The fact was he had sustained a most disastrous defeat, and was seeking an opportunity of laying the blame on one of his subalterns, which he succeeded in doing, resulting in the cashiering of one of the best corps commanders there was in the Army of the Potomac, retiring him from service, but after a lapse of twelve or fifteen years after the war ended, the case was re-opened by Congress, and upon an unprejudiced examination of the court marshal proceedings he was restored to full rank. In accordance with General Pope's wishes, General Halleck issued orders for his retirement to the fortifications in front of Washington, and Pope on the 2nd of September issued orders directing the routes to be taken by each corps. We remained in position all day the 2nd, expecting an attack, but none occured. When night came on I was detailed to go on picket. Mose Maybin was detailed as Sergeant and was put in command of the squad. I was Corporal of the guard which was my first duty as such. We proceeded down the Little River turnpike about one mile in the direction of Germantown, a little village not very far away. We were conducted by an officer on a horse, and arriving at a house we halted, and the officer instructed that two men should be put on post at a time, alternating every two hours. At a late hour I, with two other men were on post, when we heard some horsemen coming from towards the enemy, one was whistling. We let him come as near as our orders would allow, when I ordered him to halt. He laughed and said he had been expecting to be halted for some time, and that we could lie down and sleep, for there was no danger, the Yankees had retreated and were then safe within their entrenchments around Washington City. He lit from his horse and told us of his narrow escape that evening. He said "Boys, I got into a hornet's nest before I knew it, and I tell you I had to put spurs to escape." He was jolly and jovial, full of fun, and cracked several jokes, and at last complimented us on our victory, when he bid us good night and left us, to find General Lee and Jackson. This was no other than J. E. B. Stuart, our cavalry commander, we knew him at first and felt no danger of a surprise. There were no disturbance that night, there was not even the sound of a gun to be heard. What a change! But there was another venture lying before us, many more battles were yet to be fought. We had won the crowning victory in Virginia, the gates of Richmond had been freed from Federal soldiers and pushed back to the entrenchments of their own capital. Our adventures had been so daring and our achievements so great that the Yankees thought there was nothing too hazardous for troops of Jackson. I fell out with General Pope when I read his first order that he issued to his army when he took command down in Culpepper County, and if you have been a close reader of my letters on this campaign, you would have observed that I have been after General Pope all the time, and now, gentle reader, I have followed him under "Stonewall" Jackson to his stronghold in front of his capital, there I leave him, as a defeated braggart, chaffing under disappointment. On his arrival he relinquished the command of the army and little Mc was restored and begun at once to re-organize it, which he did and soon had it up to a high state of proficiency. The reports and orders of the prominent officers of both sides relative to this campaign have already been written, and is interesting reading matter for an old veteran that was there. I will not give any figures in regard to the losses, as they are matters of history which you can find if you so desire. Well, on the morning of the 3rd, it was ascertained that all the Yankees had gone, and we were ordered off picket to join our command, and soon we were on the road that led to Dranesville and Leesburg, camping on the night of the 4th near the big spring between Leesburg and the Potomac, which was nearby. Now, kind reader, this chapter closes my account of "Stonewall" Jackson's campaign against the Federal General John Pope in the summer of 1862. I have made many errors, I have not told half of what I do remember of this campaign, for it was one of the most brilliant and frought with more dangers than any that had occured up to this time. There were many acts of bravery by our officers, and some of the boys that I would like to mention, but fearing it might be too invidious, I have refrained. I pass from this now, and will endeavor to give my recollections of "Stonewall" Jackson's campaign in the State of Maryland.

CHAPTER XLI

AN OLD VETERAN'S RECOLLECTIONS OF "STONEWALL" JACKSON'S CAMPAIGN IN THE STATE OF MARYLAND, 1862, NO. 1.

DEAR FRIEND:

It had been the talk for a good long time that, if General Lee would march his army into the State of Maryland, that the strength of his army would be increased several thousand, and after we had done enough for General Pope in Virginia, it seemed that the accepted time had come for Lee to march his army into Maryland. As I said in the last chapter that our division camped on the night of the 4th of September near the big spring between Leesburg and the Potomac, which was nearby. Some time during the next day (the 5th) we fell into ranks and marched to the banks of the Potomac, which was but a short distance, where there was a ford, and there we were told that we had to cross by wading. What! wade the Potomac river? Yes, wade the Potomac river. How strange! Had any one told me in my school days that the Potomac river could be waded, I would have been ready to have disputed it, for our fiery Southern orators very often in their speeches referred to the Potomac and the Rio Grande, and I was led to believe that the former was some large stream that divided the North and South, and the latter was another large stream that divided the South from the West. So you can see that I knew but little about the geography of our country. I only knew that there was two rivers somewhere by that name at that time, but as I have grown older I have learned where they are, and that at certain seasons of the year either of them can be waded. Now then here we are, at the water's edge, ready to cross. What next! We halt! We see the Virginians who are leading the division crossing. We receive orders to strip ourselves of our lower garments, roll them up along with our ammunition and hold them up out of the water and go in, and thus we went in. The water did not part for us on either side to enable us to cross on dry land, but we hit it up to our waist and we had to be careful to keep from falling down, and I have no doubt but some did, but I don't remember any one falling and getting ducked. Our division, which was Ewell's, but at that time commanded by Brigadier General Lawton of Georgia, was in the advance and the Virginia Brigade preceeded ours (Trimble's.) As I have already said, the Virginians were the first to cross, and I have learned since that it was done for effect, as Virginia and Maryland joins, it was as a voice from Virginia speaking to her sister State, saying, here we are, we have come at last to assist you in throwing off the yoke of tyranny that have held you down since the riot in Baltimore in 1861. We have come that you may be allowed free speech and enjoy the liberties of other American citizens. Did they come? The sequel will show. When our regiment reached the other side of the river, there on its banks was stationed a band playing, "Maryland, My Maryland," and as soon as we could dress we gave a yell and proceeded on our way we knew not where. Nobody seemed to be in a hurry and the march was at leisure. Everything passed off pleasantly all the evening, and when night came we went into camp. There was no excitement, no disturbance of any kind, and we rested quite well during the night. The next morning we fell into line and pursued our journey, until we arrived at a little town called Frederick City, which is situated on the right bank of the Monocacy River, where also the Baltimore & Ohio R. R. crosses. On our march from the Potomac to this little town, we saw but very few men. At some of the houses we were greeted with cheers and smiles, and the waving of hats and handkerchiefs by the women, girls and boys, which was a token of our welcome, but at others the doors would be closed which was a token that we were an unwelcome guest, and we generally knew that they were "Yank" inclined. The apple trees in the orchads along our route fairly groaned under the weight of ripe apples, and under some of the trees the ground would be half covered, so we could get the best from off the ground. The people did not object to us getting just as many from off the ground as we wanted, and we were not prohibited by our officers, although an indiscriminate straggle to get apples was prohibited. In a short time, two or three men could get enough to supply his company. They were a great luxury. We arrived at Frederick City on the 7th and went into camp on the east side, or the Washington side, of the river opposite the town. Our camp was near the railroad and wagon bridges that spanned the Monocacy at this place. I don't suppose we were more than twenty miles from Washington City, where a mighty army was being organized to take the field under their old leader, G. B. McClellan. At the same time General Lee was concentrating his forces to resist an advance of the Federals until certain things in other quarters could be done. We privates did not know anything, and was only there to answer and obey all orders from Lee and Jackson. We didn't see much of Lee and Jackson while in this camp, but couriers and staff officers were constantly on the go. Stuart, with his cavalry was between us and Washington, watching every move of the enemy, and keeping Lee posted. Next.

CHAPTER XLII

AN OLD VETERAN'S RECOLLECTIONS OF "STONEWALL" JACKSON'S CAMPAIGN IN THE STATE OF MARYLAND, 1862, NO. 2.

DEAR FRIEND:

While in camp at Frederick City, the weather was as pleasant as could be desired. The sun shone out beautifully in the day-time, sending forth his rays of warmth just right to make us feel good. The nights were dark, except for the light of the stars, which shone with all their brilliance and glory from a clear blue star-lit September sky. The nights were a little cool, but with a gum-cloth and blanket spread upon the ground and two bunking together covering with a blanket and gum on top to keep off the cold dew, made it comfortable enough. Those of us that had no guard duty to perform, strolled around camp, waiting and wondering what would turn up next. The line officers knew that something was brewing, but could not surmise as to a certainty. As for me, I only wondered, and give myself no concern as to what would be next. One night while here, after I had ate my supper, which consisted of fried bacon, biscuit, hard-tack and coffee, and answered to roll call, I lit my pipe and sauntered off to the camp of the 31st Georgia, which was not far away, to see my old friend, Ed Roach. I soon found him sitting around his camp fire, eating his grub, which consisted of fried bacon, biscuit, hard-tack and coffee. I had just partook of the same variety and refused to eat with him. I sat down, leaning against a tree and continued to smoke my pipe until Ed and his mess-mate was through with their supper and cleaning up the dishes, etc. After he got through he lit his pipe and we went on a stroll. Some two or three hundred yards out of camp we came to an old uncultivated field where we sprawled down upon the ground to smoke, rest and talk. We soon began to relate to each other the incidents of the hard marches, and battles that we had passed through over in Virginia since last we met. We talked of our acquaintances in each others commands and those of other commands; some of them our school-mates that was fast dropping out. We talked of our people at home, not excusing the girls that we had told good-bye. God bless them, there are but few of them living now. Occasionally I can see one, her once ruddy cheeks are furrowed by wrinkles of time, and her once beautiful hair is now silvered and gray, and like myself began to show age, which suggests a thought. A few more years and then. After staying out as long as we wanted to, we returned to camp, to find that some of the boys had "turned in," while there were others sitting up, some singing, some smoking, some telling war stories, while there were others listening and laughing, and having fun generally. My bed-fellow, Barnett Cody, had retired and I crawled under the blanket and gum with him and was soon in dreamland. Our engineers in the day time were busy drilling holes in the rock piers that supported the railroad bridge, preparatory for its destruction, and occasionally during the day we could hear sounds like cannon when they would touch off their charge of powder. We did not know and cared less about what the enemy was doing. We only knew we were near Washington City, where Pope's demoralized army had fled, and it was reasonable to suppose that hasty preparations were in progress for its re-organization, and sure enough, in a few days it was known that Pope had been releived and McClellan had been placed in command of his old army again. This restored confidence in the ranks and among some of the subordinate officers, but there were two Federal officers occupying high positions that were continually punishing McClellan, accusing him of tardiness, viz: Halleck and Stanton. Mc was a democrat, purely American, and waged the war on American principles—that of humanity and fairness, but this was objected to by such men as W. T. Sherman, John Pope, Phil Sheridan, and one General Hunter, of Shenandoah Valley fame. One lady of Virginia published him in one of the Richmond papers as being a persecutor of helpless women and children, a hunter of pig-pens, cow-stalls, chicken-roosts, horse-stables and corn-cribs, and what he could not appropriate to his own use he applied the torch to destroy. McClellan would not tolerate such in his command, therefore his mode of warfare was not approved of by the extreme Southern haters of the North. General Lee had a high estimate on McClellan, as an able commander and as a conscientious gentleman. Pardon the digression. If my recollection serves me right, early on the morning of the 10th we were ordered to be ready to move at a moment's notice, and at about 9 A. M., A. P. Hill, with his division, begun to pass and cross the river on the wagon bridge, entering the streets of Frederick City. Our division came next following Hill on the Hagerstown turnpike, Jackson's old division, following us. Frederick City was full of Southern sympathizers, as Bradley T. Johnson had raised a large company of cavalry in that neighborhood at the outbreak of the war, and were then serving with J. E. B. Stuart. We marched pretty rapid for several miles as if there were something ahead that was about to "drop." I straggled out to get two or three canteens filled with water; when I had a chance to hear some friendly words pass between one of our cavalrymen and a young lady that he was acquainted with. Our troops were passing by at a quick step, all stained with rain, dust and dirt, and was devoid of all pomp of war. We were so unlike soldiers that she had been used to seeing that she exclaimed: "Why, John, how can such a dirty, filthy set of soldiers defeat the neatly dressed boys of the Army of the Potomac? Such clothes! All ragged and filthy." John was sitting on his horse with one leg thrown over the pommel of his saddle, listening. When she got through, John remarked, "Bessie, we don't put on our best clothes to kill hogs in." This was a stunner to Bessie and it caused an outburst of applause from those that were listening. I immediately left the crowd and hurried on to catch up with my command. "Stonewall" Jackson was a great curiosity to some of the people of Frederick as his men, for it was said that crowds of people were contiuously hanging around his headquarters peeping through the windows, as if anxious to catch him at his incantations. A correspondent in one of the Northern papers wrote of him, and our appearance while in Maryland; he said that "Old Stonewall" was the observed of all observers; he was dressed in the coarsest kind of homespun, seedy and dirty at that; worse still, he wore an old slouched hat which any northern beggar would have considered an insult to have offered him, and in his general appearance was in no respect to be distinguished from the mongrel bare-footed crew who followed his fortunes. He said that he had heard much of the decayed appearance of the Rebel soldiers, but such a looking crowd! Ireland in her worst straits could present no parallel; and yet they glory in their shame." I only mention this quotation for the purpose of showing you the estimate that some of the Northern critics had of Jackson and his men at this time. We cared nothing then for good looks, all we wanted was plenty to eat—plenty of ammunition—a good gun, and plenty of game, which we found in a few days further on. Our first day's march brought us on the west side of South Mountain, where we went into camp on the Hagerstown turnpike. Here was issued one roasting-ear to the man, another luxury. I roasted mine with the shuck on, and would rub it with a piece of fat bacon, then sprinkle on a little salt and then what I did was enough. We rested well all night, and the next morning we started again, we knew not where nor for what purpose, but I will tell later on.

CHAPTER XLIII

AN OLD VETERAN'S RECOLLECTIONS OF "STONEWALL" JACKSON'S CAMPAIGN IN THE STATE OF MARYLAND, 1862, NO. 3.

DEAR FRIEND:

I said in the preceeding chapter that our first day's march out from Frederick in the direction of Hagerstown put us on the west side of South Mountain, which branches off from the Blue Ridge in the neighborhood of a little village called Boonsboro, forming what was called Pleasant Valley. This was a beautiful country, level and the large fields of corn and the large fields of red bloom clover, with its luxuriant growth was evidence of the fertility of the soil. The beautiful residences, with their surroundings along our route toward Hagerstown, denoted wealth and happiness. The people along our route did not seem to realize what was going on, or what was soon to happen among them not many days hence. At many of these houses, women, girls and boys had assembled to see "Stonewall" Jackson's Corps pass. At nearly every place we were greeted with cheers and hoozas for Jeff Davis and the Southern Confederacy. Of course, we acknowledged by giving the "Rebel Yell." It was strictly against orders to straggle or molest anything the citizens had, and as well as I remember the order was obeyed except as to straggling, for it was said that on this account General Lee came near loosing the battle of Sharpsburg, which took place a few days after the time that I am now writing about. As well as I remember, we didn't know where we were going, or what was in store for us to do, but one thing that we all knew, and that was that old "Stonewall" had his head set on something which would develop in a few days, and all we had to do was to march when ordered, and halt when ordered, and if we wanted to know what was to be done it was our business to be there, and sure enough, in a few days we found out what was "in the air." As I have already said we were marching on the Hagerstown turnpike, but before we reached that little town (which was just over the line in Pennsylvania), we turned to the left, leaving Hagerstown to our right, and pursued a direct course toward Williamsport, a town on and near the bank of the Potomac. Our march was of moderate gait, giving plenty time to rest, and was unattended with any excitement or incident to have caused uneasiness or alarm. We camped for the night and remained until the next morning, when sometime during the day we were ordered to recross the Potomac. This we did by wading at the ford opposite the town of Williamsport. I am only guessing when I say that this crossing is about fifty miles above Leesburg, where we crossed over into Maryland on the 5th. After crossing we made a hurried march out to the B. & O. R. R., which leads westerly to Wheeling in West Virginia, and eastwardly to Baltimore, running through Martinsburg, Harper's Ferry and Frederick City, where we had left the balance of the army. We were near Martinsburg, a beautiful little town, pretty evenly divided in sentiment between the North and South. It was no trouble for us to get up a scrap between the little boys as we passed through, as they would gather on the sidewalks to see us pass, some of the little fellows would hollow "hurrah for Jeff Davis," another would answer by saying "hurrah for Abe Lincoln;" we would say, hit him Jeff Davis, or Abe Lincoln, as the case might be, and thus the scrap would begin, the Jeff's and Abe's would gather from every direction, when a general melee would begin, lasting until the mothers and sisters would interfere, which generally caused a hasty retreat of the beligerants, but it was fun for us. A. P. Hill's Division was in the lead, and as they approached this little town, the brigade of Yankees that was there fled to the stronghold of Harper's Ferry, which augumented the garrison at that place to eleven thousand. Subsequent events shows that it was known by Lee and Jackson that there was a force at each of those places and it was supposed that the advance upon Frederick would cause those places to be evacuated which would open up his line of communication with Richmond by a shorter route. This, however, did not occur, and it became a matter of importance that those places should be captured. We knew nothing of General Lee and the balance of the army that we had left at Frederick, but by the 13th we could begin to see the cause of our tardiness. General Lee had to send a force to occupy Maryland Heights, and a force to occupy Louden Heights on the South side of the Shenandoah, while Jackson's Corps occupied the front, stretching from the Potomac on his left to the Shenandoah on his right. Thus you will see that we had them bottled up at Harper's Ferry, and it was only a question of time for their surrender or a terrible battle to take place, for escape was impossible. There we were in plain view of Bolivar Heights, about one mile distant, which was occupied by the enemy, and had been so well fortified, and the timber all felled with the tops toward us, which gave it a fearful appearance, and would naturally put a fellow to thinking seriously to have to attack such a looking place as that, but if "Stonewall" orders, that's enough, we are ready to obey. On account of the movements of some of the other troops, the attack was delayed and we allowed to look and wait, for we were ready to assault.

CHAPTER XLIV

AN OLD VETERAN'S RECOLLECTIONS OF "STONEWALL" JACKSON'S CAMPAIGN IN THE STATE OF MARYLAND, 1862, NO. 4.

DEAR FRIEND:

In the preceeding chapter I said that on account of the movements of other troops the attack upon Harper's Ferry was delayed, and now I will proceed to tell the cause, but I didn't know then. It has been made known that before we left Frederick City, General Lee issued a general order for the movements of his army, directing Jackson to pursue the route that we did pursue, thereby driving the Yankees that were at Martinsburg into Harper's Ferry, where the "whole crowd could be bagged"—and directing McLaws with his division to proceed in the direction of Harper's Ferry and occupy Maryland Heights, which commanded the town from the Maryland side. The heights were occupied by the Yankees and McLaws met with a stubborn resistance, and there was considerable delay in getting his infantry and artillery in position, but when once in position he had complete control of the town from that side. General Walker with his division, was ordered to recross the Potomac below the Ferry and occupy Loudon Heights on the Virginia side, where he could enfilade their line of fortifications on Bolivar Heights from the left. Harper's Ferry is situated in the fork of the Potomac and Shenandoah Rivers, thus you see that McLaws occupied a position where he could rain shells on them from the rear, while Walker could do the same thing on their left, and as I have already stated, Jackson's Corps of three divisions occupying the front or Western side, reaching from the Potomac on our left to the Shenandoah on our right. The order directing the movements of the army from Frederick was sent to General D. H. Hill, and it is said that this officer, in a moment of passion, threw the order on the ground, and when our people evacuated the place and the advance of the enemy reached there, this order was picked up by a Yankee and no time was lost in conveying it to General McClellan, as it revealed to him much needed information as to General Lee's plans. McClellan's first object was to relieve Harper's Ferry by sending a force to attack McLaws in the rear, but McLaws held the gaps in the mountain passes long enough to aid Jackson in capturing the place, although it took considerable time to get ready, and no doubt that Jackson was in great suspense. Late in the evening of the 14th, it was made known by signal from the Maryland and Loudon Heights that McLaws and Walker were ready and were only waiting for the signal from Jackson to commence the bombardment. Jackson began to make preparations for the attack at early dawn the next morning. It is said that he issued but one order, and that was in a simple and blunt way when he ordered A. P. Hill to "turn the enemy's left flank and enter Harper's Ferry." And in order to gain some important advantage for the attack the next morning he observed a hill on the enemy's extreme left occupied by infantry without artilley, and protected only by an abbattis of felled timber. He ordered General Hill to seize this crest, and in compliance with that order, Hill ordered Generals Pender, Archer and Colonel Brockenbrough, with their brigades to seize this crest, and at the same time he ordered Generals Branch and Gregg, with their brigades, to march along down the Shenandoah, and taking advantage of the ravines intersecting its steep banks, and establish themselves on the left, and rear of the enemy's works, holding his other brigade in reserve. This was all accomplished during the night, and at the same time Colonel Crutchfield, Jackson's Chief of Artillery, was not idle, for he succeeded during the night to drag ten guns belonging to our division across to the South side of the Shenandoah, so as to enfilade the enemy's entrenchments on Bolivar Heights, thereby taking his nearest and most formidable work in reverse. We infantry fellows were not allowed to build fires that night, and we lay in rear of our guns, to sleep if we could, or lie there and imagine the result of the events of the morning. I have no doubt but that there were many prayers offered to the Almighty that night imploring his protecting care and divine assistance to pass safely through the fiery ordeal that stared us in the face, which semingly to us we had to pass. At early dawn, in strict obedience to orders the attack upon the garrison began. As soon as it was light enough to distinguish objects, the pickets began to fire on each other. We were aroused from our slumber and ordered into ranks, and there we stood in suspense, waiting for orders. As the sun began to shed his light from the East, the firing became more rapid, the fight was on. There was a signal station near us, where couriers were constantly dashing to and from. This station was in communication with McLaws and Walker, and I happened to step out of ranks a few minutes and went near the station and I heard the signal officer say to a courier, "Tell General Jackson that McLaws and Walker are ready," and the courier dashed off and soon returned with a message, as I supposed, from Jackson, and soon a rapid and vigorous fire was opened from the batteries all along our line, and those on Maryland and Loudon Heights, and also the batteries of Colonel Crutchfield, down on the Shenandoah. The shells rained in on them from every direction for about two hours, when a courier came dashing along shouting "The white flag is up, the white flag is up!" We could see it from our position, and I tell you, reader, there was a proud set of boys. The firing ceased all along the line and the agony with us was over. Seventy-three pieces of artillery, about thirteen thousand small arms and eleven thousand prisoners, besides a large quantity of military stores fell into our hands. General A. P. Hill was left with his division to receive the surrender and secure the captured property. Jackson with his other two divisions set out for Sharpsburg, Maryland, and McLaws and Walker was ordered to follow without delay.

Our command did not have the chance of going over to Harper's Ferry as there seemed to be a pressing need for us in another direction. We marched that evening about twelve miles, when we went into camp and cooked three days rations, and ordered to be ready to march at five o'clock the next morning. We were all glad that Harper's Ferry had been so easily captured with so little loss of life on both sides, but we were sorry that we were not allowed to go over into the place. That was our second time to look upon Bolivar Heights and it was our last, Sept. 15th, 1862.

CHAPTER XLV

AN OLD VETERAN'S RECOLLECTIONS OF "STONEWALL" JACKSON'S CAMPAIGN IN THE STATE OF MARYLAND, 1862, NO.5.

DEAR FRIEND:

We were up pretty late on the night of the 15th on account of having to cook three day's rations. We were ordered to be ready to march at five o'clock, and reville sounded in time to get us up and attend roll call, and be ready to march when orders came. After putting on our accoutrements, getting into ranks and answering to roll call, we were ordered to stack arms and rest until further orders. Of course, we were glad to here order to break ranks and rest, and we did so by sprawling ourselves on the ground and so many of us were taking a morning snooze. We had not heard of the hard fighting that had been going on over in Maryland between the balance of General Lee's army and the advance of McClellan's, neither did we know where they were or what was next to be done, but we soon ascertained that McClellan had pursued Lee vigorously from Frederick City to Boonsboro gap in South Mountain, where Lee had halted Gen. D. H. Hill's Division for the purpose of delaying the enemy until Harper's Ferry was captured by Jackson. McClellan lost no time in assaulting Hill's position at the pass, and a sanguinary engagement ensued. Hill, with his small command, repulsed the repeated assaults of the Federal army, and held him in check for five hours. This resistance had secured sufficient time to enable Jackson to complete the reduction of Harper's Ferry, and Lee, knowing his weakness, determined to withdraw from the gap and retire in the direction of a little town called Sharpsburg, which was near the Potomac, where he could more reeadily unite with Jackson's Corps and McLaws' and Walker's Divisions, who had aided in the reduction of Harper's Ferry. As well as I remember, at about 10 o'clock, we were ordered into line and marched off in the direction of the Potomac, arriving between 12 and 2 o'clock. This ford was shallow, with a good bottom, and was near a small village on our side called Shepherdstown, and was about midway between Leesburg where we had crossed over on the 5th, and Williamsport, where we had re-crossed back into Virginia on the 12th in coming around to Harper's Ferry. We were ordered to pull off and wade again, and of course it took some time to undress and then dress up after we had crossed over to the Maryland side. When we got over and dressed, we struck out at a rapid gait to overtake the troops that had preceeded us. The little town of Sharpsburg was not more than two mile, or hardly so far away, down in a bottom on the Hagerstown turnpike surrounded by hills or small mountains. We marched up a long slant for some distance, then quitting the road, turning to the left we were marched into a heavy body of oak woods, large oaks with little under-growth. As each division arrived, it was marched in and stacked arms, and ordered to rest. I guess it was something like three or four o'clock and all was "calm and serene" with us, but it was not long to remain so. Shortly the sounds of cannon could be heard in a northerly direction; and as time passed the sound became more distinct and we could tell that it was getting nearer, which was evidence that Lee's troops were falling back and McClellan advancing. The booming of cannon increased so that it seemed that a battle was in progress. Listen! the crack of a carbine is heard! Listen boys! Stuart's Videttes are giving away, and the Federal cavalry are advancing. Presently "Boom, boom, boom" went the sound of our cannon, now I guess you will halt, but in a few moments more th ecrack of Enfield rifles are heard. One, two, three, the fire increases and becomes more rapid. Lee has halted his forces and about faced as if to say to McClellan, you will have me to fight before you can proceed further. McClellan knew it, and begun to feel all along our line that evening and concentrating his forces for a general attack the next morning. Lee was not idle in making his preparations to meet the mighty host of ninety thousand, well-fed, well clothed and well armed army that was to be thrown against his forty thousand dirty, dingy, ragged and jaded veterans, with the Potomac at our backs not three miles away. Just think of it! Ninety thousand against forty thousand! but we could "lap water like a dog" and were true, tried and trusty and were not to be driven into the Potomac. At dark our brigade was moved in the direction of the firing that we had heard before the sun went down. We were marched through a field and a large body of oak woods, passing what is known in history as Dunker's Church, a frame wooden building situated on the North-east side of this belt of woods, near the Hagerstown and Sharpsburg pike about half a mile from the latter place. This church was used that evening for a hospital, and there were a few wounded in it as we passed, but they were all removed that night, as the house was riddled with bombshells the next day. We were not allowed to talk above a whisper, and in fact, not much of that was going on anyway for the time began to be serious, no noise of any kind was allowed. We moved slowly, as if creeping up on something, and presently we come to troops in line of battle, and upon enquiry it was ascertained that they were Hood's Brigade of Texans. They told us that they had been fighting the Yankees that evening, and that they were in line of battle not very far away and in heavy force. We took their place and they retired. There we lay all night on the ground, not allowed to unbuckle, nor undo anything we had on, only to wait and see what the next day would bring forth. We had not been in line but a short while before one man from each company was detailed to go on picket to relieve the pickets of Hood's Brigade. Our company had to furnish a seargeant, and it was Scargeant Mose Maybin's time, and he went, and I never saw him again. The pickets out in the woods in front were shooting at each other all along during the night, and they were so close that occasionally we could hear a bullet go singing over us, which had a tendency to keep us awake. Thus we lay on the cold ground all the night of the 16th, waiting for the dawn of that memorable day, the 17th of Sept. 1862. In the next chapter I will tell what happened as I now remember. I had forgotten to tell that all our brigade and nearly all of the regimental field officers were either killed or wounded in the engagements over at Manassas, and we were without a brigade commander, but Captain Oates and several others of the line petitioned the proper authorities for a commander for the brigade, and Colonel John A. Walker of the 13th Virginia was assigned to command. Our Colonel (Lowther) was as usual, sick and back with the wagon train. Colonel Walker was a fine commander and filled the bill. We all had confidence in him. He afterwards became to be a brigadier. We were always glad to see him after his promotion, and it always seemed that he had a kind recollection of Trimble's Brigade, and felt to some degree that we had contributed to his promotion. Our regiment was ably commanded by Captain J. B. Feagan of Co. "B," afterwards Colonel Feagan. I will say something of him in the next chapter.

CHAPTER XLVI

AN OLD VETERAN'S RECOLLECTIONS OF "STONEWALL" JACKSON'S CAMPAIGN IN THE STATE OF MARYLAND, 1862, NO. 6

DEAR FRIEND:

At early dawn on the 17th, or as soon as objects could be distinguished, the skirmishers of both sides began to fire on each other, and as the sun in the East began to throw his reflecting rays of light over the top of South Mountain, the firing increased and it was in this early engagement that Seargeant Mose Maybin of my company received his death wound. General Lee was now prepared to deliver battle, and meet the mighty host that he knew would be thrown against him that day. General Lee did not intend an advance upon McClellan, but took position to resist any further advance of the Yankee army. Our skirmishers, after a spirited contest for an hour or more was driven in and followed by heavy lines of solid infantry. We remained in line, ready and waiting for the general advance. The batteries of both sides opened a furious fire all along Jackson's front, under cover of which the enemy advanced his masses to attack. Our corps occupied the left of General Lee's line of battle, extending far to the left in the direction of the Potomac. Our right joined the left of Longstreet's forces. At about 7 o'clock the enemy advanced his double and tripple lines against us, and we met them with the utmost resolution and for several hours the conflict raged with great fury and alternate success. My regiment, the 15th Alabama, was on the extreme right of Ewell's Division, and joined Longstreet. We were without any protection whatever; we had sit or lain on the cold ground all night with no covering to protect us from the cold dew of a September morn in that cold climate, and our limbs had become so stffened and benumbed that would have prevented an active movement by us unless there had been some urgent necessity which occurred about eleven o'clock, which I will endeavor to explain later on. About two hundred yards in our rear, and opposite Dunker's Church, there was a hill that our people had crowned with artillery. It seems to me now that there were not less than twelve guns there which done the most of their firing over our heads, and as many, if not more of the enemy's guns were replying all the time, and shot and shell from both sides were constantly passing, not more than ten feet above our heads, and I tell you, reader, that was a very unpleasant place to be in. Longstreet's Corps stretched back to our right and rear, occupying the crest of a hill overlooking the slope to the Antietam Creek, and the valley beyond to the base of South Mountain. The Yankee batteries over there could enfilade our lines, and had it not been for the burning of a large house on our right, I have always thought that we would have been driven from our position by the fire of their cannon, but the smoke from the burning house obscured our position from view while we were engaged with the infantry in front. It was a face to face combat between the 15th Alabama and the 10th Maine. This fact I ascertained some sixteen years ago, through a correspondence with Maj. John M. Gould, of Portland, Maine. He had the kindness to invite me to meet with them at a reunion of the 1st, 10th and 29th Maine, to be held on the battlefield by the above named regiments on the 17th of Sept. 1891, and had I been able I should have went, for I was satisfied that that fellow would have made it pleasant for me, barring the recollections of the loss of some of the best men in my company. Our correspondence was entirely without bitterness or partisanship. He addressed me as his friend in Gray and I would reply as my friend in Blue. Our correspondence has long since terminated and it may be that he has "crossed over." In this engagement the positions of Co.'s K, G and B was protected to some extent by a slight rise in the ground in our front. We loaded and fired on our knees just raising high enough to miss the ground in front. There was a fence about fifty yards that run diagonally across our front, and it was at this fence that the 10th Maine lost so heavily. They made repeated efforts to cross, but each time they would be met with such a shower of "buck and ball" that would cause them to run back to the woods where they would re-form and come again. When they would reach the fence they were so near that I could see the buckles on their caps and buttons on their coats. They would mount the fence and with each volley from us I could see them tumble forward and backward at such a rate as to check their determination. Their colors would go down, but there was always some one to raise it again. They were a brave set of fellows, but they could not drive us. They fought us long and hard, and finally they retired to the woods for a more complete organization, and to be re-inforced for a renewal of the attack. While we were thus engaged, the battle on our left was raging with great fury. The main assaults were being made on Jackson's Corps. Hood's Brigade of Texans had been sent to re-inforce Jackson, and they became hotly engaged. Our ammunition was running short, and Capt. J. B. Feagan, who was in command of the regiment (Colonel Lowther being absent sick), ordered details to be made to go to the ordnance train and bring ammunition. The firing in our front had slackened, and we were lying idle holding our position waiting for ammunition, when Gen. D. H. Hill rode up in our rear and asked "What regiment is this lying here?" Captain Feagan replied "the 15th Alabama." "My God," roared General Hill, "is this an Alabama regiment lying here?" "We are out of ammunition," says Captain Feagan. Hill roared out again, "Haven't you got bayonets? Take rocks and go forward." At this juncture several officers rose up, and men in the ranks protested by exclaiming in loud voices, "Don't you do it, Captain," and Captain Feagan remained quiet and Hill rode off. He afterwards preferred charges against Captain Feagain for disobedience of orders, and upon a trial the court exhonorated Captain Feagan and complimented him for his good judgement, a rebuke to General Hill's rashness. General Hill did not know what was in front as well as Feagan and the men did, but he soon found out, for he ordered Colquitt's Brigade of Georgians, who belonged to his division, to re-inforce that part of the line when really we were not being pressed at that time. They came up in fine style and passed over us, and as it happened, little Johnnie Mathews, who was known by some of us before the war, belonged to the regiment and company that passed over ours, was recognized and he paused long enough to shake hands with a few of us that he knew. He bade us good-bye and broke off in a run to overtake his company. Soon they encountered Hooker's Division of Sumner's Corps when the firing for a few moments was extremely heavy, and a stream of wounded Georgians came pouring to the rear. We never saw little Johnnie Mathews again for we afterwards learned that he was killed in that engagement. I knew him before the war, and had cultivated a friendship for him that old mother time will never efface. Peace to his ashes. The Georgians met with such overwhelming numbers that they had to give way, and here they came pell mell, and our joints that had been so stiff and benumbed now became limber, and I tell you, reader, we "got" with the Georgians. My individual line of escape lay directly across the hill that our artillery was on, and as soon as our infantry had passed out of the way, they turned loose a sower of grape and cannister that put a check on the pursueing enemy. The Yankee batteries that was posted on the other side of Antietam Creek had a direct flank fire on the right of our battery on this hill, and as soon as the infantry got out of the way, the batteries in front turned loose and I can't see how man or horse got away from there. I had to pass through, or near by, to our battery, and it was like running the gauntlet, for as I passed the shells and solid shot was playing havoc with our battery, but we lost no guns. When on this hill I looked back to my right where the left of our line lay, and I distinctly saw three line of battle advancing on Lawton's Georgians, commanded by Colonel Douglas. The Georgians were lying behind a little breastwork made of fence rails, quietly waiting for them to come near enough to deal a death blow at a single volley. I and others had no time to halt around that battery, and hurried on to get out of range. As I passed I turned to the right, coming to the rock fence that was on one side of the Hagrstown turnpike, I fell over as quick as I could, others doing the same. About this time McLaws' and Walker's Divisions arrived from Harper's Ferry and a part of each division was thrown forward to meet the mighty host that was trying to crush Jackson's Corps. Lawton's Georgians had turned loose upon the advancing Yankees and put a check on them, such a roar of musketry was seldom heard and there I was, away from my command, without ammunition, not knowing where it was or what to do. The solid shot and unexploded shells kept knocking down the rock fence, and my position soon became untenable, so I concluded that I would move on down the pike in the direction of the little town of Sharpsburg, which was not far away down in the bottom. When I got down there I found General Colquitt and several other officers of distinction standing in the road begging men to halt and fall into ranks, of what looked to me as a straggler's brigade. I told them that I was without ammunition, and they cited me to a place where I could be supplied. I filled my box and pockets and went where they directed and fell into line. I asked the lieutenant commanding for a certificate of my presence and detention in that command, he wrote on a small slip of paper the following: To whom it may concern: I hereby certify that Corporal W. A. McClendon of Co. "G" 15th Alabama Regiment, was detained to do service in front of Sharpsburg, to assist in checking the advance of the enemy near the bridge across the Antietam. Signed Lieut———Ga. commanding." I folded the slip and put it in my pocket and felt some easier. Our position was behind a fence, with a corn-field in front. The corn was in roasting-ear, the rows running at right angles to the fence, which enabled us to have a fair fire at the Yanks as they advanced down the rows. The contest up on the hill, in the direction from which I came, and on the left of Longstreet's front, was raging with great fury. Somebody's children were being hurt. We were not long in waiting before they showed themselves in our front, and commenced to advance down the corn rows, and as soon as they came near enough we gave them a volley which sent them back disorganized. We kept firing as long as we could see one in range, and at last the smoke became so thick that we could not see anything. I quit shooting and lay down, for I could not see anything to shoot at. They ceased their attack on us, and fresh troops coming in they fell back, consequently we were idle and some of the men began to leave the ranks to hunt for their commands. This was objected to by the officers, and I made no attempt to leave and remained there fully two hours, ready to do whatever I was commanded to do. The contest for the possession of the bridge across the Antietam was in progress, and the slaughter was something like to that of Bonapart's passage of the bridge of Lodi. It was defended by that unreconstructed Georgan Bob Toombs, with two regiments of his brigade. They repulsed five different desperate assaults made by greatly superior numbers, but the Georgians maintained their position with distinguished gallantry. The enemy began to extend his line to the left down the creek as if to cross below, and Toombs withdrew his command when the enemy began to cross, but was met by General Jones, which put a check to their advance from that direction. After this the emergency of our detention passed, and we were ordered to break ranks and go to our commands. I set out at once, and passing through the little town, I entered an apple orchard and there helped myself to all I wanted from those that had fallen from the trees. I passed by some straw stacks that were two feet above the ground and several men had taken refuge under them. I knew only one of them, and that was Johnnie Nelson, an Irishman that belonged to Co. "K." I asked him if he knew where the regiment was and he replied "No" and looked so indifferent that it left the impression on my mind that he did not care. I did not know which way to go or what to do. What bothered me was being away from my command, and did not know but what they were in the heavy fighting that was going on in front. I had understood that Gen. A. P. Hill, with his division from Harper's Ferry was momentarily expected to arrive. I went up a long slant toward a heavy belt of woods and sat down. Soldiers were passing to and fro, some lost from their commands the same as I was. I enquired often for the 15th Alabama, but no one could tell anything about it. The sun was about two hours high when General A. P. Hill arrived with his division. He threw forward his batteries along with Gen. D. R. Jones and reinforced him with three brigades of his division, and the progress of the enemy was soon checked and his line began to waver and began to fall back. I was an eye witness to this fight, and it was animating to me to see Hill's troops advancing and firing in such fine style. The enemy fell back in confusion, pursued by the troops of Hill and Jones, until he had reached the protection of his numerous batteries on the opposite side of the creek. It was now nearly dark when the firing ceased. I moved on up the hill where I saw a line of men, but it proved to be men belonging to several commands lost like myself. They began to call out their commands and I began to call for the 15th Alabama. I called several times as loud as I could, and at last some one answered "Here." I called again, receiving the same answer. I moved on in the direction of the voice, until I came up to the man that had been answering, and I found it to be Daniel McClellan of my company, who had been sick and had fallen behind. He had not been in the engagement, consequently he could give me no tidings of our company. It was dark and after consulting over our condition and the situation of affairs, we concluded to stay there until morning. We spread our guns and blankets at the root of a large oak, and there undisturbed we soon dropped off to sleep, not however, until I had told him of our hard fight that day, and the loss of four or five of our best men.

CHAPTER XLVII

AN OLD VETERAN'S ACCOUNT OF "STONEWALL" JACKSON'S LAST DAY IN THE STATE OF MARYLAND, 1862.

DEAR FRIEND:

All Confederate veterans know how easily it was to sleep, after a hard day's fight, when an opportunity was offered. He would only have to be still a little while before he would fall into a doze, even under bursting shells, and the sound of small arms he would fall asleep. Thus it was with myself and Daniel McClellan on the night of the 17th. At early dawn we started to the front in search of our command. Other soldiers were moving in the same direction, some in squads commanded by an officer, all moving to the front, bent upon the same mission as ourselves. We came out of the woods into a large field where we could see a mile to the front, and in the far distance I discovered a line of troops, which I recognized by their colors to be Virginians, occupying pretty much the same position of the day before. This proved to be Jackson's old division on the left of his corps. We hurried on in the direction of our position of the day before, until we came near the belt of woods that Dunker's Church was in, and not far away I recognized the colors of the 15th Alabama, and we proceeded directly for them. When we arrived, as well as my memory serves, there were about sixty men with them, and they were commanded by Lieut. C. V. Morris of Co. "G," who is familiarly known to us as Colonel Morris, an aged and honored citizen who now resides at Ft. Gaines, Ga. Lieut. L. L. Guerry of Co. "C" was second in command; he has crossed over. The boys were telling of yesterday's battle, who were killed and who wounded, and what they did. They all had been more or less engaged after we left our position of the early morning. Of course, I had to tell my experience, that I had fought in what I called a straggler's brigade. I produced my certificate of detention, which eliminated all doubt, if any existed of my unfaithfulness. I was proud to get to my command, but was made sad when I learned that our Orderly Sargeant Joe Balkum had been killed and Sargeant J. J. Carr had lost his right arm from which he died; either of them would have made fine officers. Others kept coming in and by nine o'clock we had a pretty good regiment, considering the arduous service that we had lately performed. All the regiments of the brigade were gotten together, and took position in line in the division and made ready to meet a renewal of the attack that was expected would be made that morning. Desultory firing had been going on between the pickets all the morning and an attack was momentarily expected but happily for us none came, for we were tired and worn out and needed rest, but we would have obeyed and would have hurt the Yankees worse that day than we did the day before, as our position was better. About 11 o'clock a truce was ordered for the purpose of removing the wounded and burying the dead. I was not on the detail, but straggled over as near to our position of the morning before as I could, looking for Orderly

Balkum, but I did not find him. I passed through a low rocky bottom in the woods, just in the rear of the position of Lawton's Brigade of the morning before and there I saw boys in Gray and boys in Blue, cold in death, lying close to each other, almost touching each other in some places, and I am sorry to say that some of them were partly denuded. Colonel Douglas of the 13th Georgia was one of the slain that I recognized, and he was partly nude also. Ghastly spectacles were abundant as the eye ranged over this scene of mortal strife. The scene was so sickening and the cries of the wounded so pitiful, and I so powerless to help that I turned away in silence and wended my way back to my command, wondering how and when this cruel war would end. During the day the wounded were removed, and the dead buried. General Lee had special reasons for not renewing the battle that morning, in consequence of the arduous service that we had done, having been deprived of much rest, making long marches and many without shoes and all these things together had greatly reduced our numebrs before the battle commenced. Our ranks had been greatly diminished in the terrible action of the day before, so much that he was too weak to assume the offensive, and he preferred to wait for a renewal of the attack upon him. The day passed without any demonstration by the enemy and it was reported that he was waiting for re-inforcements. General Lee could not expect any, but had formed his line with what he had, and was ready to receive them in a much better position than of the first day. History says that Fitz John Porter's Corps of the Yankee army did not fire a gun the first day, and that a strong division under General Couch arrived that evening from Washington, and these facts being known by General Lee, he did not think it prudent to wait for another attack, consequently during the night of the 18th we were quietly withdrawn to the South side of the Potomac, crossing at the same ford near Shepardstown where we crossed over on the 16th. Our crossing was made quietly, without loss or molestation, back to Virginia once more. Thank God! with whole hide and bones. I just naturally felt like I had been a long time from home and had to my joy returned. I was just simply tired out and no one but myself knew how glad I was to recross the Potomac. I was glad that we were not attacked as was expected that day. Our loss in field officers had been heavy. Several brigadiers and colonels had been killed, but the loss of the Federals had been greater than ours as they were the assailants. Major Generals Mansfield and Reno were killed, each commanding a division in Sumner's Corps and several brigadiers and colonels were killed and wounded. Major General Hooker was also wounded. History gives our loss at eight thousand. The sacrifice of officers on both sides had been serious. I give it as my opinion that the battle of Sharpsburg or Antietam (as some called it,) was the hardest battle that was fought by Lee's army during the war. I base my opinion upon the general condition and numbers of both armies at the time. It was an all day fight. The Confederate line was weak, but the Federal line was strong, and they could re-inforce their line whenever and wherever they wanted to. We could not do it, but would have to stand with our depleted ranks and meet every assault made upon them without flickering, which was characteristic of the Veteran Corps of "Stonewall" Jackson. 'Tis true, our line was broken in several places, but at no time did we become panic stricken and desert the field. They had the numbers, we had the courage and confidence to meet them in every attack. With but two or three exceptions we held our same positions on the 18th, that we did on the 17th, and thus we stood with our depleted ranks staring the Federal army in the face ready to meet the increased host that could have been thrown against us that day, but the Yankee's general hesitated, he was afraid to venture. It has been conceded by impartial histroy that this was a drawn battle, but the Federal commander had to say something to appease the wrath of his government; and on the 19th, after Lee had re-crossed everything back into Virginia, he telegraphed his government "that he did not know if the enemy were falling back to an interior position or recrossing the river, but we can safely claim the victory as ours." But in a very short while after this despatch he ascertained that Lee had recrossed the Potomac, he consoled his government with another telegram saying, "The victory is complete, Lee has been driven back into Virginia, and Maryland and Pennsylvania are safe." McClellan wa stoo badly hurt to push his advantage if he had any. He knew his condition better than any one else, but his government was chafing under disappointment. It had long been the talk that if Lee's army could advance into Maryland that there were thousands of Marylanders only waiting for a chance to join our army to assist in throwing off the yoke of tyranny that had so long held them down. At Frederick City about the 8th of September, General Lee issued an address, (which is somewhere in history) directed "To the People of Maryland." In this address he told them the object if his visit, and giving them an opportunity of rallying to our colors if they so desired, not to oppress or wantonly destroy anything they had, but I think they were sorter like some of Jubal Early's men were in the Valley in the summer of '64. It was said that when his lines were broken at Fisher's Hill, he would dash around on his horse commanding the men to "rally, rally men, for God's sake rally," and some of his men, to guy the old fellow by replying, "narry rally, General, narry rally." So that was the way with the people of Maryland, with the exception of a few, they didn't rally worth a cent, preferring to gaze upon both armies, fearing a confiscation or a conflagration, by the Yankees. So the object of the Maryland campaign to some extent was a failure, although we had some Marylanders with us that was as true as steel, and loyal to the last. God bless them, all honor to them wherever they may be. I have disgressed somewhat from my main subject, but will return by saying that the 18th day of September, 1862, was the last day that "Stonewall" Jackson spent in Maryland. He was killed the next May, and his corps never went into Maryland again during his lifetime. As I have already said, we re-crossed the Potomac by wading and marched out about four miles and went into camp. I have forgotten to say that there was a canal on the North side of the Potomac, which was made dry by cutting the lock above. The banks were dug down which made it easy to cross, and in the next chapter I will tell you what use the Yankees made of it when they started in pursuit.

CHAPTER XLVIII

STONEWALL JACKSON'S CORPS BACK IN VIRGINIA IN CAMP AT BUNKER HILL BY AN OLD VETERAN.

DEAR FRIEND:
If my memory is not at fault, our division (Ewell's) was the last to recross the Potomac and Lawton's Brigade of Georgians was the rear brigade. As a matter of precaution the skirmishers were left in front to conceal our movement. I don't remember seeing any soldiers, or any property of any description abandoned on our route down to where we crossed the Potomac. When Lawton's Brigade crossed a company from the 38th Georgia was detailed as pickets to guard the ford. This company was called "The Irvin Invincibles" and was largely composed of men from this county, (Henry.) During the night the pickets that had been left in front was quietly withdrawn and the way was clear for the Yankees to advance, if they wanted to. Early on the morning of the 19th they discovered our adsence and began to advance. Colonel Pendleton, our chief of artillery, had planted four guns on a hill above the little town of Shepherdstown, for the purpose of resisting their advance, and the Yankees soon engaged him with a number of guns to overmatch, and under cover of their fire they began to advance their infantry. There was an obscure way by which they could reach the canal unobserved by our artillerymen, and they didn't fail to take this advantage, and passed down by small squads until they had no less than a brigade in solid column in the canal. They then moved down in the canal by their left flank unobserved by our pickets until they became opposite the ford, and all at once the command forward was given, they rose up out of the canal as though they had come out of the ground, and immediately made a dash for the river, and began to cross by wading. They began cheering, with their familiar Yankee brogue by yelling "hooza, hooza" as if to frighten our pickets away. Our pickets were on the opposite side, stationed behind trees, and everything

else that afforded protection and immediately began to fire on them while crossing, killing and wounding a great many of them while in the water. The fire from our pickets were insufficient to check them. There were too many for our boys, and those that lived come right on, and our men had to back and let them cross. It was said that they crossed over a division when they formed line of battle, threw out skirmishers, and began to advance slowly for the purpose of ascertaining our position. Jackson being always on the alert, was knowing to all this, and he sent A. P. Hill down with his division to meet them and according to his custom, he was not long in finding them, and his attack was so sudden and furious that the Yanks broke for the river, but Hill crowded them to the water's edge, and many of them found a watery grave, many of them surrendered rather than run the risk of being shot down in the water. (I would have done the same thing.) The fight being over, Hill established his pickets and began to move his wounded and bury his dead, and then marched his division back, and went into camp. I don't know when or how the dead and wounded Yankees was disposed of, for the battle-field was three miles away, and I never went back to see, but I suppose they were properly attended to as was our custom. Peace and quietude then reigned supreme, and the usual interchange of visits among the soldiers of different commands commenced. One of my visits was to the 38th Georgia, and to the company that had been left on picket at the river when the Yanks crossed on the night of the 18th. I had several acquaintances in that company, one in particular that I will mention, and that was no less than our good old man, W. W. Kirkland, who still lives an aged, honored, Christian gentleman, and is loved by all that know him for his manly bearing and virtue. He is familiarly known as Uncle Wilce, with not an enemy on earth, or in heaven. He knew me when a boy, was glad to see me and delighted to tell me his experience while on picket at the river, when the Yankees come across. I was an intent listener and took great delight in his story. He said, "they just come right on, hoozaying and hoozaying, as though they were driving a drove of cattle or trying to scare us with their noise. I loaded and shot them as fast as I could and I certainly must have downed some of them. If I didn't, the fault was in my gun, but we couldn't keep them back, and to keep from being captured we had to retreat." Uncle Wilce hasn't forgot it 'till this day, and enjoys to tell about it yet. When he crosses over, surely a good man will be gone. Our camp was in a thick woods where fuel and water was plentiful. We were ordered to cook two day's rations, and we had to wait until our "pot" and "spider" wagon came up, which was momentarily expected. When it come, a rush was made by one from each mess to get a spider; I represented my mess, and luckily I seized on to a spider and started to camp with it, and on my way I discovered that it was marked, which indicated that it had a special owner. It was marked on the handle by having three notches filed in the handle, and it was up to me to disfigure it so that the rightful owner would not recognize it. When I arrived at my camp I laid the handle on a rock and with another I intended breaking it below the notches, but just as I raised my rock to come down on it, some one says, "Don't break it, it's mine." I looked up and saw that it was Lieutenant Strickland of Co. "I." I withheld the blow and surrenderd the spider as gracefully as I knew how, but not without remorse, for I knew that I had done wrong. My messmates guyed me considerably, but I could say nothing, only for them to do better if they could, consequently we had to wait until some of the rest of the boys fininshed their cooking before we could cook a mouthful. This, however, was frequently the case, for cooking utensils was very scarce. While at this camp, I went out foraging for honey one night. One of my company ascertained where some other soldiers were going to rob some bee gums at night, and his plan was to play officer with a guard and fain a capture of the whole crowd and get the honey. After roll call he donned an officer's uniform and the three or four others that he had let on to it, got our guns and quietly, unobserved, slipped out of camp. Our leader knew exactly the spot of woods that the gums was to be brought to, and we hastened on for a mile or more. Suddenly we halted, no one speaking, but gazing intently down into a piece of woods where we were informed that the gums was to be brought. This is rather a squeamish piece of business, thought I to myself. I had just begun to realize the perilous position I might get into, and the more I brooded over it to myself, the more serious it became, until I was on the eve of dropping out and retracing my steps back to camp, but all at once the light of fire flashed not fifty yards away.

"That's them" whispered our leader. Directly a knocking commenced, as if to lift the lids off the gums. More light was made. Much laughing and talking in subdued tones were heard, and the constant passing around the light represented half, or a dozen men, a pretty good crowd for us to tackle, thought I, but I am going to stick if I am captured myself. After a reasonable length of time, we marched on to them briskly. We came up from different directions. There were only five or six of them and as luck would have it we had no trouble in getting rid of the whole crowd. Each one had an excuse for absence until the last one left, the very thing we wanted them to do. The night was cool and the bees being of the good kind we had no trouble with them. They had robbed about three gums and their honey were in camp kettles and our commander thought it wise to get away from there as soon as possible. We picked up the three or four buckets of honey and hastened back to camp. On arriving we concealed it the best we could, and for several days enjoyed eating good honey. We expected the next day that the citizen who owned the gums would be around looking for his honey, but none came, he might have been in the war. We didn't know what house they came from, the other fellows did. We remained in this camp for several days. I did not know what was going on in the balance of the army. After a few days we broke camp and marched in the direction of Winchester, halting, and going into camp about five miles North of Winchester at a large spring near the turnpike. This place was called, and is know by the men of Lee's army as "Bunker Hill." There was no town, nothing but a large spring surrounded by a beautiful level, fertile land. When we were first there, in the early spring the surroundings indicated wealth, but the ruthless invader had been there, and had laid waste to everything that could not be appropriated to their use. The famous "Stonewall" Brigade of Virginians were mostly raised in these parts, which intensified the hatred of the Yankees against these people. The spring alluded to above afforded enough pure water to supply Lee's army without muddying it. While at this camp we turned in our old smooth bore muskets, and was armed with new Enfield rifles out of the lot that had been captured at Harper's Ferry. Ammunition to suit was issued (56 calibre minnie ball), and we were all glad of the change, for we felt like we would be more on equality with the Yankees at a long distance than we were with our old muskets. As well as I remember, we spent twenty days of October at this camp, and the next move we made it was to cross the Blue Ridge in the direction of Culpepper Court House.

CHAPTER XLIX

AN OLD VETERAN UNDER "STONEWALL" JACKSON IN THE BATTLE OF FREDERICKSBURG DECEMBER 13TH, 1862.

Dear Friend:

The weather during the latter days of September and all during the month of October was ideal for the movement of troops. There had been but little rain, and the roads were good. We knew nothing of the movements of the Yankees and cared less. They seemed to be idle, waiting for reinforcements. Our ranks, after the battle of Sharpsburg, and up to the battle of Fredericksburg, had received considerable strength by the return of the absentees from hospitals and otherwise; notwithstanding all this we were out-numbered by the Yankees two to one, as we generally were. Our march from Bunker Hill to Culpepper Court House was made with leisure, nothing to molest or impede our progress. History says that the government at Washington was chafing with impatience at the tardiness of their commander, McClellan. He began to concentrate in and near Harper's Ferry, but made no forward movement. On the 6th of October President Lincoln ordered an immediate advance, recommending that he should take the interior line between Washington and Lee's army and make an early battle, but McClellan still hesitated and weeks wore on without any decided movement. The beautiful weather of September and October had finally passed without any demonstrations of moment being made. The cold, bleak November winds begin to whistel over the fields and mountains, and it was getting about time for something to happen. McClellan's hesitation and timidity became so evident to his government at Washington that he, to his surprise, was relieved of the command of the Army of the Potomac and General Burnside assigned to command. He found at his command a splendid army under good discipline, such as it's former commander always had. It was divided into three grand divisions, each consisting of two corps, and were commanded by Generals Sumner, Hooker and Franklin. Of course the Yankee generals of that army had all been planning to defeat Lee, and capture Richmond and Burnside at once proposed to go to Richmond via Fredericksburg, by crossing the Rappahannock by means of pontoons, and with his one hundred and ten thousand men brush Lee with his sixty thousand out of his way and proceed to Richmond by Hanover Court House, but let's see how near he came of carrying his plan into execution. About the 18th of November General Lee received information that confirmed the impression that Burnside was moving his whole army in the direction of Fredericksburg. He had already occupied Stafford Heights, had fortified and planted seige guns which commanded the town, and was making every preparation to cross. General Lee had already moved some of his army down there to resist a sudden attempt at crossing. Our corps was some twelve or fifteen miles below, near Port Royal, a little town on the river. General Lee concentrated his army, took position on Maryea's Heights, and began to fortify. Longstreet's Corps occupied the left of our line and our corps the right. Cold weather had set in, and we were without quarters. As the days wore on each army was preparing for another "spat," one to advance and assault, and the other to resist. General Lee had stationed Barksdales with his brigade of Mississippians in the town, and along the edge of the river to impede their progress as long as they could when the Yanks began to lay his pontoon to cross. From our position we could hear more or less cannonading every day, in the direction of Fredericksburg, and about the 10th of December we received orders to cook three day's rations, and be ready to move at a moment's notice. We knew something was going to happen pretty soon, as orders of that kind was always a prelude to a battle or a long march. It was said that Burnside had a powerful artillery force attached to his army, of which no less than one hundred and forty guns, overlooked the town of Fredericksburg, and commanded the course of the river and the opposite bank. The corporate authorities had been summoned to surrender the city with a threat that in case of refusal the city would be bombarded at a certain hour the next day. The women and children began at once to leave their homes, carrying with them only what they could on their backs. The bombardment did not take place at that time. At early dawn on the 11th, our signal guns announced that the enemy was in motion. Some time early in the morning he commenced to lay two pontoons, one opposite the city and the other about one and a quarter miles below, near the mouth of a little creek called Deep Run. From an early hour until 4 P. M. our troops that had been stationed to resist, sheltered themselves behind the houses on the river bank, and repelled several efforts of the enemy to lay his bridge opposite the town, driving them back with great slaughter. At the lower place there was no protection for our men, and they could only keep up an annoying fire from whatever protection they could find, and for a moment the enemy retired. Then they turned loose not less than one hundred guns upon the city. Houses fell, timbers crashed, dust rose from brick houses, flames from the burinig buildings ascended, while there poured out a stream of unlucky citizens who had remained too long. Our troops, unable to withstand the fire of the batteries, and a superior force of the enemy's infantry that lined the banks on the other side, were withdrawn and left it free for the Yankees to cross and come on. They began at once to lay their bridges, and when completed they sent up a cheer and begun to cross.,General Lee had accomplished his design in delaying them, until he could concentrate his forces. Burnside, availing himself of the dense fog on the river, continued without molestation to cross his army over. It taken nearly all day of the 12th, and late in the evening when he had formed his line, he fell along Lee's front, only to find him in compact lines ready to receive him. While all these things were taking place at Fredericksburg, our corps was on the march to take our place in line. A. P. Hill had preceeded us, and his divisions had been placed on Longstreet's right and extended to Hamilton's crossing on the railroad. Our division, commanded by General Early, and Jackson's old division, composed Jackson's second line, while D. H. Hill's Division was our reserve. This was our formation when we arrived on the A. M. of the 13th. Jackson had numerous batteries posted all along his front so that he could fire on their advancing columns whenever they attempted an advance on his line. Early in the morning, the plain between our position and the river where the Federal army lay in great force was enveloped in fog, and it was under cover of this fog that he formed his three grand divisions for assault. Only occasionally in the morning part of the day could his lines be seen in consequence of the dense fog, but all the while loud commands could be heard on the plain that indicated that troops were marching and counter-marching, forming to advance. All was feverish with expectation. Between nine and ten o'clock the sun lifted the foggy veil from the valley and there stood the Yankee army in plain view just ready to advance. Our batteries at once, from the left to the right (where we was) began their murderous work upon the long lines of their densely crowded infantry that occupied the level plain between us and the river. More than a hundred pieces, and some of large calibre, was turned loose upon our position under which their infantry advanced and assaulted Longstreet's position with great determination, but was repulsed with great slaughter. Their attacks upon Longstreet was repeated, after redoubling their forces, but the last assault was attended with no more success than the first. While these attacks were going on he extended his left far beyond Jackson's right, and began to make preparations to attack Jackson in front and on his right flank. J. E. B. Stuart, with his fine division of cavalry, and the gallant Maj. John Pelham who commanded the Stuart Horse Artillery, protected our right so they could not reach our flank and had to assault us directly in front. Sumner, who commanded the right grand division, and Hooker the center, had met with such slaughter that any further attempt upon Longstreet was abandoned, and now it was up to Franklin to attack Jackson with the left grand division. My brigade was commanded by Col. R. F. Hoke of North Carolina, and was directly in the rear of Gen. Maxey Gregg's Brigade of South Carolinians, were attacked with such overwhelming numbers that caused them to fall back, and in General Gregg's effort to rally his men he was shot and killed almost instantly; this caused some confusion, but they never broke but kept falling back, contesting every inch of ground the advancing enemy gained. Colonel Hoke called us to attention, and ordered us to fix bayonets. A perfect stream of wounded was passing to our rear. The firing in front was of the heaviest kind. The cheers of the advancing Yankees could be plainly heard. They were following and crowding the South Carolinians with perfect joy, but poor fellows, they did not know what they were soon to meet. Capt. W. C. Oates (Now General Oates), was in command of my regiment, and was eager to order an advance but had to wait until Colonel Hoke ordered. When everything got right, Hoke ordered us forward, with orders not to fire until we had passed our men in front. We soon came upon them when we halted and was ordered to fire, and immediately we raised the "Rebel Yell" and rushed on to the Yankees with the bayonet. They could not stand. They were not expecting such a deadly volley. They broke and we after them down the hill to the cut in the railroad where we overhauled a goodly number of them crouched down, waving white handkerchiefs to surrender. Our troops on the right and left charged simultaneous with us, and had the same success. The railroad made a curve at this place and as far as I could see to the right and left there were Yankees and our men all mixed up together. The South Carolinians had killed and wounded a great many when they advanced upon them, and they were lying scattered about, some beyond the railroad. We were ordered to halt, after we had crossed over the railroad. The Yankees went to the rear in a hurry. I believe they were really anxious to get out of it. Captain Oates ordered us back to the railroad and there we remained awaiting orders. There was a powerful army just in front, and we made ready to meet an attack from them. Our artillery just in our rear, commanded by the youngest artillery officer in Lee's army, was dealing destruction to their infantry all the time. Their seige guns from Stafford Heights tried in vain to silence him. This was the only assault made upon us that evening, and dark coming on, the firing ceased "except now and then a stray picket." There was a little broom sage in our front and the fire from the enemy's bombs had set it on fire and several of the wounded Yankees were unable to get away, and the blazing straw swept over them like a hurricane. Those that were able fought the flames manfully with their caps, and those that were not able to fight was considerably singed. Cruelty to their own men. About dark we received orders to lay off everything except our canteens and cartridge boxes, load and fix bayonets, and be ready to move at a moment's notice. What does all this mean? It was soon reported that we were going to charge the Yankees. We were not to speak a word and was to be preceded by our artillery which was to be drawn by hand. I had seen what was in front before it became dark, and in my imagination I conceded it to be a hazarduous undertaking. I had been in one night fight over at Manassas which satisfied me, and somehow I had a peculiar horror for night fighting, and could picture in my imagination the most horrible things. It was "Stonewall" Jackson's plan to drive them into the river and doubtless we would have succeeded if General Lee had not opposed it. General Lee thought that they would surely attack him the next day, and he did not want to lose his advantage by risking a night attack. The order was counter-manded, and I was detailed to go on vidette. I was told to advance out in front about twenty-five yards, and there watch until I was relieved. I knew by going that far out I would be near the Yankees. It was dark, except the star-light. I did not know then that any one else from the regiment had been sent out, but I afterwards ascertained that similar details had been made from each company. I crawled as low as I could in the scattering broom sage as far as I thought I was ordered to go. I kept looking back to see if I could, how far I was out. I was in constant dread for fear I would crawl into the Yankee lines, for I knew they were nigh, and I had to be cautious. When I decided that I was far enough out I halted and crouched down until I could just look above the top of the straw. I was not there long before I discovered something dark just ahead of me lying on the ground. I decided that it was a Yankee lying there in silence to take me in. I cocked my gun, and took position to shoot at the first word or movement that might be done. I sat and watched for a minute or more without discovering any movement from whatever it was. I had a thousand thoughts in a minute. I would look back occasionally. I was not going to surrender without a difficulty. I eased up a little nearer, near enough that I punched him gently with my bayonet, then it was that I ascertained that it was a dead Yankee that had been killed about four hours. I eased up to where I could lay my hands on him. The thought struck me to rifle his pockets, and take off his shoes, but upon examination I found his pockets wrong side out, and his shoes gone. He had been robbed by his own people. There I sat beside my dead

—11

enemy in the dark, one who had lost his life in trying to subdue a people who asked for nothing more than "Equality in the Union, or Independence out of it." While there, meditating over our condition, the thought entered my mind that neither our parents, kindred or friends at home, could draw the picture in their imaginations of our condition and situation at that time. Nothing but the "All Seeing Eye" could do it. I was near enough to the Yankees to hear them cough and clear up their throats. We had no orders to shoot unless they advanced. There was wounded Yankees lying between our lines sending up the most pitiful cries for help I ever heard. Some were calling for water, some calling the names of his friends, but none answered or went to their relief. Neither side could help. The night was cold and there is no telling how some of them suffered. Some of them may have died during the night by freezing. 'Twas here that I heard the Masonic word of distress given, but I did not know what it's meaning was then. Such was the condition in our front on the night of the 13th of December, 1862. We fought the brigade of the Pennsylvania Reserves; one young fellow that belonged to the 13th Pennsylvania lay wounded at the rail road and it was from him that I got my information from as to what troops. I remained out on post about two hours, when I was relieved by a man of another regiment which had come down to relieve ours. I went back to my command, and we soon after moved out quietly to the rear, about two hundred yards and after rectifying our line we were ordered to rest. It was after midnight, cold and damp. We were not allowed to build fires and the only way to keep warm was to huddle together. This we did, and slept as best we could 'till daylight, when we were aroused and put in shape to receive the attack that was expected to be made. When night closed in the shattered masses of the enemy took refuge in the city, leaving their dead and wounded scattered all over the battlefield. The Yankee army was now at an appalling extremity, crowded in the city with a river in their rear, and I always thought that if we had crowded them that night according to Jackson's plan we would have been successful. It was said that General Lee candidly confessed his error in not ordering the attack as Jackson had suggested, and gave as a reason that the attack on the 13th had been so easily repulsed, and by so small a portion of his army, that he did not suppose that the enemy would limit his effort to one attempt and preferred to wait for another attack. It would have been a suicidal policy for us to have advanced on them in the day time, for they had at least one hundred guns planted on Stafford Heights on the opposite side of the river, that commanded the entire battle-field. We lay all the day of the 14th in the rear, expecting to be called into action at any time. There was no demonstration made by the enemy that day, and each army lay still, and only sharpshooting and an occasional shelling was indulged in during the day. The 15th passed off quietly without an attack. We were necessarily ignorant of the extent to which the Yankee army had suffered, and was only made known to us when on the morning of the 16th we found that he had availed themselves of the darkness of the night and the prevailance of a violent storm of rain and wind to recross the river. A great victory had been achieved by us with the small loss to that of the Yankee's, and with this engagement ended active operations of both armies during that year, and each commander began to take positions to go into winter quarters, with the Rappahannock River intervening. Our corps was moved down the river about twelve miles, where we went into winter quarters and there remained until my brigade was broken up, and each regiment was transferred to other brigades composed of troops from the same States. I don't mean to say that the organization of the brigade was completely destroyed. My regiment, the 15th Alabama, was transferred to Law's Alabama Brigade in Hood's Division, Longstreet's Corps. Another regiment from another State took our place, and Colonel Hoke of the 21st North Carolina was promoted to command it. Law's Brigade was composed of the 4th, 15th, 44th, 47th and 48th Alabama regiments, and when we broke up from our old brigade, which was Trimble's, we marched back up toward Fredericksburg, going into winter quarters where some other troops had moved from. We were sorry to leave our old comrades, for we had gained an envious reputation while together, and we did not know what kind of metal we were going to be attached to, but we found them all O.K. Now, kind friend, with the battle of Fredericksburg ended my career under the immortal "Stonewall" Jackson and the next two years of my service was in Longstreet's Corps from here to Appomattox. Many were the battles and skirmishes engaged in before the end came, the 9th of April, 1865, of which I will undertake to tell in the next volume, should life last to write it.

PART SECOND

CHAPTER I

REMINENCES OF AN OLD VETERAN OF THE 15TH ALABAMA REGIMENT, LAW'S BRIGADE, HOOD'S DIVISION, LONGSTREET'S CORPS, FROM FREDERICKSBURG, VA., TO APPOMATTOX COURT HOUSE.

KIND FRIEND:

It has been two years since I finished my narrative of events while under "Stonewall" Jackson, and as I have been spared to nearly see my 64th birthday, I assume the arduous task of telling only a part of my service in Longstreet's Corps from Fredericksburg to Appomattox, and this will be from memory, therefore it will be replete of many things that occurred. My regiment, the 15th Alabama was transferred from Trimble's Brigade, Ewell's Division, 2nd Corps, (Jackson's) to Law's Alabama Brigade, Hood's Division, Longstreet's 1st Corps, A. N. Virginia, some time in January, 1863. We were sorry to separate from our old comrades and have to fight under a new commander. We were greatly attached to "Stonewall" Jackson, for he had never known defeat, but the law requiring State troops to be brigaded together had to be obeyed, and we bid farewell to our old brigade and marched to take our place in Law's Alabama Brigade. We had constructed comfortable winter quarters, and we thought it a hardship to leave them not knowing that we would find any in our new position, but when we arrived at our new command we were assigned to a position that had been occupied by another regiment that had been transferred to another command. They had constructed rude huts as we had done, and had to give them up to be occupied by other troops. At that time there was a general moving among the troops for the law for brigading the troops applied to all the

States as well as Alabama. I don't suppose that any regiment experienced any inconvenience by having to leave their quarters, and going to others, for the whole army had gone into winter quarters and had built huts as a protection from the cold wind, rain and snow, and I think the Yankee army had done the same thing. As well as I remember the weather was intensely cold, and snow was on the ground four or five inches deep. Our camp was on Maryea's Heights, near the battle-ground of the 13th of December, on the left of General Lee's army. The timber had been cut away and we were in plain view of the city of Fredericksburg, two miles away, with the open plain extending to the city. This plain was occupied by the two grand divisions of Burnside's army. The right was commanded by General Sumner, fronting Longstreet, the left commanded by General Franklin, fronting Jackson. It was Hooker's Division of Sumner's Corps that made such a desperate and determined assault on a part of Longstreet's forces, which resulted so disastrously to what was afterwards known by us to be the "Irish Brigade," commanded by Brigadier General Maher, an Irishman. It was said that their attack was resolute and determined, causing such a loss that there was not enough left to organize any more. Their brigadier was killed and nearly all the other officers. It was Cobbs' Georgians that these Irish Yankees were butting against, which resulted in putting them out of business the balance of the war. It was this assault that the gallant Brigadier General Thomas R. R. Cobb of Georgia was killed. No truer patriot ever drew blade than he in defense of the South. The position of Cobbs' Brigade was well nigh impregnable, and could be held against great odds. Such was the opinion of General Hooker, when General Burnside called him into council the night after the battle. It was said that they were discussing the propriety of renewing the attack the next morning, when General Hooker expressed his doubts as to his ability to accomplish anything, as it would only add a greater slaughter of his men and vigorously protested against a renewal. With this protest offered by General Hooker, General Burnisde decided to withdraw, which he did, greatly to the disappointment of General Lee. Pardon the disgression. I will now return to our doings in camp. I said the snow was four or five inches deep, yes; and it frozed over, and remained so for several days. We soon became reconciled, and applied ourselves to the new order of things that the change had brought about. Those of us who liked the sport of snow-fighting fell in with the balance of the division and made a vigorous attack on McLaws' Division. Our division was commanded by Colonel Little of a Georgia regiment. I don't know who commanded McLaws' Division, but it was a colonel. He and Little were on horses, and it's useless to try to tell how severely they were pelted. It was a sport that I enjoyed although I would be roughly handled at times, occasionally some great big Georgian would down me, and get astride of me, and would fairly bank the snow in my face, and around my neck. I would hollow for help, and if none came the fellow would get sorry for me and let me up, when I would begin pelting away at some one, trying to retaliate for the treatment I had just received. I don't thing if I was to say that there was three thousand engaging in that snow-fight I would be exagerating. Hood's Division, vs. McLaws'. There were small engagements every day between regiments, and sometimes brigades, as long as the snow lay on the ground. I was worsted pretty badly at times, but summing all up, I guess I come out as well if not better than a great many others. In a few days the snow melted and the ground became to be slush and remained so until a cold North wind would come and dry off everything, when camp would be pleasant. A part of the time while we were at this camp, late at evening we could look away North beyoud Fredericksburg and across the Rappahannock River over in Yankeedom, and see Prof. Low's balloon with a man in it, overlooking our army. He was too far off to be reached with a shot from our cannon. At last it came our company's time to go on picket, to be gone one day and night. We had to go down on the Rappahannock below Fredericksburg, near where the Mattaponix creek empties into the river. We relieved a company that had been there twenty-four hours, occupying the same quarters the did, which was a large brick dwelling house which had been deserted by its occupants on the approach of Franklin's Corps about the 12th of December, for it was near this house that he laid his pontoons and crossed over, occupying the left of Burnside's army. At this time the weather had moderated so as not to be unpleasant. There were only three post to keep up, and the vidette would only have to remain on post two hours, consequently he would not suffer with cold before he was relieved. Those of us that did not have to go on duty, would pass the time off most pleasantly by singing old time sacred music songs, while others would be patting and dancing. The house was large enough so all these things could go on at once, and one would not disturb the other. Our officers enjoyed the fun as well as the men. The Yankees had their picket post on the other side of the river opposite to ours. We were only sent to guard against any sudden attempt that they might make to lay their pontoons and recross. We were not allowed to shoot at them, nor have any communication with them whatever. From four to six A. M. it came my time as corporal to go with three men to relieve the three that had been on from two to four. After I had went the rounds I returned to quarters and when the streaks of day began to light up in the East I sauntered off up the river a short way, and took my seat on the trunk of a small oak that had canted over by the roots near the edge of the water. The bank in my rear hid me from view. The river at this place was so narrow that by talking a little loud we could understand each other. When it got light enough to distinguish objects on the other side a Yankee emerged from the bushes that skirted the outer edge of a sand bar, he must to have seen me as he came down to the water's edge, and began bathing his face and hands. When he rose he looked over at me, and in a subdued tone said, "Good morning, Johnnie." I nodded to him. Continuing, he says, "Johnnie, have you got any sugar and coffe over there?" I shook my head. Continuing, "Have you got any tobacco?" I nodded yes. He then said, "If you will send me over a plug of tobacco, I will send you over a cargo of sugar and coffee." I nodded all right. He stepped back a few steps and picked up a piece of plank ten inches wide and about two feet long, sat down on the sand and began doing something, I could not tell what, but I afterwards found out. He had bored three holes, one at each end and one in the middle, he did this with his pocket knife. He set up three little sticks, in these holes and put pieces of newspaper tied with strings on them, which imitated a three-master schooner, the paper answering for sails. He was but a few minutes at it, and when he finished he put a sack of ground coffee about six inches long, mixed and proportioned with sugar just right to sweeten any quantity you would like to make, on the little craft and he pushed her from shore. I sat and watched the little craft with a great deal of anxiety, for I began to get uneasy for fear I would be caught by the officers. It was curious to see how it would tack in different directions, and ripple along on the small waves, all the while drawing nearer to my side of the river. It finally landed about thirty yards below. I was ready to unload the ship and did, without asking the permission of a government officer. I rolled up a plug of tobacco in a copy of the Richmond Examiner and put it on board. He motioned to me to go above and shove it off; I did as directed and in a few minutes it landed below him. He was proud and so was I. The paper that I sent him had a scathing rebuke to the U. S. government for enlisting negroes to fight us Southerners. I had marked the article, and it caught his eye as soon as he opened it. He read about a minute and says, "Pretty good." About that time some of his friends called him and told him that the officer of the day was coming and that he had better get away from there. With this notice, he rose up, and taking a handful of cartridges from his box, threw them into the water, looking at me he said, "Don't you wish you was at home this morning?" I nodded yes. He hurried off and was soon lost to sight and I sauntered back to quarters feeling shy with my sack of sugar and coffee. I did not use any of it until I returned to camp, and then I kept it a secret from all except my mess-mates. I always thought if I and that fellow ever met and recognized each other he would have offered his hand as a token of friendship for his acts proved to me that his heart was not in the war, and he was in it only by the force of circumstances. The celebrated Texas brigade belonged to Hood's Division, and I had several acquaintances in the 1st and 5th Texas that I had not seen since June, '62. I visited them and found but few of them there, some had been killed and others permanently disabled since last I saw them. These were boys that left Henry County with their parents to make their homes in Texas several years before the war commenced, and I was glad to meet them. As well as I remember it was some time in the early part of February that we had to abandon our winter quarters and march with the division in the direction of Richmond. It seems to me now that we were on the march two days. We marched through Richmond, and went into camp about three miles South of the city, on the Petersburg road. It was reported that General Lee apprehended an attack upon Richmond via of Petersburg, and we were in position to repel any assault that might be made from that direction, and to be nearer our depot of supplies. About sundown, Jackson, Ward, myself and Lieut. Brainard started back to Richmond The lieutenant was our passport to pass us over the bridge that spanned the James river. There were guards stationed at each end, and all the lieutenant had to do was to show his stripes, and that was enough to pass us along with him. It was a dark, cold, cloudy night threatenting snow. We went into a theatre and remained about two hours, and when we came out everywhere was covered in snow and it still snowing heavily. We strated back to camp and after crossing the river and passing through Manchester, we were in the broad road. The snow had so completely covered the ground that every where looked like a road, until we began to come to a fence on each side, but until then, one or the other of us would miss our way, and go into a ditch nearly waist deep. When we arrived at camp some of the boys were up standing around a fire with their oil cloths spread over their shoulders. They were in a bad humor, and said things that I will not undertake to repeat here. That was one of the trials of the life of a soldier that we frequently encountered after that. The question with me was, what am I to do. Snow all over the ground, and nowhere to lie down. I was tired enough just to pile down anywhere. I could see little mounds about covered with snow. It was two, sometimes three men would be covered up with their blankets and oil cloths, all covered with snow under there sleeping soundly. I called for my bed fellow and he answered several yards away. I had some difficulty in reaching him in avoiding stepping on, and blundering over some one that was covered up and asleep. everything looked level after I left the fire. I found my mate and eased under the blankets with him, and I was soon sound asleep. When I woke up the next morning I could look at the little mounds and see a little volume of smoke ascending from the heads of each, caused by the breath of each one as he breathed through the snow. After awhile we rose, shook our blankets and brushed away the snow, gathered some dry brush and sticks around and went to building fires preparatory to cooking breakfast. This was generally done through the whole camp, and by the middle of the afternoon the snow had disappeared only in shady places. We remained here a few days looking and expecting all the time for something to turn up. All at once, one day we received orders to draw two days rations, cook them, and be ready to move at a moment's warning. We hardly got done cooking before the drum beat for us to fall into ranks. Colonel Oates formed the regiment and we took our place in line with the brigade, and it was not long before we was in what seemed to us, as a forced march back in the direction of Richmond. We passed through hurriedly, and took the road that lead out toward a little town called Ashland, some twenty miles away. We arrived in its neighborhood about dark and went into camp. The next morning we fell in again and retraced our steps. The dirt road was all slush and the marching was extremely bad. After awhile we came to a railroad that led to Richmond and General Hood ordered the division on to it. Then it was a short step, and a long step the balance of the way until we struck the paved streets of Richmond. We passed right through, and moving again on the railroads towards Petersburg. After marching ten or twelve miles we went into camp on the right side of the railroad, camping in a large body of oaky woods minus of any undergrowth. We afterwards learned that the forced march out to Ashland was made to be in striking distance to aid General Lee at Fredericksburg, should the enemy attempt to recross again, which General Lee had reason to believe that he was making preparations to do, but it proved to be a false alarm and we were ordered back. We remained in this camp pretty much all the month of March, and about the first of April we were ordered to Suffolk. We marched through the city of Petersburg and took what they called the Jerusalem plank road. This was good marching as far as the plank lasted. As well as I remember they lasted until we came to a small village called Jerusalem, near a small river called Black Water. We were three or four days on this march, and when within a few miles of Suffolk our advanced guard encountered the outpost of the garrison of Suffolk. It resulted in a running fight then by our advance, until they reached the environments of the city. We approached as near as we could on one side, and formed a long line around all of one side, and sharp-shooting was the order of the day on through the month of April. That was a sport that I was fond of (If you call it sport), and I could indulge in it every day. One day I shot at a Yankee standing on his breast-works, he hollowed back at me, "You shot too high." The next shot I lowered my sights and fired, he never told me any more of the range of my bullet. C. L. Renfroe, who now resides in Marshall, Texas, was behind a big pine log with me, and is a witness to the incident. Not long since, in our correspondence he reminded me of the incident, a circumstance that I had long forgotten until he mentioned it. I made some very narrow escapes sometimes. I would have close calls by bullets from the Yankee pickets. Several of our regiment was killed and wounded while here. I could not see, then, the object in sending our division off down there, but I afterwards learned that that country was likely to be run over with the Yankees, and it was the object of our commissary department to gather the supplies for the army before the Yankees could pillage the country, which they soon would have done had it not been for the arrival of Hood's Division. We were as a guard for our wagon trains and I suppose there were an immense amount of supplies collected and sent to a railroad that came down that way from Petersburg. We remained a few days in our position that we took when we first arrived. We moved around what seems to me now on the North side of the town, and immediately entrenched ourselves. Our breastworks were not very strong, but strong enough with other advantages that we had to make us feel secure. We invited attack, but could never draw the Yankees beyond their picket line. Firing was going on somewhere on the line of the division nearly all the time. It become to be monotonous and was hardly noticed. One evening, Captain John Cousins of General Law's staff called for volunteers to go with him at night to undertake to capture a small steam boat that lay in the Nansamond River below Suffolk. The river was narrow and the boat was tied up on our side. Cousins had spied out the route where as he thought it could be captured by making a sudden dash upon it. Some twenty-five or thirty from the brigade had volunteered to go with him. I obtained permission from Lieut. C. V. Morris who was at that time in command of the company to go with him, and according to an understanding we assembled at Law's headquarters about dark. Here the Captain give instructions haw he wanted us to act. Getting through, we started off, not allowed to speak to each other. When we arrived at a certain point he halted us, and had us to get down on our knees in single rank, that being done we began to crawl, on one hand, and knees for we had our gun in the other, and could not use but one hand. It seemed to me that we crawled at least half a mile, sometimes in briars and bushes and occasionally a gulley would have to be crossed. We had got near enough to the boat to see the lights and to hear the bells ring. We halted, and lay flat on the ground for a considerable time. I could not imagine the cause of delay, but I afterwards learned that our leader had to do some reconoitering before we could proceed further. I heard the sentinel hollow out twelve o'clock and all right. After a considerable lapse of time our leader came crawling down the line ordering us to about face and move off in the direction from whence we came. The undertaking was a failure, and we went back to camp. The captain explained to us that the boat was too well guarded for us to make the attempt to capture it. In 1894 when the Confederate Veteran Reunion was at Birmingham, I met him for the first time after the war. I made myself known to him and in our conversation I mentioned the incident. "Oh yes! I now remember," said he. "I had forgotten it long ago." He smiled and said, "Well Mc you boys didn't know how near we all came to being captured that night." I replied no, I didn't know anything about it. "Well," said he, "we were nearly surrounded when I ordered a retrogade movement." The fact was that some deserter that knew of the undertaking had informed the Yankees of it, and they made preparations to take us in. I would have volunteered to go with Cousins anywhere, for he was a man of courage and fine judgment, and a noted scout. He was an Englishman by birth and education, and a man of note in the brigade. We all called him Law's wild man, on account of the dress he wore, and manner in which he wore his hair. He was a strange looking man altogether from any one that I had ever seen. He resides at Glenn Allen, Va. A few days before we left Suffolk he said something that give offense to Colonel Connelly of the fifty-fifth North Carolina regiment, and he asked Cousins for a retraction, Cousins refused and the colonel challenged him for a duel. Cousins promptly accepted, and the colonel mounted his horse and rode away. Major Belo volunteer to take the colonel's place, and came over and informed Cousins that he would take the fight off the hands of Colonel Connelly. Cousins told him all right, and agreed to use Mississippi rifles at forty yards. Their seconds arranged for the time and place, and the next morning they met and everything being arranged according to the "Law Duels" the word was given. They both fired and the major was seen to wince a little, Cousins stood erect, folded his arms and remarked to the major that they were doing d—n bad shooting. The major was snicked a little about the neck and blood was seen to trickle down his breast when a parley between the friends of each commenced and the matter was amicably adjusted. I only heard the guns, but my captain (Oates) was a witness. About the first of May General Longstreet received an urgent order to proceed at once to the relief of Lee on the Rappahannock. The foraging teams were out and Longstreet delayed his move until the next day, but in the mean time for the purpose of holding us there the Yankees made a heavy attack with their skirmish line all along our lines. Their loss was considerable, as we fought under cover. Some time during the night we abandoned our position and moved hurriedly to Ivor Station on the railroad. The march was extremely tiresome on account of the deep sand. That part of Virginia is a low flat piney woods country, land very poor with bad water. We reached the station about one o'clock, P. M. The sun shone brightly, no breeze stirring, with the heavy sand, and without cool water the march became necessarily slow before we reached the train. There was a great deal of straggling done, men sick and faint, fell out of ranks and flanked off to one side to hunt water, and I was one of them. I flanked off through the woods in search of a house, and after going half a mile I found a house with only women and children as its occupants. I asked for water. They had none at the house fit to drink and I gave one of the boys three cartridges to take my canteen to a spring and fill it. They were good Southern people and were willing to relieve my suffering. I unbuckled my trappings, pulled off my coat, and lay down in the shade of a tree in the yard and waited for the boy to bring the water. He came in about half an hour, but the distance to the spring was so far and the sun-shine so warm, untill the water became warm in the canteen. However, I was greatly relieved, rested and cooled off, and I was ready to pursue my journey to the depot. They gave directions so that I took a near cut, and was not long in getting to the train. The company had got aboard of a flat and when they saw me coming they hollowed to me to run. I would be left. I did run as fast as I could; I was sick and exhausted and was not fit for service then. Pretty soon the train pulled out for Petersburg. It ran slow and I don't remember exactly at what time we arrived, but it was dark, and we were marched out a piece and went into camp. It was here that we heard of the heavy fighting that was going on at the "Wilderness." The next day we marched rapidly for Richmond, and boarded a train there at the Fredericksburg depot, and went up the Orange and Alexander railroad as far as a station called White Hall, where we got off and marched in the direction of the Rapidan River. The fighting at the "Wilderness" was all over with, and Lee had gained a complete victory over the Yankee army commanded by Joe Hooker, without the aid of two strong divisions of Longstreet's Corps. Sadness prevailed in the 15th Alabama when we heard of the death of our former corps commander, "Stonewall" Jackson. This was his first battle without us, and the idea prevailed that had we have been there it might not have occured, but such was fate. The division encamped about two miles of Morton's Ford, on the Rapidan, and our regiment was sent there with orders to resist at all hazards any attempt the Yankees might make to cross at this ford. We were most pleasantly situated, and had nothing to do only to guard this ford and drill a little. While at this camp I became feeble, and began to wane, and some time in June I took the fever. There was a grand review of the whole army, and I was left in camp, not able to go. I always protested going to the hospital, and Dr. Wilson, our assistant surgeon, treated me in camp. At this time, the middle of June, there was being made great preparations for a grand move somewhere soon, and the grand review of all the army was a preliminary to the move. Lee's army at that time had never known defeat, and began to think that it was invincible. After the battle of the Wilderness (Chancellorsville) and the death of Jackson, Ewell succeeded to the command of the Second Corps. The army was well organized into three *Corps de arme*, Longstreet first, Ewell second, and A. P. Hill third. I lay for several days in camp under my little tent with a scorching fever, and at last, one evening about the middle of June I was aroused by a man bending over me with a paper in his hand with my name on it. He told me that I was billed to go to the hospital, get up, and get into the ambulance, and he would take me to the nearest station, which was Rapidan Station on the

Orange and Alexander R. R. I rose up on my elbows and discovered that all the tents had been struck and the regiment gone. I had awaken from my delirium, and then become cognizant of the fact that I was a sick boy. The fever that day had rose to such degree that, that and the medicine had caused me to become delirious and I knew nothing about the time the regiment fell into line to move. The first word I spoke after I had sorter come to, was to ask where the regiment had gone. He replied that he did not know, as the whole army was on the move. There now. He assisted me to and into the ambulance and drove around to other little tents to get others that was left sick as I had been. After getting his load of sick he drove off to the station, arriving there just before sundown. There I saw some evidences of a fight that had occured near Brandy Station between J. E. B. Stuart's cavalry and the Yankee cavalry. I saw a few prisoners, arms and accoutrements that had been captured and was then on their way to Richmond. We did not have to wait long for a train. We were assigned to the genral hospital at Lynchburg. All that I have written in this chapter has been entirely from memory. The dates are only approximately correct. I will tell more in the succeeding chapters.

CHAPTER II

REMINENCES OF AN OLD VETERAN OF THE 15TH ALABAMA REGIMENT, LAW'S BRIGADE, HOOD'S DIVISION, LONGSTREET'S CORPS, FROM FREDERICKSBURG, VA., TO APPOMATTOX COURT HOUSE.

The train carrying the sick of Hood's Division arrived at Lynchburg some time in the night. It was met by the ambulances, and the sick was conveyed out about a mile west of the city where there was many buildings constructed for a general hospital. The buildings were new, well ventilated and surrounded by a large grove of oak trees, where the convalescents would resort to, for recreation and rest "under the shade of the trees." On arrival I was assigned a "bunk" about midway the building. There were two rows of "bunks" and an aisle between. It was well lit up with candles, and I soon discovered that I was surrounded by sick men from various commands. It was not long before I was visited by the surgeon in charge, accompanied by a man called the "Hospital Steward." He was a South Carolinian and he did everything possible to hold his job. I still had fever. The doctor called it camp fever. It was intermitting, or remitting, sometimes would cool down, and then reach to a hundred and four or five degrees. The first thing they did was to bathe me all over in cold water and give me a change of clean underwear. Then came the quinine. Oh my! A hospital! Is this the place that I am to die at? Miserable! Miserable! Far away from a loving word of sympathy or a caress from the lips of mother or loving sisters. A touch from no one except from the rude hand of a man. These were the thoughts that flitted through my mind while lying prostrate on my bunk. Men were dying and being removed to the "dead house" constantly. One night, a fellow that occupied a bunk next to me died. We talked to each other in the early part of the night, and little did I think that he would die before another sun. I dropped off to sleep, and sometime after midnight I awoke and to my surprise they were fixing to carry him out to the dead house. In about a week my fever gave way, and I began to eat solid food. I regained my strength rapidly, and was soon able to go down to the shady grove and loll around with the other convalescents. In strolling around one day I came across Ben Singletary and Rance Kirkland, men that I knew at home. They both were afflicted with bone scurvy, which afflicted their legs so that they could not march. There was a young fellow there that belonged to the 16th Mississippi by the name of Bill Couch. I and him soon became chums and strayed together a good deal after he got able to walk. His large toe nails had tucked down and wouldn't grow no other way, and the doctor pulled them out by the roots with a pair of forceps. Talk about a painful operation, that will do to be called one, but he stood it like a man and was soon well. The doctor said that was the only remedy. I left him there, and never saw, or heard of him again. There came a young fellow in my ward one night that had been wounded in the head. The doctors examined him and found that the ball had hit him square in the forehead and came out at the back of his head. They

—12

told him that nothing could be done for him, and that if he had any preparations to make, he had better be at it, for he could not live. The fellow disagreed with them about that. The doctors left him, and went about their business, leaving the fellow grumbling because they had no hopes for him. He grumbled four or five hours and became loud in his denunciatory remarks about the doctors. At last the doctors came, and told him just to satisfy him they would probe his wound, and in doing so, found that the ball had just run under the skin over the skull and came out on the other side in the back part of his head. There! said the doctor, you will be all right in a few days. The fellow replied "By G——d, I told you so." The doctors laughed and went on. While at this hospital, as well as I remember, it was the 28th I received a letter from one of my sisters conveying the sad intelligence of the death of my father, which occurred on the 23rd. This was sad news to me, for I had a great desire to see him, and recount to him the many incidents of my life as his soldier boy. He was an old soldier himself in his boyhood days, and well do I remember how interesting his stories would be when he would relate of his thrilling experiences he had with the Indians, but fate had decreed otherwise, and I had to accept it as the inevitable I was getting along splendidly, and began to feel like going back to the army, but where was it? No one at the hospital knew, if they did they kept it a secret. About the first of July the doctor announced that all that wanted to go to the army to fall into lines outside the hospital. There were fifty or sixty besides myself fell in. There were some turned down, and was not allowed to go, the doctor pronounced them unable. I was passed and told with others to get our belongings and march in line down to the depot, where transportation would be obtained for each of us, and be ready to board the first train to Staunton, a beautiful little town at the head of the Shenandoah valley. We did so, and arrived in due time. There we found five or six hundred soldiers that had accumulated there on their way to the army. We were held there two or three days, and with the arrival of each train the crowd was augumented to about one thousand. While here we learned of the great battle of Gettysburg being fought. Having different reports they created no little excitement. We were informed that we would have to march as an escort or guard for a long ammunition train that then was getting ready to start to General Lee's army. We were all supplied with a bran new Enfield rifle with cartridge boxes, bayonets and forty rounds of ammunition to match. I often have thought of the pretty little short Enfield I drew. It was made at Salisbury, N. C., and was a dandy. I was anxious to try it, but opportunity never offered before I had to give it up. About the fifth of July the long ammunition train drove out onto the pike and we formed in single rank on each side. When all was ready, we moved off down the pike that leads down the beautiful valley of the Shenandoah towards Winchester, and the Potomac. The distance to the latter being one hundred and ten miles. We had plenty of rations and the march was only frolic for me, I enjoyed it. We were four days making the trip. We left the train packed on the Virginia side of the Potomac, opposite Williamsport, in Maryland. I had already met some of my company that had been wounded at Gettysburg, but they did not know much as to who, and how may was killed and wounded, for they left as soon as they were wounded. We crossed the Potomac on a pontoon bridge that spanned the river below Williamsport. We were partially organized and commanded by commissioned officers that were on their way back to the army. We marched in the direction of Hagerstown, some eight or ten miles from the Potomac, when we began to meet some of the army. The officers could not hold us in line any longer, each man was anxious to find his command, and we dispersed in every direction. The first man I met that I knew was my old friend, Dick Trawick. He was a member of the Henry Greys and belonged to the 6th Alabama. At that time there was a great difference in our dress. I was what was called a hospital rat, let out with fair skin and clean clothes. Dick was barefooted, his pants torn off half way to his knees, his shirt black and dirty, with half dozen canteens full of water. He was detailed to go for water the day before, and his command moved off while he was gone, and he got lost off from them. When he saw me he hollowed at me and asked me if I had seen Rodes' "foot cavalry." I told him no. He went his way and I went mine, hunting my command. Dick was a good soldier and still lives in Geneva county. After wandering about through the different commands, I at last found Longstreet's Corps, then Hood's Division, then Law's Brigade. After I found the brigade I was not long in finding my regiment and company. I reported to my

Colonel, W. C. Oates, and from him I learned of the terrible battle, and the losses of our regiment and my company. My Captain, H. C. Brainard, 1st Lieut. John A. Oates and 2nd Lieut. B. H. Cody had been killed or mortally wounded. Brainard was killed. Oates and Cody mortally wounded, from which they died in a few days. The ranks of my old company had been so depleted since they left me sick on the Rapidan, that it was a mere skeleton. It was sad to me to think of some of the boys and to know that I would never see them again. My company was commanded by our 3rd Lieutenant, T. M. Renfroe, a noble, brave officer. He recounted to me the particulars of the battle and it was nothing short of a miracle that any escaped. The company was without non-commissioned, as well as commissioned officers. My colonel called me to his quarters and told me he would promote me to be Orderly Sergeant of my company, so I began to act at once in that capacity. The army had fell back to near the Potomac, and formed line and built breastworks. The Yankee army had pursued, and when they ascertained that we had halted, they only felt along our line with skirmishers to find out our position. They formed their line paralel to ours and only skirmished the few days we remained there. I have since ascertained that General Lee was anxious to be attacked in this position, but Meade declined. Our command shared with him in the desire to be attacked, for we felt like we had a position that could not be carried by assault, although the Potomac was near to our backs, and a defeat at that time and place would have been most disastrous. We only had one pontoon across the river to pass the immense wagon train to the Virginia side. We invited attack every day but it was refused. It was said that Meade's army was so crippled at Gettysburg that he would not hazard an attack. Notwithstanding, the heavy losses of Lee's army, they had not lost its morale. After remaining in position three or four days we crossed the river unmolested, and mrached in the direction of Winchester. We camped for a few days at Bunhill Spring, and then marched on through Winchester and took the left hand pike leading to Culpepper Court House, crossing the Shenandoah by wading near Front Royal. It so happened one day that our regiment was leading the advance of the infantry and the Yankee cavalry got in our front and run back our cavalry Videttes that was preceding the infantry. Colonel Oates threw out Co. "D" as skirmishers and brushed them out of the way, but not without the loss of their gallant commander, Captain Head. He was a fine officer and his loss was irreparable to his company. The whole regiment was sorry that Captain Head had been killed. Colonel Oates had him wrapped in a blanket, put in an ambulance and conveyed to Culpepper Court House and there buried him by the honors of war. We camped near the Court House in a fine shady grove, remaining there all the balance of July. I don't remember the exact day we moved from there, but it was some time in the early part of August when we moved in the direction of Fredericksburg. We did not know anything about the movements of the Yankee army, and cared less. It was reasonable to suppose that J. E. B. Stuart, our great cavalry commander, would keep General Lee informed, and we would be moved at the right time and place. We were marched down the Fredericksburg pike, crossing the Rapidan at Morton's Ford, and camped seven or eight miles South of Fredericksburg. Since the death of my father in June, I wanted to come home and told Colonel Oates if he saw any chance to get me a furlough, I would appreciate it; he promised that he would. All through the month of August there was nothing doing with us, only moving to a new camp occasionally, which was good for our health. Some time in the latter part of August General Lee issued a general order that one man from each company would be granted a furlough for thirty days to go home. This man was to be the most meritorious man of the company, and was to be selected by the officer commanding the regiment. Two applications from each company was to be sent up by the officer commanding the company. Lieut. T. M. Renfroe was commanding the company and Col. W. C. Oates the regiment. There was three selected from my company, John Shepherd, G. C. Renfroe and myself. The lieutenant would not decide what two, from the three, and he proposed to us to draw. We agreed, and proceeded to draw when it fell to my lot and G. C. Renfroe as the ones to be recommended to the Colonel. Renfroe, who was a brother to the lieutenant, was a transferred man from the Barbour Greys, 5th Alabama. I was one of the originals of the company. According to orders, our applications was forwarded to the colonel and he to decide between Renfroe and myself. Applications of a similar character from the other companies were flooding the colonel's desk, and he had a job on his hands. Somebody was going to get mad, and cuss the colonel for partiality. These were momentous times with Renfroe and myself, both waiting the decision of the colonel. A day or two passed without any hearing. I was under great suspense. I had no claim as to merit, for Renfroe had always done his duty and was as good soldier as anybody. I had only one claim on Colonel Oates, and that was he was my captain when I volunteered and Renfroe was a transferred man. What would he do? Which one of us would he turn down? That was the question. At last one day the orderly call was sounded and Sergeant Lingo went to the colonel's quarters. I and Renfroe, and others of the company was watching. Who would, and who would not get it had been the chief topic for discussion since the applications had been forwarded. We see Lingo coming back, with a paper in his hand. There was a considerable gathering at Lieutenant Renfroe's tent. I kept my distance. Lingo handed the paper to Lieutenant Renfroe, he glanced over it a moment and read, "Respectfully returned, disapproved, W. C. Oates, Colonel commanding." "Here Green, here is your application disapproved." "Just as I expected," exclaimed Green, "that's what a transferred man gets, it matters not how faithful he may have been." He poured out vials of wrath on the colonel and the lieutenant, his brother, was not at all pleased. My friends were rejoicing that I had won the plum. I said nothing in an exulting way, but my heart within leaped for joy at the thought of going home to see my mother and sisters that I had not seen in over two years. The next thing with me was, how long will it be before I start? Days and nights wore on, I became uneasy, fearful that we would have another battle and that I might get wounded or killed. These were my thoughts and I was in great suspense again. We moved from this camp, camping in a piney grove near Hamilton's crossing on the Richmond and Fredericksburg R. R. The warm days and nights would pass, and I could hear nothing from my furlough. One man from each company of the regiment was having the same experienc that I was. Couriers to the colonel's tent would come and go, but nothing would be said about our furloughs. As well as I remember late at night of the tenth of September, the orderlies call was sounded, which I promptly attended, and when a representative from each company had reported the colonel announced that the furloughs had come, and gave orders for the man to go to the commisary and draw three day's rations, cook them that night, and be ready to take the train the next morning at Hamilton's crossing, where transportation would be furnished us to Richmond. The colonel then began to call the sergenats from the different companies beginning with Company "A" and so on down until he came to "G," the letter of my company, when he skipped to "H" and so on down to Company "L" the last company in the regiment. Well! I drew long breaths, wondering what was the matter, what had become of my furlough, I stood still and said nothing. As the furloughs would be handed to the sergeants, they would disperse and go to their companies. After all had left the colonel invited me into his tent, and after repeating the orders about rations and transportation, he told me he would get from General Law an extension of six days on mine if I would arrest some deserters from our company, and send them back; of course I gladly accepted that offer. He told me to call at his tent the next morning before I left. I went back to my company and my mess-mates were ready to assist me in getting rations, and helping me to cook them. I was ready in time the next morning and called at the colonel's tent as I went by. He handed me an order from General Law permitting me to stay at home six days after the expiration of my furlough, which kept me from being molested at home by the provost guards, he also gave me some letters to deliver to parties at home. I bid him good-bye, and with a whole host of others hastened to the depot. There I found a great many from my division that was coming South; Alabamians, Georgians, South Carolinians and Texans. All of Hood's Division, starting for home, but the poor Texans could not cross the Mississippi, and they stopped along with relatives in other states. We all got transportation and the long train pulled out for Richmond. Then we had to obtain transportation home. We could not leave until the next day, and we lay on the beautiful lawn in Capitol Square. The guard tried to rout us out but we would not be routed, and remained all night. After the police found out who we were and our business, no further effort was fade to run us out of there. The next morning we went hunting for the Quartermaster and the place to get our transportation. What we said to the fellow in charge had but little effect. Time was precious with us, and we was in a hurry. We were told that the office would not open before twelve o'clock; that didn't suit, for that was the time for the train to leave for the South. General Hood, that was wounded at Gettysburg was there and some of the Texans made known to him our condition, and after roaring out a few oaths, repaired to the transportation office and we all followed. After a few sharp words of command from Hood, the Quartermaster increased his clercial force and began to grind out our transportation. Mine was to Ft. Gaines, Ga., and return. We left that day on time, and I had a pleasant trip of three days to the point of destination; coming through the Carolinas and Georgia, the Texans dropped off except those that went up by Lynchburg and on into North Alabama and Mississippi. I arrived at Ft. Gaines late in the evening, crossed the Chattahoochie on a flat and walked out seven miles to Mrs. Tom Knight's, where they were delighted to entertain a Confederate soldier. Besides Mrs. Knight there were three grown daughters, one son in the war and one too young to go. They were strong Southern people, and they were glad for a good rebel to stop with them that was fresh from the army. I was in twelve miles of home, and I was anxious to move on, but they said stay all night, and they would send me over to Abbeville the next morning. I consented, but I felt rather cramped when I went in to supper. It had been a long time since I had sat down to a table for a meal, especially with a refined family as they were, and I suffered with no little embarrassment, but they did every thing to relieve me, and I put on as bold a front as possible. The longer I stayed and talked the better I got, and by morning a great deal of my timidity had worn off. After breakfast, young Knight hitched a horse to a buggy, I told them good-bye, and started for Abbeville. I was glad to see my old town once more and meet some of the old men that was staying at home. After resting awhile I set out for home only four miles. I met several on the way, and had to stop and talk with every one, and lost so much time at this until it was late in the evening before I got home. There was a lane two hundred yards long down a gradual slant to the old homestead. Things on every side looked lonely and desolate. I felt sad, for I knew there was one absent that I would not meet. I approached slowly wondering how we would meet, as I drew near the yard fence one of my sisters came in the front yard. I knew her, but she did not recognize me in some time. I slowed up, my other two sisters and mother came in the front piaza, stopped and looked. About that time a little negro boy named Pete came dashing out at the front gate, and drawing near he turned around, calling to Miss Polly, saying its Mas——, calling me by name. I then advanced quickly to the gate where I was soon captured by mother and sisters. No one can imagine the joy we had in meeting. Caroline, my old nurse when I was a baby, came running to meet me, she was as proud to see me as mother and sisters. Well, I was at home to rest for a short time with mama. It was not long before they begin telling me the particulars of father's death, and how anxious he was that I might go through the war safe, and return home to see him, but fate had decreed otherwise. In a day or two, my home coming was known for miles around, and the old people and a great many of the young people began to drop in to see me. Several came making inquiries about their relatives in the army. The young boys, and the girls of all ages came to see me, and it was not long before I was beseiged by the latter. A soldier of my age was a great curiosity and they enjoyed hearing my camp stories, I was fresh from the army then, and memory good, I was well loaded, and could tell a great deal. During my stay at home, I saw all my relatives that were living, and had a good time with them. There was a little girl in the settlement that had moved into it since I had been gone, and some of my people had become so impressed with her, that they had picked her out for me, and had even wrote of her while I was in the army. I was anxious to see her and sure enough in a few days I did, and she caught me at once, but I never let her know it, for I had another girl that I had left behind. I said that this strange girl caught me, and to tell you the truth, reader, I stayed caught, until the war ended in April 1865, and in November following I caught her and she is with me today. I had been at home some ten or twelve days, when I began to make arrangements to carry into effect the instructions I had received from Colonel Oates when I left camp for home.

CHAPTER III

REMINISCENCES OF AN OLD VETERAN OF THE 15th ALABAMA REGIMENT, LAW'S BRIGADE, HOOD'S DIVISION, LONGSTREET'S CORPS, FROM FREDERICKSBURG, VA. TO APPOMATTOX COURT HOUSE.

There was a little squad of cavalry stationed in my town, commanded by a Lieutenant Bolling. I conferred with him, and asked him to go with me and aid me in capturing the men that was at home, absent without leave. He readily consented, and told me that that was his business, to arrest all absentees and return them to camp. We set the day, and appointed the place of meeting. Promptly on time he with six of his troopers met me at the designated place, and we set out for a half-day's ride to the home of the men that I was after. I had but little trouble in finding them, and met with no resistance when I told them my business. I informed them to get ready they would have to go with me to Abbeville that night. They complained a little, and said they were making preparations to return in a few days. That was not satisfactory, as that was not in accordance with instructions from headquarters. When they fully ascertained that I meant "business" the wail from their wives and children began. My heart almost melted within for the sorrow that I had for their wives and little children. Their entreaties for their husbands and father, were enough to move the heart of the Duke of Willington, or Bonaparte, the Emperor of France. I had to assume a spirit of austerity though without harshness. I endeavored to conceal my sympathy and in a plain manner made them understand that they had to go voluntarily if they would, otherwise forcibly. The fact was they thought they would be tried by court marshal for desertion, and be condemned to be shot. I succeeded in consoling their wives and children upon that fear, and we soon got ready, bid farewell and moved off for Abbeville arriving there about ten o'clock at night. I turned them over to Lieut. Bolling with instructions to send them to their commands as soon as possible, for it was a time when every able-bodied man was needed at the front, and there was no time for sulking. They were sent back to the army through the proper channel, and was finally pardoned by an amnesty proclamation from President Davis, when they entered immediately on duty with the company, and fought well until one of them was severely wounded at Fussle's Mill, August 16th, 1864, which disabled him from further service. The other deserted, and went to the Yankees one night while on post in January, 1865. They both came home, and were respected citizens in the settlement in which they lived. I have no harsh words for them now. They have long since crossed over, and all I have to say, "May they rest in peace." In a few days after this, news came that a hard battle had been fought at Chickamauga, Ga., and that a part of Longstreet's Corps had been sent from Virginia to reinforce Bragg's army, and was engaged in that battle. This was startling news to me and I was inclined to discredit the report, for I neither saw nor heard of any preparations being made for that move when I left the army only a few days before, but in a day or two the report was confirmed, and that Hood's division was there, and engaged in the battle and that Gen. Hood had lost his leg. This made me extremely anxious to hear from my regiment, especially my company, for I had a brother-in-law, and some cousins in the company that I was deeply interested in their safety. In a short time I received word that my Lieutenant, T. M. Renfroe, was at home wounded, and wished for me to go over to see him. This I did, and found him suffering with a fractured elbow. He was lively, and free to talk and he gave me a full history of the part taken by the regiment and company. The loss of our company was heavy, and among the slain was my brother-in-law, Wm. G. Moore. This was sad news to me, for I would have to be the one to tell my sister when I returned home. My cousins went through safe, but several of my comrades that I left in camp in Virginia were killed, and others maimed, so that it rendered them unfit for further service in the ranks. He told me that the corps followed in three days after I left camp, so as in other instances, I was fortunate to be absent from that battle, as well as that of Gettysburg. A kind providence provided. After remaining with him till late in the afternoon, I returned to my home where mother and sisters were in waiting to hear what news I had from the battle of Chickamauga. I did not know how to break the news to my young widowed sister. When I returned I was met at the gate by all of them anxious to hear the news from the battle. I could not help from observing a look of fear in my sister's countenance, and they detected a glimpse of sorrow depicted upon my countenance, "What news! What news! have you from the battle." We whipped the Yankees, and drove them from off the field back into Chattanooga, said I; but not without serious loss to my company. Then addressing my sister, I said to her, "Sis, I am sorry to have to tell you that your husband, Billie Moore, was killed." O, God! may I never experience just such a scene again. Of course I consoled her all I could, and the few remaining days of my stay were wrapped in sadness and gloom for her, and his family, that did not live far away. This was a sudden check to my joy at home, and I longed for the day to arrive when I would take my leave for the army. There was no more pleasure at home for me as all pleasure had banished, and my home that for a few days had been one of joy was now by the cruel hand of fate had been turned into a home of weeping and mourning. A few days before the expiration of my furlough I started back to the army, taking the train at Ft. Gaines, Ga., via Macon through Atlanta and on to near Chattanooga, where I found my command entrenched on the extreme left of Bragg's army which was comamnded by Lieut. Gen. Longstreet. During my absence my company had elected our Adjutant, Captain, our First Lieutenant refusing the honor of promotion. I was his Orderly, having been promoted by Col. Oates just after the battle of Gettysburg. I reported to him for duty and entered immediately upon duty devolving upon the First Sergeant. I also reported to Col. Oates, who was proud to see me, and he gave me an interesting account of the part played in action of the 15th Alabama Regiment. These were the first days of October and we only remained in this position a few days when the regiment with the brigade was ordered across the Lookout Mountain, taking position in Wills' Valley, and picketing on the Tennessee River nearly in the rear of Chattanooga. While on this duty I had some thrilling experience as a scout, making narrow escapes, which I will undertake to tell. There were six regular scouts in Hood's Division, that carried Whitworth Rifles. They were Texans, Georgians and one Alabamian, and he was from the 4th Regiment of Law's Brigade. They came to our camp early one morning, and asked permission of Col. Oates to allow them to cross over to Williams' Island. This island contained one or two hundred acres, and was surrounded by a split in the Tennessee separating above our camp towards Chattanooga and coming together below our camp. The man who owned the island was a strong Southern man and the Yankees had a habit of crossing over the other prong and going to the old gentleman's house, and taking what they pleased, and it was this kind of a party that these scouts wanted to meet. I wanted to go with them bad. I obtained the consent of my Captain, Waddell, and Col. Oates and I asked one of the scouts to let me take his place. He consented, and turned over to me his Whitworth and a 44 revolver. To cross was the next thing to do. There was two "dug outs" (or canoes as we called them) lying down at the water's edge opposite our camp, and as there were only two boats three of us had to get in each boat. No sooner done we pushed from shore, and the man in the stern with his oar fought the swift current manfully, and landed us at the designated spot. We went ashore, making as little noise as possible, tieing up our little crafts to trees, we went in search for a path that would lead us through the thick cane to an opening. Sergeant ———— Champion of the 4th Texas, was in command and after rambling around awhile, a path was found. He formed us in single rank, and enjoined secrecy. "Notice Me," was his order. When I wave my left hand around move to the left, and when I move my right hand around move to the right; if I move my hand quick you move quick. Such was his orders, and I don't know if they would have been necessary had not it been that I was a new man, and needed instructions, for I supposed that the other scouts had been with him so long that they understood him thoroughly. It did not take me long to catch on, and we could be thrown into a skirmish line to the right or left by the wave of his hand as if he had given it by the word of mouth. After receiving instructions we proceeded on slowly, in single rank without even a whisper. We had not gone far before we came to an opening at the lower end of Mr. Williams' large corn field. Here Mr. Williams' son, 14 years old, came to us and the Seageant got all the information from him that he wanted. He told how many generally came over, and the time of day, and where they landed. That was enough. We moved a little down toward their place for landing, and took our position about two steps a part behind a very large log that was resting on another giving it a raise of about a foot from the ground. I was on the extreme left next to——— Chandler of the 1st Texas, on my right. I crouched down upon my knees and done my watching under the log. Sergeant Champion was twenty yards to the right stationed behind a large beech where he could observe everything passing. Presently he motioned, look out! I looked to the left, and saw a Yankee alone coming in our direction, and his line of march threw him on the opposite of the log that we were behind. He came slowly along with his gun carelessly on his shoulder, not dreaming he was so near to a Confederate prison. I watched him, until he passed, and gave the nod to Chandler when he all at once rose up within six feet of the Yankee with gun presented, in a low tone, told him to cross over the log. The old Yank seemed perfectly bewildered and could hardly realize "where he was at." He could only see five of us and he made inquiry as to our number, but got nothing from us, but told us that sixteen were making preparations to cross and if that was all the men we had we had better leave from there, but we let his suggestion go unheeded, and waited for the coming of the others. He was made to understand that loud talking would not be tolerated, and what talking he did he did it in a subdued tone. He was greatly excited as he imagined the most fearful of consequences. We were not long in waiting before we heard the chain rattling, as they were being pulled out of the canoes to make them fast. "Listen," said the Yank, that's them now. All was silent, and something soon was to happen. Yonder they come, in single rank. I, on my knees watching under the log, but there is a high rail fence between us, only twenty yards from us. Now what to do? The Sergeant shook his head, and motioned silence, let them pass; the fence is in our way. So we permitted them to pass on without being discovered by them. They went up to Mr. Williams' house and moved around in his yard, little thinking that a few Johnnies had their eyes upon them. We assembled in a thick place where we could not be seen, but were in plain view of them watching every man. There was one of them, and a woman took positions opposite each other in a door seemingly for a talk, when Sergeant Champion laid his rifle up against a tree, and sighted at him, then taking it down, looked around and said, "Must I?" I can kill him as dead as h—l. One fellow said no, don't shoot, you will scare that woman to death. We were about one hundred and fifty yards from them, and the Sergeant said, lets fire on them in the yard, and recross the river. They were pretty thick in the yard and we took good aim with our Whitworths, and fired and we witnessed only a few making a hasty retreat through the corn field to the opposite prong of the river. We retreated in good order to where out boats were, and recrossed to our side in safety. We had our Yankee prisoner along, and that made it necessary for four to occupy one of the boats. The Sergeant ordered that four of the lightest should go in one boat, the heaviest three in the other. I and the Yankee were two of the light ones, and with two others we came over, but not without experiencing some trouble. Our boat dipped water and it looked at times as if we would sink, but the Yankee was familiar with such, and he kept the water bailed out with his cap. I was awful scared, the water was deep, swift and cold, but I had unbuckled all my accounterments and was ready to swim if it became necessary. I thanked God when I landed in safety on our side, and promised that I would never go on such an expedition again. In a day or two there was another expedition organized to cross over in the night, but this time I was not one to volunteer for I had had enough of Williams' Island. After they had matured their plans and had gathered two other boats they pushed off about dark for the other side. Everything went well until they began to pull the bushes that lined the bank on the other side in order to land, and all of a sudden Bang! Bang! and the fire from the Yankee guns could be seen plainly from our side. The Yanks had discovered our crossing place, and had placed a picket there to visit it. Fortunately, no one was hurt, and a right about was made by the oarsmen, and they came back a wiser set than they were when they first started. After they landed Col. Oates directed a volley to be fired over the river, after which all became "calm and serene" at that place. We had a pleasant place to camp, and had no duty to perform, only to picket along the river where the Yankees might be expected to cross. One of our post was a half mile below our camp and below where the converging streams came together. The Yankees had their picket post opposite ours and by mutual agreement between the pickets, there was no firing done at each other across the river. It became my duty one morning to have to carry our pickets their day's rations to them. I wended my way along an unobserved narrow path at the foot of Raccoon Mountain, until I reached the place where the boys were on post. It was my first visit down there, and I could not help feeling a little shy, not knowing but what I would be shot at from across the river if I was seen. There were five on post, four privates and a Sergeant, all from my company. After delivering the rations and looking around awhile I started back to camp. I had a splendid Enfield rifle with plenty of ammunition, and I was anxious to try it. When I reached an abrupt declivity in the mountain I ascended by going from rock to rock, until I reached a place where I could overlook the whole of the Yankee camp on the other side. I took position behind a large rock that completely hid me from the Yankees only when I would peep around to see what they were doing. There was their camp in full view, their tents up, and squads of them in different places standing around a log fire. It was rather cold that morning and it looked to me that they were enjoying the warm, barring the smoke. All old soldiers who reads this well knows what it was to be smoked. I sat there watching their movements some time wanting to fire on them, but I was afraid, fearful that it would be a violation of orders. They were about five hundred yards distant, and my gun was amply effective that distance, and I at last decided to try them. I selected a squad that was standing around a fire as my first target. I was considerably above them, and I had a fair shot. At the crack of my gun there was old hustling to get away, and go into their tents which hid them from view. When I would shoot the smoke of my gun would be so dense until I could not see whether I had made a hit or not. After each round I would fall back in the crevice of the rock, and reload. I enjoyed it so well until I became so bold as to hollow, "Look out!" and then fire and fall back behind the rock and reload. I repeated this half dozen times, and it finally got so that I could not see a Yankee nowhere. The Yankee pickets down opposite ours made complaint to our pickets, and told them if they didn't have that firing to cease, they would open on them. They didn't know what it meant, and our Sergeant told them that it was a fool that was shooting and was always doing something he had no business to do. There was a Yankee that kept blowing a horn, and it sounded to me that it was a signal station, his sounds were peculiar, and would be answered by the same sort from the direction of Chattanooga. I looked for him in the trees of the other side, and if I had found him I was going to try to topple him out. I discovered where the headquarters were, and I directed a few at the tent. I had not fired many rounds before they discovered my position, and occasionally they would throw a shower of balls against the rocks near my position. As a blind, our sergeant burst in a rage with oaths at me, and told the Yankees to "Kill him if they could, he couldn't stop him." That was all right for him to say so, as it kept the fire off of him, we laughed about it afterwards one of the balls that they shot at me struck the rock above me, and fell down near where I picked it up. It was mashed flat, and pretty warm. I became alarmed in my feelings when the thought struck me as to how to get away from there; I was in constant dread that they would bring their cannon to bear upon my position, and batter down my shield and expose me to view to their sharpshooters. I imagined that for once I was in a precarious position. It was time I was at my company; now what shall I do? I can't undertake to go down right now, for my position is known, and they may be watching for me to come out. All these things flitted through my mind, and I finally decided to keep hid and be quiet for an hour or two, and it may be that they would cease their vigilance and that I could descend unobserved. After waiting two hours, I ventured out and began the perilous task of making my escape. I succeeded beyond my expectation, for not a single shot was fired at me, and I returned to my company all OK. This was October and the nights were cool, with frosty mornings, but we had plenty covering to keep us comfortable. Each company of the regiment had its particular place to camp and was well supplied with small tent flies, gum cloths, and blankets that was picked up on the battle-field of Chickamauga, where they were thrown away by the fleeing Yankees. Each company was sent alternately on picket to guard the river front, each remaining twenty-four hours. Sometime near the twentieth of October our pickets discovered signs of an unusual character among the Yankees, and every indication

—13

were that they were making preparations to cross in force, and bag the whole regiment. This was communicated to Colonel Oates, and he forthwith communicated this intelligence to the higher authorities, but it seemed that his reports were unnoticed, and in due course of time the expected happened. The Yankees did not cease their activities, and each day brought nearer the conflict that ensued. Our pickets increased their vigilance, so as not to be taken by surprise, but we felt sure that we could defeat any attempt to land that the Yankees would make, but preparations among them still went on and at early dawn of the 27th here they came. Co. "B" commanded by Capt. N. B. Feagan was on picket at what was afterwards ascertained to be Brown's Ferry, the place selected by the Yankees to make their landing. It was at early dawn when we felt secure in our warm beds, that the cracking of guns began in rapid succession. A runner from Capt. Feagan was dispatched to Col. Oates with the intelligence that the Yankees were crossing in large force, and that he could not maintain his position against such odds. Our company, commanded by Captain Waddell and Company "A," commanded by Captain Schaaff was formed, and hurried to the support of Co. "B" in double quick time. We left all our camp equipage, including our tents, oil cloths, blankets, cooking utensils and clothing, except what we had on, as prey for the Yankees. When we arrived at Co. "B," they were contending against great odds, and our two companys deployed and went at them firing volley after volley into their crowded ranks, but there was a whole brigade of them, eighteen hundred strong, commanded by Brigadier General Hazen, and they had landed and had gained a foot-hold so strong that we could not drive them back. We fought at close quarters for awhile. The left of my company were in the woods and advanced to the bluff and fired on them in their crowded condition on the sand-bar as they would get out of their boats. My position as first sargeant was the right guide of the company, and joined to the left of Co. "A." That part of our line was in an open field with no protection, the Yanks in the woods behind trees between us and the river. Two or three of our men were killed and several wounded, and among the wounded was our gallant Colonel Wm. C. Oates, and had to be toated from the field on a litter. Orders soon came for us to fall back as the Yankees were in force below us and our capture for a time seemed a certainty, but we made our way out without any confusion, and recrossed Lookout Creek, and took position at the foot of Lookout Mountain, exposed to the harrassing fire of the Moccasin Bend battery stationed across the river in the outer edge of Chattanooga. We moved from this place in a more secure place, out of the range of this battery, and remained a few days waiting developments. It was ascertained that Hooker, with two strong divisions had crossed the Tennessee at Bridgeport, and was marching up the valley to get in our rear, but Hazen's movement was a day or two too soon, so we got out in that way. Hooker's advance came in sight of Lookout Mountain with a large wagon-train. As far as they could discover it was only guarded by a brigade. It went into camp about three miles and Longstreet was anxious for its capture, and to do so he ordered General Jenkins with his six regiments of his South Carolinians to proceed after dark and capture it if he could, and at the same time he ordered our brigade (Law's) to recross the creek and form his brigade in Hazer's path in order to prevent him from sending reinforcements to Hooker, and gaining Jenkins' rear. Law crossed over his brigade quietly and took position as directed and waited for further developments. We were not long in waiting before we heard the advance of Jenkins' troops began to fire. The moon shone bright, and Jenkins attacked with great fury. He succeeded in getting in among the wagons, but Hooker hurled the whole of Howard's Division against him and he had to abandon the project after sustaining a heavy loss of some of his valuable officers and men. Longstreet has been heavily criticised for its failure in not sending reinforcements to Jenkins when he was hard pressed. The position of our brigade that night was attacked with such numbers that we had to yield our position and fall back to where we started from, but not until we had inflicted a heavy loss on the Yankees when they tried to over-run us. We held them in check until it was ascertained that Jenkins could not carry his point, and gave him time to fall back to his original position on the slope of Lookout Mountain. All of these operations were on the left wing of Bragg's army, which as General Bragg said, was entrusted to General Longstreet. I don't know by what authority these moves were made, but one thing I know now, they were "triumpant failures," for the want of proper support and resulted in losses to us for no good.

We occupied the crest of Lookout until sometime in November, when our corps was withdrawn and sent against Burnside in East Tennessee, who was then occupying Knoxville. We encountered many delays before we reached Knoxville, the first at Cleveland, about twenty-five miles from Chattanooga on the E. T. & Go. R. R. We remained there a day or two waiting I suppose for a train to carry us to Louden, a little town on the north bank of the Tennessee, We traveled on the cars from Cleveland to a little place called Sweet Water, and there we found a pontoon train with horses hitched, ready to move. That meant that we were going to cross the Tennessee. The bridge had been burned at Louden, and we could proceed no further by rail. In a short while after our arrival the teams that were hitched to the pontoons were driven off, and we remained two or three hours before we were ordered to move. We were awful sleepy when orders came to fall in, but we had to go. We were marched off in a Western direction, and at last came to the pontoons where they had been launched and laid across, so that we could cross without any difficulty. The guard that had preceeded us said that the Yankees offered no resistance when they commenced laying the pontoons, but rather invited us to come over that they would see us tomorrow. After crossing we marched until one or two o'clock, halted and ordered to rest, without making any fires. The nights were real cool. White frosty mornings and the loss of our blankets over in Raccoon valley were greatly missed, and we were anxious for a scrap with the Yankees in order that we would supply ourselves again with such things as we had lost. We lay down and slept as best we could, until about day-break the guns in front began to pop. We were ordered into line and with the balance of the brigade we were moved off rapidly in the direction of the firing. We marched two or three miles before we overtook the troops that was doing the shooting, although we had passed several dead and wounded Yankees in the road. It was our advance cavalry that was driving the Yankees in on their reserve, understood to be at Lenoir Station, on the railroad between Louden and Knoxville. It was a running fight, until the Yankees reached their entrenchments around Knoxville. I don't remember how long it took us to reach Knoxville, but we captured many things on the route that we were in need of, which to some extent and in some particulars repaid us for our losses. On arriving in front of Knoxville, Longstreet, with his two divisions, and some cavalry, proceeded at once to lay siege to the place, but our forces were not strong enough to completely surround the place hence its capture was a failure. We had no regular engagement with them, but was sharpshooting and skirmishing every day. My company, as well as the other companies of the regiment, would have some hard skirmishes with the Yankees, in our efforts to establish our position to vantage, but sometimes we would fail, and at other times we would be successful. I well remember the hardest fight my company had. It was on the 25th of November, when we were detailed to drive the Yankees from their position, and to establish one for ourselves. We drove them nicely until we reached a certain place when they received reinforcements, and gave us such a reception that caused us to halt and seek such protection from their fire as the situation afforded. We kept them back until the Texas skirmishers came up on our left, which drew the fire from our front on them. The Yankees kept reinforceing until it looked awhile like we were all going to be captured. There was no help for us in supporting distance, and our gallant Captain Waddell, seeing that nothing could be gained by remaining there, ordered us to fall back, but not without the loss of one of our best men, second Sergt. John T. McLeod, he was shot through the head while standing up encouraging, and showing some of the men where to direct their fire. He was killed instantly and in our retreat we left him in the hands of the enemy. In falling back we halted in the woods and took shelter behind trees (as skirmishers had a right to do) and began firing back at the Yanks who had advanced to, and halted at the position that we had left. While engaged in the woods, J. O. Dell of my company received a mortal wound from which he died that night. Night coming on put a stop to the skirmishing, and each beligerent fell back and occupied their former positions. All this occurred to the South of Knoxville, and on the South side of what was then called Holston river, as I understood it at that time by that name. An improvised crossing was made for us by pulling in wagons and laying a floor on the bolsters. The water was not more than three feet deep, but was too cold to wade. As a last resort to caputure Knoxville Longstreet decided to storm Fort Sanders and we were hurried back across the river in supporting distance, and in sight of the devoted Georgians of Woffords and Bryans Brigades of McLaw's Division, who had been ordered to make the assault. It was a strong fort built upon a commanding position and the large and small timber had been felled with their tops outwardly, making the route to the fort almost impassible. The fort itself was well nigh impregnable, and could not be occupied from the front unless the assaulting column was well provided with ladders to scale the wall after the large ditch in front was occupied. We stood in position under arms, and watched the brave Georgians as they moved out to the assault. I knew from what I could see that it would be a desperate undertaking, and many a brave Georgian would bite the dust. The blood within me became chilled with fear of the result of that charge as I imagined the carnage to be in the ranks of them brave fellows, but I kept silent and made no comment. The Georgians moves on, until they come in range of the numerous cannons that could be brought to bear upon them when they began to send forth missles of destruction into their ranks. Without wavering they move on, until they become entangled in the brush, when they lost their organization, and each man picked his own way to advance, but they move on, shot, shell, grape and cannister dealing death at every step, but they move on, until they get near enough to receive the fire from the small arms in the fort, they gave the "Rebel Yell," and firing as they advanced they made a dash for the fort. They reached the ditch and could go no farther, and all the commanding officer could do was to order a retreat. There was no effort as I saw, made to reinforce them, and they were repulsed with heavy loss, but the charge upon "Fort Sanders" by them Georgians will ever live in the memory of the living, and will adorn a page in history testifying to the devotion of them Georgians to the "Lost Cause." There was no other effort made to capture Knoxville, and upon information that reinforcements were coming to Burnside, Longstreet raised the seige, and moved off up towards Bristol. General Bush, Rod, Johnson with two brigades from Braggs' army had come to us just before we left Knoxville, and was known as Johnson's Division. They moved with us and shared all the hardships of the East Tennessee campaign during the latter winter of '63 and the early winter and spring of '64. General Hood, loosing his leg at Chicamauga, was unable to command and Brigadier General C.

W. Field was promoted to major general and by order of President Davis was assigned to the command of Hood's old division, and thus it was that we were called Fields' Division. Lieutenant Renfroe being disabled, it became necessary for us to have another lieutenant and while at Knoxville Captain Waddell got an order to have an election in our company, to elect a second lieutenant. I was solicited and with two opponents entered the race, a ballot by the men was had and upon an official count it was found that I had received a majority of the votes cast; I was declared elected, and on dress parade orders were read to that effect. Officers of the regiment came and congratulated me upon my success, and bid me God's speed, hoping that I would be as faithful as an officer as I had been a private and orderly sergeant. So I turned in my rifle, and donned a sword with one stripe on my collar I entered immediately on my duties as lieutenant, but I never did feel right in battle with only a sword, and always provided something to shoot with. Our march away from Knoxville was attended with nothing worthy of note more than to say that the weather was cold, roads were muddy and a great many were barefooted and bare for clothing. We passed through several little villages on the railroad, inhabited by people that was divided in sentiment as to the North and South, but we treated all alike and soon made friends, and could get a meal from the union girl as quick as we could the Southern. We had two scraps with the Yankees during the winter, one at Bean's Station, the other at Dandridge, both resulting in the discomfiture of the Yank, but in each engagement we sustained losses that we could not restore.

CHAPTER IV

REMINISCENCES OF AN OLD VETERAN OF THE 15th ALABAMA REGIMENT, LAW'S BRIGADE, FIELD'S DIVISION, LONGSTREET'E CORPS, FROM FREDERICKSBURG TO APPOMATTOX COURT HOUSE, VIRGINIA.

Our new commander, General Fields, was from Virginia and before his promotion commanded a brigade in A. P. Hill's Division and was perfectly familiar with the tactics of "Stonewall" Jackson. The division admired him very much, and he soon had the confidence of his men. We went into winter quarters above Morristown, and near to Greenville, the home of Andrew Jackson and the place where the Yankees murdered John H. Morgan. This was the hardest winter that we had ever experienced. It rained, sleeted and snowed so much that the earth became so full of water until a little stomping around our camp-fires would cause the water to rise, and the earth around would become to be a perfect loblolly, and there was but one remedy, and that was to gather brush or any other kind of wood and stand on it, but the worst of all was that it would rise on us at night in our beds, and everywhere our hip-bones rested water would come to the surface. Ditching around our tents done no good. A good supply of wheat straw gave some relief, but that would only be temporary. One evening I took my blanket and started out to hunt straw, and after walking several miles I came upon a stack, and I approached the lady of the house and made my wants known. She at first refused, and said it was an unusual hard winter and that was all she had to feed her cow on. I laid my condition before her and offered five dollars for as much as I could carry in my blanket. She consented, I give her a five dollar Confederate bill and went to packing my turn. I would pile up and then pack and continued in this way until I had a right respectable pile when it was made loose. When I got as much as I thought I could carry, I tied the corners of my blanket together, shouldered it up, and started to camp. I don't remember now, how far out I was, but I do remember that it worried me awfully before I got to camp. Others from my company had been out and brought in straw and continued as long as there was any to be had in a reasonable distance from camp. It was said that there were plenty of bushwhackers in that country, and when they caught a Confederate soldier they would hang him or put him out of the service in some cruel manner. One of my company straggled on the march up there and he never was heard of afterwards, and it was thought that they caught him and executed him. The Yankee cavalry kept making threats all along during the winter and we would be called out occasionally to brush them away. Their excursions did no good more than to find out where we were, and what manner of men we were, and they certainly found us out at Dandridge one day, for we killed lots of them and they let us alone afterwards. The soldiers of Longstreet's Corps, who were present in his East Tennessee campaign will never forget its hardships. There were many men with bare feet, others thinly clothed, perfectly unfit to stand the rigors of such a winter only by remaining around a fire, and wrapped in a blanket. Carry us back to old Virginia was the constant cry of the men, but at that time we had not the remotest idea where we would go when the spring opened, (but I will tell you later on.) After the wounding of our Colonel Oates in October, the regiment was commanded for a while by Maj. A. A. Lowther, and about the time we left Bragg's army in November he took sick and went home much to the delight of many of us. Our Lieut. Col. I. B. Feagan, who had lost his leg at Gettysburg was still a prisoner, and the regiment was commanded by a captain all through the East Tennessee campaign until early in March when Col. Oates returned to us and found us in winter quarters. My old company rejoiced at his coming, for he brought a large box from our home, filled with good substantial home-made clothing that our people had made up for him to bring to us. We were perfectly delighted, for it went a long way in relieving our want for clothing and shoes, besides that, we were glad to be under his leadership once more. During the month of February my captain had been furloughed home for thirty days and I commanded the company during his absence. He and the colonel returned about the same time and many of the sick and wounded that had become able for duty returned until it swelled the ranks of our much depleted regiment to about four hundred effectives. On the march we had the appearance of being a brigade. The middle of March brought spring weather and we left our winter quarters and took up the line of march toward Bristol. As well as I remember we moved about ten miles and went into camp on an elevated ridge which was more pleasant than the low grounds that we had left. While here our regiment was detailed to go as a guard to our wagon-train over among the hills, across a stream called Big Pigeon, for the purpose of gathering corn as it was understood that there was corn in abundance over there, subject to capture by the Yankees. Our march was pretty brisk and led us through the little town of Dandridge. A company from this town belonging to the 60th Alabama regiment was camped in the place and as I had relatives and friends in the company, I flanked to one side to see them. I could not remain but a few minutes and bidding good-bye I ran on and soon overtook my command, but while there with my friends I learned that small-pox was prevalent in their camp and one of my acquaintances had died only a few days ago. This give me a scare and I had no further use for Dandridge. It was getting late in the evening when we come to the little river. We crossed over in the wagons without much delay. I began to feel badly, I had a violent headache, and fever rose high. I marched on, suffering in that way some four or five miles. We halted to rest, and I reported my condition to the captain and he sent to the head of the regiment for the surgeon. After examining me he gave me medicine and a pass to return to camp the next day. I didn't like that at all, but it was the best that could be done. The sun was about half-hour high, and the country was reported to be full of deserters and bushwhackers and it looked to me a doubtful chance. The captain told me to choose any one that I wanted from the company to stay with me, and I chose Will Phillipp. We saw a single-story log house over on the side of a hill, and after the regiment moved off we made for the house, arriving we found it occupied by three females an elderly woman and two robust likely girls. They met us very coolly, and I suspicioned something immediately. I told her that I was sick and wanted to stay in her house that night, to this she peremptorily refused. I told her that I would not disturbe her nor nothing she had, all I wanted was shelter to keep from lying on the ground. She still refused and said no Rebel should take shelter under her roof. I told her that I would pay her anything reasonable to let me stay. She replied that she did not want any of my Rebel money and that she would not let me stay. Turning and looking her in the face, I said "Madam, I am going to stay anyhow, you may say what you please; Will make my bed down by the fire place, I want to lie down." Will spread down our oil cloths and one blanket and down I lay. About this time the least of the girls was taken with a violent toothache and had as an excuse to run over to a neighbors and have it pulled. I and Will was watching all that. All at once, I became very sick and had to go out to vomit; Will followed and while out there we agreed upon a plan of defense in the event the bushwhackers was to come for us, for we were sure that that was the girl's business off, to inform on us. I had a good Remington 44 revolver and Will had his gun and bayonet. There were two doors to the house and I was to guard one and he the other. We agreed to fight to a finish and not surrender for it meant death, if we were captured and that we would sell out as dear as possible. Will was true and trusty and I had implicit confidence in him. We went back in the house and about dark the girl returned without having her tooth pulled, telling her mother that no one was at home that could pull it. I and Will took all that in. They sat down and ate their supper and then took seats and coversed in a low tone until bed time. They had two bedsteads in the house and they completely stripped one and piled all the bedding on the other. Will was setting up watching every move and I tell you, reader, I was not asleep. I looked at them secretly, so that I would not be discovered, and I thought there was the highest bed I ever saw, three or four large feather beds with mattresses to match all piled up on one another. Will ate his snack of cold beef and bread and asked me if I wanted anything. I was too sick to eat, had a violent headache with high fever. After awhile all three without undressing piled up together on one bed. Will fastened the doors as best he could and as the soldier expresses it, turned in. Before dark Will had provided enough fuel to last nearly all night and he kept it chunked up pretty much all night. I would drop off in a doze occasionally and lie awhile awake and listen. Will would do the same thing. Thus we pased the night without being disturbed.

I was much better the next morning and relished a good cup of coffee that Will made while I was taking a morning nap. When I awoke the bedding had been removed back upon the naked bedstead and they were stirring around cooking breakfast. We offered them some of our coffee, which was readily accepted for they had not had nor seen any in months. After the sun rose to an hour's height we started back to camp. I asked her what county that was, and she said it was Tennessee county. Said I, "That is the name of the State." She insisted that she was right, and I didn't dispute her and computed it to her ignorance. I thanked her for all the kindness shown and bid them good-bye. Will and I retraced our steps and arrived at camp about sundown. We stopped at a house about twelve o'-clock to rest awhile and soon we were invited into dinner. It was a fine dinner and was greatly appreciated. The man of the house was too old for service and had two sons in Pat Cleburn's Division, and treated us royally. We told our experiences of the night before and he expressed wonder that we lived through the night. After dinner we chatted and rested awhile, thanked him for his kindness and bade him good-bye. As I have already said we reached camp about sundown, and found all "calm and serene." The regiment remained off two days and came in with the wagons loaded with corn. While at this camp, Lieutenant Renfroe came to us fresh from home. He had a stiff arm, and did not come for duty, he only come on a visit to see the old boys that were living once more. Some time in the early part of April, orders from corps headuarters were issued, that a furlough for thirty days would be granted to an officer where there was three officers and the company did not exceed fifty men. It struck me at once that if I could get Lieutenant Renfroe to report for duty, my chance was good for a furlough. I approached him on the subject and he readily consented to be reported for duty three mornings all right. I went over to Colonel Oates' quarters and laid the matter before him, and he readily consented to approve my application under the order. I hurried to get it off, with other officers, and in due time theirs came back approved and they started for home leaving me to wonder why my application was delayed. I waited a reasonable length of time, and still it didn't come, and I summed up courage enough to go to the several headquarters to make inquiry. I went first to General Law's, then to Division

Headquarters ascertaining that it was not at either place where I had been, I ventured to General Buckner's quarters (for he was in command of the corps then) he being a strict West Pointer, I felt a little shy in approaching him, I inquired for the Adjutant General, introduced myself and told my business, explaining the circumstances. They showed every courtesy, and the clerk began to search for my application, and sure enough he found it "pigeon-holed" in his desk. He approved it at once, and I carried it back through the proper channel, and each one approved it. I began at once to get ready, drawed and cooked three day's rations, had the quartermaster to give me an order on the quartermaster at Petersburg for two months pay, and the next day Colonel Oates dated my furlough and I started for home. I took the train and came via Bristol, Lynchburg and Petersburg, Va., Weldon and Wilmington, N.C. Branchville, S. C., Augusta, Macon and finally landing at Ft. Gaines, Ga., seventeen miles from home. In company with Cade Lee, a member from Co. H who was coming home on sick furlough, decided to make the trip that night on foot. It was sometime after dark that we were ferried across the Chattahoochie river, when we struck boldly out for Abbeville. I knew the road, and came on without being bothered anywhere, arriving at Abbeville about two o'clock. The place looked lonesome, and as Pollard remarked about the city of Richmond the night after its surrender; I can appropriately apply it to Abbeville at that hour. He said: "That there was not a cheerful fire to dispel the gloom, and darkness brooded over the great city." That truly applied to Abbeville, my home town. We came out about three miles and an old neighbor of mine would have us to stop and take breakfast. We rested with him until about nine o'clock, when we started for our homes. We did not go far together before the roads forked and we had to separate, he going to his home near Newton in Dale County, and I to my home half-mile away. I took my people on surprise. They were not expecting to see me that time. Oh! how glad we were to meet again. Much fighting had been done since I left home in the past fall, but one casualty had happened to any of our relatives, and that was that one of my cousins had lost one of his eyes at Knoxville and was then a prisoner. His young wife at home came to see me to get the particulars. She was greatly disturbed over it, but she had hopes of his recovery, and that he would be exchanged and come home to her some time. He was kept in prison until the close of the war, when he come home but was never well afterwards. The older he got, the worse he was, and at last he began to have epileptic fits, and only a few years ago, while sitting on the bank of Choctawhatchie river fishing he had one of them spells, fell in, and drowned. Thus ended the life of J. N. Trawick, a good soldier. I didn't enjoy the stay at home much for there were no one to associate with but old men. The girls was in full force and was as patriotic as ever. The old citizens had almost despaired of the success of our cause, but I held up the other side and told them General Lee's army was still in the field, and in good spirits. "Yes, but Bragg's army has lost its morale and can't be relied upon with Bragg in command," but I held out to them that things would change now Bragg had been removed, Johnston had been put in command, confidence had been restored, and he had as good soldiers as anybody, and that they would defeat Sherman yet. Such was the line of argument that I would use to hold up our cause. I was glad when the time came for me to start back. A few days before the time come I heard that my command had joined General Lee's army in Virginia, and that heavy fighting was going on. We received news every day which kept us posted as to how the battles were going, and with each dispatch, the news was favorable. The time come for me to return. I kissed mama and sisters good-bye, turned my back upon them and my face towards Ft. Gaines, Ga. to take the train for Virginia. Two of my neighbors had packed two boxes with clothing and provisions for me to carry to their sons. One of them belonged to the 4th Alabama, the other to my company, and what a burden they were before I reached my final destination. I was informed before I left home that W. A. McAllister, our A. Q. M. wanted me to carry back to him one thousand dollars, and accordingly my mother made a pocket to some of my underclothing, where I could secrete it, and when I arrived at Ft. Gaines a man was there with it securely packed. I took it, and that caused an uneasiness all the way. When I landed at Richmond, there I learned that my regiment had been engaged and the losses were considerable. I lost no time in getting my boxes on, and had them checked to Hanover Junction, as I had been informed that my command was near there. It was only fifteen or twenty miles by rail, and I was not long in landing. I put the boxes in the depot, and ran out in search of my command. I was not long in finding them and at once informed the two boys what was at the depot for them. We went back immediately and broke them open and got out the contents and hastened back to the line. One of the boys made me a present of a large, well smoked ham that his father had sent him, saying as he handed it to me, "Here take this for your trouble." The other boy offered nothing, but I did not blame him for he saw that I had as much as I could take care of. All the while the skirmishers were popping away at each other, and a battle was expected at any time. Everything was in a hustle, and there was no time to parley. We hastened back to the line as soon as possible, to be ready for the expected attack on our lines. I reported to my captain and colonel, and they were glad to see me. In a brief way they told me of the hard fighting they had done since their arrival from Tennessee the third of May. They had fought more or less every day up to that time, the 15th, and many of the boys that I left in Tennessee had been killed or wounded. There was not more than twenty-five men in ranks, commanded by Captain D. B. Waddell. The ham that had been given me had a beargrass string to it, and I carried it hung around my waist, and in passing some Georgians they saw it, and began to yell "Here's a ham! ham! ham!" One said, "Never mind old fellow, I will watch you today in battle and if you get killed, its mine sure." The next thing to get rid of was McAllister's money. I found him and handed him the bundle just as it was given me, minus fifty dollars that I took to pay expenses on them boxes. Since the war I paid that man five dollars in good money as a charge that he made against me. I thought it unjust, as I remained to the end and he come home and had a "bomb-proof" position until the close of the war. But that's all over with, and I have lived until now without it and have never suffered for the lack of it. Since our corps had been gone, a new commander for the Yankee army had been appointed and he had assumed a different mode from the rest, to get to Richmond, and that was to increase his numbers and flank Lee out of his position, but in this he failed as history shows. Read it.

CHAPTER V

REMINISCENCES OF AN OLD VETERAN OF THE 15th ALABAMA REGIMENT, LAW'S BRIGADE, FIELD'S DIVISION, LONGSTREET'S CORPS, FROM FREDERISKSBURG TO APPOMATTOX COURT HOUSE.

I said in my last chapter that when I arrived at my command that the skirmishers in front was popping away at each other. Yes, my regiment was in line behind a small breastwork, and some of the men were engaged in strengthening them, for it was not certain where Grant would attack as that had been his tactics ever since he was defeated at Spotsylvania Court House, but he has found Lee ready to receive him wherever he come out. We remained in that position till late in the evening when my company was detailed to go on picket, and relieve some troops that was already on. They were down on, and near the South Anna Creek, and the Yanks were on the other side. We deployed as skirmishers in squads of fours, and relieved those that were there. Each squad occupying a small redoubt. We passed the night quietly until just at daylight we were ordered up to a skirt of woods that was between us and our line of battle. The officer in charge saw that our position down near the creek was untenable in case of an attack, and was easily flanked on our left. He reported these facts to headquarters, and that, I guess was the cause of our removal. We established our line in the woods and had a fine view for several miles beyond the creek where the Yankees were. We were relieved by another company, and we went back to the line. The Yanks were threatening an advance all the time. About the middle of the afternoon here they come, and in such force as to force our skirmishers in. The under-growth in our front had been cut down for about fifty yards, and a charging column would have been considerably tangled if they undertook to capture our breastworks. Every one was ready the moment they showed themselves at the edge of the fallen brush, but they halted in the woods and began to annoy us with their sharpshooters. General Law couldn't stand that and he ordered

Colonel Oates to drive them away. My company, commanded by Captain Waddell, was selected for that duty. The captain deployed us as skirmishers behind the breasworks and gave the command, forward, double quick march. The boys dashed over the works and ran until they reached the thick timber when we were ordered to halt and shelter ourselves. We received their fire, but they aimed badly and not a man was hurt. The men opened fire on them and soon had them to hustle to the rear, but they halted and kept up a desultory fire, resulting in no good more than to hold us to our position in order that other movements could be made. We took position behind trees and the men would fire whenever one would show himself. The firing finally ceased in our front, but continued heavy on our right and left. I was on the left of the company observing things on that flank near the Fredericksburg railroad. I and Barney McArdle, an Irishman of my company, were behind trees that stood near together; a Yankee had advanced unobserved and had taken position behind a tree not over twenty yards distant, all at once his gun cracked and his bullet hissed by. I located him by the smoke of his gun. I was to the right of Barney and could see the Yank better than he could. Barney had located him, and fired on him but missed. The Yank kept shooting, sometimes would hit the trees we were behind. I told Barney that I would tell him when the Yank would get ready to shoot. They exchanged several shots without effect, at last I told Barney to get ready, he was fixing to shoot. He came around slowly, exposing only a little of his side face and head. I told Barney "now" and he fired, down dropped the Yankee. Barney looked at me and winced his head, and in his Irish brogue said "I got 'im." That put an end to that. We remained silent for some time watching and waiting, presently we saw a Yankee coming slowly and to all appearance using caution. We said nothing; he was unarmed and we preferred to let him walk right up on us, and then capture him. He came near enough and Barney presented his gun on him, and he surrendered. He was utterly surprised. He was a lientenant, and only had a sword. Barney carried him back to the line and turned him over to Colonel Oates and I guess he went to Richmond sooner than he bargained for. We were relieved by a company of diffcrent command and we went back to the breastwork, took our place in line and moved by the right flank

—14

behind breastworks in the direction of the Chickahominy. On this flank movement of Grant to Petersburg, he did not fail to attack every place where there appeared to him a reasonable hope of success in breaking our lines, and ride into Richmond, as that was his objective point. It is said of him that on this move that he and his staff stopped to rest at a house and the lady asked him where he was going. He replied that he was going to one of three places: to Richmond, to Heaven or to Hell. She replied that "You can't go to Richmond for General Lee is in the way, you couldn't stay in Heaven for "Stonewall" Jackson is there, and I guess you will have to go to the latter place." He plucked straws and made no reply. The month of May was passing rapidly away and Grant said he "proposed to fight it out on that line if it took all summer," and it really looked that way, for he kept receiving reinforcements while our ranks were constantly diminishing, and could not be replaced, but the remnant of us that was there still showed a bold front and repulsed every assault he made on our lines. We kept pace with all his flank movements and was in his path every time. History has accorded this campaign to General Lee as being one of the most sublime that ever happened in the United States. One day the latter part of May (I don't remember the date) we were marching by the flank nearing Cold Harbor, that the Yankee sharpshooters were uncomfortably nigh to our line, and became a menace to our movement. Colonel Oates detailed Co. "K," commanded by the Irish Lieutenant Pat O'Connor, to drive them away. He deployed his company and sprung over the breastworks and drove them away, but it was a dear victory. Lieutenant O'Connor was killed, which was a loss to his company and the regiment that could not be replaced. We arrived at Cold Harbor the second day of June, and halted as an attack was threatened at that point. The Yankees were near and were massing in strong force. Now I will give in as concise a manner as I know how, a description of our position, breastworks, etc. Our line of works ran down a hill and across a sluggish little branch, and up a hill on the other side from us. There was a large pine sappling thicket just above where our line crossed the branch, which afforded an elegant place to mass troops, where we could not see them. All of Field's Division was on one side of the branch and Breckenridge's Division was on the other. What troops were not in the breastworks were in the rear not far away as reinforcements in case they were needed. General Law's Brigade were all in the front line and he seeing the situation, as soon as dark came the men went to work tearing down the works that lead down to the branch, and building a work down the slope crossing the branch lower down. Corresponding work were done by the troops on the other side, thus you see if you understand it, it placed the whole brigade in position to fire on the Yankees when they reached the place where our first line had been razed. It gave the troops on the other side the same advantage. The men worked all night and had completed them by the first streaks of day. From reports, the Generals were certain that an attack would be made in force the next morning. Captain N. B. Feagan, with his Co. "B" was on picket and was ordered to come in at the first appearance of an advance. Law was anxious to get them in his trap and didn't intend to throw nothing in their way to impede their progress. Colonel Oates had asked Law for a piece of artillery to place at the angle of our works, where they would have full view of the Yankees when they come in sight. The piece was a brass twelve-pounder and commanded by Lieutenant O'Flannigan (an Irishman.) Sure enough about sunrise here they came, charging through the pine thicket huzaing as they came, expecting to run over and capture all that were in the breast-works, but lo! and behold! when they arrived they found them torn down and deserted and was receiving a perfect storm of lead from both sides of the branch. The twelve-pounder, with cannister, did wonderful execution. It was Smith's Corps, closed in mass, and it was hardly possible for a ball to pass through without hitting some one. The men loaded and fired as fast as they could, and in a half-hour's time it was said they lost five thousand men. I never in all the bloody conflicts that I had been in, saw such a destruction of human lives. They literally piled on top of one another, often the dead would hold down the wounded and vice versa. In an hour's time there was a calm, except some sharpshooting. A flag of truce was raised and the Yanks was allowed six hours to bury their dead, after which General Grant began his flank movement toward Petersburg, crossing the James on pontoons below Bermud hundred, where Gen. B. F. Butler was. Beaureguard had him in check and Grant compared Butler's position as being in a jug and it tightly corked. Grant in his flank movement on Petersburg had no trouble and proceeded at once to attack the outer works which was thinly occupied by some of Beauregard's troops. General Lee had anticipated Grant, hurried our division over to put a check on Grant's advance. We went in double quick time through the streets of Petersburg, halting by small detachments just long enough to drink a cup of coffee that the ladies had in waiting for us. It was a miserable warm day and we had been on the quick step for several miles. The streets that we had to march on had been sprinkled, which added much to our comfort. The Yanks was just forming to attack Wise's Brigade in the trenches, but seeing us coming in, withdrew. Grant began to concentrate his army and entrench it at the most available points that were in his possession. Lee concentrated his army opposite and began to entrench also. In the meantime General Lee had dispatched Early with three divisions to the valley to head off Hunter, and threaten Washington. That which was accomplished by this move is a matter of history and not in the province of this narrative. Suffice it to say that it ended disastrously to Early. Grant continued to stretch his left around Petersburg, until he struck the Weldon R. R. at Reams' Station. He succeeded in tearing up some of the track, but Mahone's Division pounced down upon them and give them a glorious thrashing, and capturing many prisoners with their colors. The broken place was soon restored and the regular schedule for the trains was resumed. Fields' Division was shifted several times, first on the North side of the James East of Richmond, then back to Petersburg as the emergency of situation required. By the middle of July Lee had good breastworks, both in front of Richmond and Petersburg. I guess they were thirty miles from right to left. Several attempts were made during the summer to break Lee's lines but all failed. The most formidable attempt was made on the morning of the 29th of July. (I have reference to the Crater, and will pass on and say no more.) Grant lay regular seige to Petersburg and all through the summer, fall and winter months of '64 made repeated efforts to control the railroads that ran into Petersburg, as they were the lines that furnished subsistence from the South to Lee's army, and in some instances he succeeded, but never completely stopped us up. By the middle of June the lines of both armies were established and work to strengthen the breastworks was the order of the night, for neither side was allowed to work in the daytime, where they were the least exposed. My command would go to the front about once a week and relieve troops that were in the trenches in order that they might retire to the rear for a few day's rest, when we would be relieved to rest. About the middle of July a demonstration in heavy force by the enemy was made upon our lines on the North side of the James and within ten miles East of Richmond. The attack was so sudden in such force as to enable them to gain some foot-hold and our division was sent hurriedly from the front of Petersburg to reinforce our troops on the North side of the James. Just before we arrived at the place needed the Yankees had seucceeded in capturing Ft. Gilmer, and the works that led to the right of it towards the James. There were no guns in the fort, and our generals decided that the works that they had captured was of little value to us, and was not worth the attempt to recapture them. The Yankees did not advance any farther, and we established our line which remained permanent until the war closed, although there were repeated efforts made several times during the summer and fall to flank us out of them. We had another fort on this line to the left of Ft. Gilmer, called Ft. Harrison, which commanded a view a mile to the front and had four twenty-pounders mounted therein, ready for action. It was a large earthwork made of earth thrown from the outside, which made a ditch on the outside so deep that the top of the fort could not be reached without ladders. The Texas Brigade occupied this part of the line including the fort. My brigade was on their left, with a branch between, but the bushes had been cut down so that we had a fair view of what took place in front of and at the fort. About the middle of the afternoon brisk firing was heard in front, and presently our advanced skirmishers came in, followed by those of the Yankees. It meant that a heavy assault was going to be made on Ft. Harrison and from our position we could be spectators, if nothing come in our front to detract our attention. Presently the long line of *"Blue and Black"* debouched from the woods in fine style to the attack. Poor, ignorant negroes. They did not know what was in waiting for them behind them works that flanked the fort. Our cannon in the fort threw twenty pound shrapnel at them from the time they made their appearance until close enough for grape and cannister. All this did not check them. Great gaps would be made in their ranks to be closed immediately. When within one hundred yards, the Texans opened upon them with their Enfield rifles and such another thinning of ranks I had not witnessed in a long time. There was nothing in our front and we would yell as if we were on a charge. The attacking column was Ledly's Division of negroes, and we were perfectly delighted to see how the Texans was cutting them down. We had heard of the negro troops in Grant' army, and we wanted a chance at them. We had heard of their cruelty to prisoners, and that had made us *"mad"* and we wanted a chance to appease our wrath. We knew they were fronting a set that would do the right thing by them, and we were satisfied to turn them over to Texans and the Georgians, for they were there also. They came right on, until they reached the outer ditch when into it they went and began to climb up, but let me tell you, reader, our boys threw hand grenades over on them and lit five second fuses to them twenty pound shrapnel and tossed them over on them, until there was heaped in that ditch such a pile of dead *niggers* that no American had ever seen. What few white officers that were left and some of the *niggers* took advantage of the smoke and escaped. The night was hideous from the pitiful cries of them cruel wounded negroes, and many of their dead was thrown into an old well that was on their side. The wounded was hauled off to the hospital near the James and there received good treatment from our surgeons and nurses as they were entitled to. It was ascertained that them *niggers* were tanked up on liquor and that was the cause of them being so headstrong and going to destruction with so much recklessness. That put a quietus on that part of the line, and remained so for several days. The Yankees that were on the North side of the James at that time was commanded by General Butler. Hancock, who commanded a corps in Grant's army, came over and extended Butler's lines far to their right (our left) until our division had to move to the left to keep in Hancock's front. In establishing our lines, sharp skirmishing would occur between us, and it was kept up in this way until the night of the 15th of August revealed the fact that Hancock would attack in force somewhere on the line the next day. We were all put on the qui vive. We in the ranks didn't know where, nor when the attack would be made. As well as I remember it was ten o'clock, that we began to hear firing to our left and it grew to be sharp as if regular lines of battle were engaged. At that time we occupied New Market heights near a large spring where it was said that at one time Washington watered his army. All I can say about that is, that it affordtd an abundant supply. Our brigade had out pickets in front, commanded by my Captain, D. B. Waddell, which left me in the command of the company. The firing increased in volume and our regiment was formed in line and followed by the 48th we moved off in quick time left in front in the direction of the firing. We crossed a little branch and moved rapidly up the hill, and when we struck the level we double-quicked until we became opposite to where the works had been lost. The Georgians were scattered along the works so thin that they had to yield to overwhelming numbers. When we arrived at the place, we were needed, we halted, fronted, and forming we were ordered forward, but while forming, we were fired upon from the left, a place that we were not expecting it, which caused a little confusion in the left wing of our regiment. Order was soon restored, and looking to the left I saw a regiment of Yankees down on their knees loading and firing. Nine of my company were wounded from this fire, and Co. "B" that was on my left sustained similar loss. Two Lieutenants of the regiment were wounded who left their companies without a commissioned officer to command. Our regiment was commanded by Major Lowther, and he was wounded also. Two or three of Bennings' Georgia regiments passed to our rear, and when their right passed our left they fronted, and we altogether charged and drove the Yankeee to and past the breastworks, and capturing many prisoners. Col. Oates by special order from the war department had been assigned to the command of the 48th Alabama and while we were engaged he, with his regiment, was on our right contending with overwhelming odds for the repossession of the lost works. By their bravery and skill of their commander they retook the line, capturing, wounding and killing more Yankees than they had in their ranks, but in this Col. Oates lost his right arm, and the next ranking officer was desperately wounded. Our color bearer, W. I. Defnal, while leading the charge, hat in his right hand and the colors held aloof in his left, had the misfortune of having his left arm cut off at the elbow by a solid shot from the enemy. The colors dropped to the ground, but were still grasped by his hand. Capt. Feagan loosened the staff from his hand as it lay on the ground, and carried it in triumph to the breastworks. When we reached the works, the Yankees that were on the other side, fell over on our side as prisoners. The boys shot at them that run, until they were out of sight. Things soon got quiet, except we were the recipients of an awful shelling. While we were behind the works, a shell hit the ground on the other side and bounced over into our ditch. It was smoking and ready to burst when John D. Shepherd of my company, picked it up and quickly threw it back over the works, it exploding before it hit the ground on the other side. I fell flat on my stomach on the ground as that was the only remedy for my escape. The ground in our rear was dotted with the killed and wounded Yankees, and they were in direct range of the shells from their friends, and the wounded begged piteously to be removed, but we had no time for that, as we expected that another attack would be made on the works. There was one poor wounded Yankee that lay in our rear that was literally torn to pieces by the explosion of a shell thrown from his friends. It was here in this charge that I had the only drop of blood drawn from me during the war by the Yankees' bullets. While on the charge to the works a minnie ball struck the ground in front of me, and bouncing, struck me on the upper lip, causing my two upper teeth to become loose. It hurt real bad and I thought at first that my tongue, and mouth were shot all to pieces. It was a spent ball, and fairly sung before it hit me. I soon discovered that I was not seriously hurt, and went on, and only suffered a few days with a swollen upper lip, and loose teeth, which become tight, and I carry one of them today, having lost the other by decay about one year ago. This battle was fought on the 16th of August, 1864, and is known in history as the battle of Fussel's Mill, on the Darbytown road ten miles east of Richmond. According to the number of troops we had, and the number engaged by the Yankees, our victory was a grand success and had the effect of silencing Hancock for several days. All being quiet, troops came in to relieve us, and the next day we resumed our position on New Market Height. We remained on this line all during the month of August and September and only moved to the threatened points. We kept out pickets all the time, fronting the Yankees, and our boys would fire on them whenever one would show himself, and they did us the same way, consequently picket firing went on all the summer, and became so common that it was not noticed at the main line. There was a circumstance that happened to me over at Petersburg in June, which I should have related in my stories of the seige, but it had slipped my memory and now while I think of it, I will tell you. We had out videttes in front, occupying small redoubts, and the Yankee pickets were so close by that we could hear them cough. We could not go out, and remain in the day time, neither could the Yankees. Our pickets were made up by a promiscuous detail from our brigade, and a small branch separated the pickets of our brigade from that of Bennings. Each brigade picket was commanded by a commissioned officer detailed for that purpose. It was my time to go, and I went out very cautious, making no noise, placing four men in each redoubt, and my duty was to keep one man awake at each post. Firing on the line was prohibited. The Yankees were busily working on a large fort in my immediate front, and we could see them on top of the fort between us and their lights that were on the other side. They presented a good target, but we were not allowed to shoot. Sometime late in the night, one of the Georgians from the other side and near the branch crossed over lookfor the commanding officer of our pickets. When I was shown to him, he asked my permission to fire on the Yanks at work. I told him to go back to his post, and shoot as much as he wanted to, as far as I was concerned, I had no control over his part of the line. He went back, and in a short time I heard the whizzing of his bullet and the crack of his rifle, and at the breastworks I heard a fellow hollow, "Oh, Lordy!" He hit one, thought I, and that started a firing all along the line. It caused the men at the main line to be aroused, and get ready for action. I was really uneasy for I didn't know what would be done with me the next morning. The officer from Bennings' picket came over to consult as to the best thing to say, in the event we were called on, and we agreed not to give the fellow away, and that he fired without our consent. Just at dawn, we withdrew, and went in to the main line. I dismissed the men, telling them to report at their commands. Then I went to sleep, and slept until ten o'clock. In the afternoon Col. Perry, who at that time, was in command of the brigade, sent his Orderly to the 15th Alabama with instructions for the officer that commanded the pickets the night before to report to his headquarters. I went, uneasy as I could be. When I reported he asked me all about the firing, and at last said, "he hit one of them for I heard him hollow; if he hadn't I would put you under arrest. I dismiss you, Lieutenant." I was glad to hear that. I will return to my narrative of events as they come under my observation during the fall and winter of 1864. On the 7th of October our division was sent out on the Darbytown road to make a reconnaissance. The advance was led by some South Carolina cavalry, commanded by Gen. Gary. The outpost of the Yankees consisted of cavalry and they were easily pushed back on their main supports. My company was deployed to cover the advance of the regiment, but in maneuvering and being ordered by Gen. Gary. I was led away from the front of my regiment, and went on a flanking expedition commanded by Gen. Gary. At last we came up on the left of a company of Yankee cavalry, and my whole line of skirmishers fired on them, putting them to rout until they reached an old house when they dismounted, and took shelter, firing at us through the cracks from which two of my company were wounded, and one killed. Gen. Gary ordered us to lie down, and keep up a fire to hold them there, until he could move around, and "bag the whole concern." He only partially succeeded, a few escaped. A little further on, they had a cannon which they turned on us, and fired a few rounds of grape at us before we captured it. We advanced at a double quick, firing as we advanced, until the Yankees disappeared in the woods. But where was the regiment? I did not know, but I knew I was a long way in the advance, but kept right on. They had abandoned their piece of cannon and I made straight for that. Looking to my right I saw the brigade advancing in line of battle as if they were going to make an attack, but there was nothing there to attack but a few dismounted cavalry, and they were disorganized. As I was passing down the road, I came across a member of Co. "A" of my regiment, with two or three others. He was sitting beside a tree struggling in great pain. One grape shot had entered his face, just under one of his eyes, ranging downward, had lodged near the root of his tongue, and he was struggling to get it out but failed. It was the size of a large size marble, an iron ball, and it made an awful hole beside his nose, where it entered, and I was sure that it would kill him. I didn't have time to stay there long, and hurried on leaving him there with his comrades. I never expected to see him again, and never heard anything of him during the war, but to my surprise he was at the reunion of the 15th Alabama in November, 1902, in Montgomery, and had the grape shot with him. I told him of seeing him by the tree in great pain, and never expected to see him again. It was taken out of the neck below the chin. It left a large scar at both places where it entered and where it was cut out. The grape shot is in possession of Gen. Wm. C. Oates or in the archives. I don't remember his name, but he resided in Russell County in 1902. I was awful proud to meet that fellow, and wish I knew his name. My skirmishers passed by the piece of artillery and entered the woods. We were somewhat scattered but kept up the alignment. I was on the right, and nearing a small branch with but little swamp. Jim Rhodes of Co. "K" had fell in with me, and he was on my right and Alex Stone of my company was next to my left. My attention was on John Bray who was on the other side, among some scattering pines. John was acting as scout that day, and had gotten in our front. I noticed his slipping along half bent as if he was trying to slip up on something, but all at once right in front of me, a large Yankee stepped from behind a pine hardly ten paces away, throwing his large revolver on me, ordered me to surrender. I had nothing but my sword, and without saying a word I turned my right side to him. I expected to catch a shot from him every second, but fortunately for me, Jim Rhodes saw him just as he spoke to me, and throwing his gun on him stormed out, "Surrender yourself, G—d d—n you." The Yankee seeing that Rhodes had the drop on him, dropped his hand, at the same time dropping his revolver. We went up to him and Rhodes asked for his pocket book. The Yank pulled it out of his pocket and handed it to Rhodes. I took his sword belt, and wore it home when the war ended. He had on a pair of cavalry boots, a good hat, and a fine ring on one of his fingers. The boots, and hat were no good to either of us, so we didn't swap with him, but Rhodes commanded him to take that ring off his finger. It was hard to get off, and in the effort to get it off he remarked in a subdued tone that his mother put that on his finger when he left her to join the army. That touched me, and I told him to keep it, and hide for he might not find as honest Rebels as we were when he went to prison. I turned him over to Alex Stone, who guarded him to the rear, and turned him over to the Provost Guard. After we got through with him we hurried on to where Bray was. He had slipped on to, and had captured a Yankee in a gully. I swapped hats with him. It was a small white fur hat, and I wore it home at the close of the war. We had no orders from any one, and we kept up the forward movement until we came to some rifle pits that had but a short time been occupied by the Yankees. We took possession, and fell into them to shelter us from a severe shelling from the main line of the Yankees. While here, a battery of four pieces came into position in our rear, and engaged the Yankee battery in a regular duel. Our position was anything else but a pleasant one, and we had to lie down to protect ourselves. The Yankees had left a good woolen overshirt that was soiled a little around the collar, and I appropriated it to my use. Presently the batteries ceased their firing, and a Colonel of one of the Georgia regiments rode up and ordered me to advance to as near the works as I could and develop what strength the Yankees had behind them. I did so, but on nearing the works we received a volley from a solid line from behind the works, fortunately no one of my company was hit as we fell flat on the ground at the first intimation we had, that we were going to be fired upon. There we were under full control of the Yankees, we had gone as near as we could, and nothing remained for us to do but to fall back. I expected the Georgians to advance over us, and charge the works but they did not come, and after waiting a reasonable time, I ordered the company to fall back, and this we did in double quick time. The Yankees had a fair shot at our backs for a short distance, and fortunately for us only one man of my company was hit. That was Jackson Ward who fell just in front of me, and I stepped over him, passing two or three steps, I looked back, and he had his hands raised, asking me to help him away. Before the war, he was my playmate, schoolmate, and in the war my friend. After getting out from under the fire from the Yankees, I assembled the company and started in search of the regiment. I found them about a mile in the rear fixing to go into camp. I ascertained that they had had several brushes during the day, and had lost some men killed and wounded. Our company had lost four, two died from wounds, the others were only slightly wounded. When dark came I took with me Dave Merritt, and went and brought poor Jack

Ward out, and got him off that night for the hospital at Richmond. He died on the 9th and Col. Oates being there, wounded himself, procured a burial case, and in accordance of a promise made to Jack's father, shipped his remains home. They lie in the cemetery at this place, and I never fail at each memorial day to lay a bunch of flowers on his grave. He was a noble young man, with a noble pride, and a lofty ambition. Before retiring I put on the woolen shirt, and lay down with Dave Merritt, my bed fellow. The night was pretty cool, and it was real comfortable, but not long something began to sting me, and I became restless, so much so that Dave complained, and after telling him the cause of my restlessness he rose, and made a fire, and told me to get up and let's see what's on that shirt. He had mistrusted something. I did as he requested, and we found thousands and thousands of "Body Creepers" (every old soldier knows what they were.) I pulled it off and laid it in the fire and done about to get rid of the others so that I and Dave could sleep.

CHAPTER VI

REMINISCENCES OF AN OLD VETERAN OF THE 15th ALABAMA REGIMENT, PERRY'S BRIGADE, FIELD'S DIVISION, LONGSTREET'S CORPS, FROM FREDERICKSBURG, VA., TO APPOMATTOX COURT HOUSE.

Brigadier General Law, after receiving his wound at Cold Harbor the 3rd of June, never commanded us any more. He was promoted to Major General, and assigned to command somewhere else. Col. W. F. Perry of the 44th being the senior Colonel, was promoted to the command of our brigade, therefore, I now call it Perry's brigade. After our spat with the Yankees in October we fell back, and established a line on more favorable ground, and began to fortify. The Yankees to find out our position on the 13th attacked our position with Birney's division. They drove in our pickets, and came huzzing through the woods. Our works was nothing like half complete, but we repulsed their attack implicating a havy loss on them. Co. "K" was on picket when the Yankees advanced, and was driven in by a heavy line. They had no commissioned officer to command them and Lieutenant Glover of Co. "B" was detailed to command them, and in this skirmish he received a wound that in a few days ended his life. Another noble officer was lost. There was a calm for a while, and one of our cavalry advanced down the road toward the Yankees, and it was but a short time before we heard the sound of horses coming up the road. We thought it was a cavalry charge, and the left company of our regiment that was nearest the road made ready to receive them. The right companies of the regiment on our left made ready also. The sound came nearer, and all at once our cavalryman that had advanced half an hour before came running at full speed, with his legs clinched tight to the sides of his horse, sticking his spurs. Here come a Yankee sitting half bent in his saddle, with a drawn sabre in his hand, in close proximity to our fellow. In another half minute's run the Yankee would have overtaken him, but when the Yankee reached the gap in our works there must have been fifty guns fired at him, and down come the rider and horse, both lifeless. Our fellow did not slack his speed, and one of our men remarked that he had gone to Richmond to tell Jeff Davis how near he had been run down by a Yankee. It was real funny to see the fellow running so fast with no one in pursuit. All the time we were idle, we were busy strengthening our works. The under brush had been cut down in front for a short distance. We could hear the Yankee officers giving commands in their formations, and presently we heard the command, Forward! given, and then we knew they were coming. It was a momentous time with us, for we did not know how strong they were, but we were sensible of our weakness, and the inadequacy of our works. The men resolved to stand to the last, and give them the bayonet in the event they came near enough. There was no thought of surrendering or retreating. Our men held their fire until they reached the point where the bushes had been cut down, and as soon as they reached that point our men poured such a deadly volley into their ranks as to cause them to waver, and become confused. They lost their organization, notwithstanding the living officers were among them urging them forward. All the while our men kept pouring a furious fire into their crowded ranks, and the commands of their officers to advance were in vain. There was an old Major on his horse for a short time among his men with a drawn sword in hand, ordering his men to advance, but his orders were unheeded. I had a Remington 44 revolver that I emptied at them at close range. I fired four shots into their crowded ranks, and two at the Major on his horse. The Major didn't last a minute after he made himself so conspicuous. He and his horse went down about the same time, riddled by many bullets. What was left, broke and run until they reached their main line of works. Our skirmishers pursued until they reached a place of safety from us, and each party went to work in establishing their outer lines, which were used by each party all during the winter. After the battle was over I went out among the dead and wounded that lay in my front, and examined as well as I could to see if any of the 44 calibre balls had taken effect. I think I found two. Adjutant Camp of the Yankee regiment, lay dead with a small bullet hole in the corner of one of his eyes next to his nose; the other was shot through the breast from left to right, the ball going clear through. Julius Wicker of Co. "K" always said that I killed them two Yankees. I examined the Major, only found two small holes through his cape, but several large ones in his body. The next day the wounded were removed and the dead buried, and we resumed our position on the left, and went to building breastworks. We finished them in November, and the weather became cold and rainy so that the roads become so bad that active operations ceased, and both armies, where we were, contented themselves in watching each other, but it was not so over and around Petersburg for they fought more or less every day over there, but it didn't bother us. In December orders came for us to build huts preparatory to spending the winter there. We were glad to hear that, and the boys went to work in earnest, and soon had comfortable huts to protect them from the sleet and snow. We were just in the rear of our breastworks and in plain view of the Yankee works of their outpost. It was an admirable position and I always wanted the Yankees to attack us there in heavy force, but they never came. We spent Christmas in quietude but our head commanders had not forgotten the old custom of having a dram on Christmas morning, consequently unexpected to us a small quantity (but enough) was issued to each man. There was some that refused, and his share was prorated, in order that all would share alike. Rations were scarce, and some days we would get real hungry. They had been reduced, and it caused hunger. We had not been paid off in eight months except for two months, and the amount being so small and had to pay such high price for anything we bought, until it was soon gone. One day a wagon come in with some sweet potatoes to sell. General Perry rode up on his horse. Several of the boys were standing around the wagon and among them Bryant Skipper, Bryant looked up at the General and said, "My God, General, ain't they never going to pay us any more money?" The General replied that he didn't know, and pulling out a five dollar bill, handed it to Bryant, and he gave it for two potatoes. The scarcity of money and rations caused some good men to become despondent and lost all hopes of our success. Consequently, all through the months of January, February and March desertions became to be frequent. While in winter quarters I was cited to appear before an examining board of military officers to be examined for promotion to a First Lieutenancy of my company, as Lieut. Renfroe had been retired, which caused a vacancy. I passed all right, but for some cause never did receive my commission from the war department and was only declared so by order of the Colonel commanding. The Yankee picket post where our men would desert to at night, was half a mile away, and was guarded by Yankee cavalrymen as we could plainly see. I conceived a plan to capture him at night, and quietly went to our Colonel, Lowther, to obtain permission to make the attempt that night, and to lay my plans before him. He consented and dealt out a great long string of advice in the way of caution. His lecture almost caused me to decline as he depicted to me some horrible circumstances that would follow a failure. I went back to my company, and thought over the whole matter, but I never could agree with his suggestions, and finally concluded that I would make the attempt. I crossed over the breastworks before dark and proceeded to a piece of woods where we had a picket post. It was in command of a Georgia Lieutenant and I selected this as the place from which I would approach the Yankee picket. I put him in possession of my plan, and obtained his consent to pass through his line but I bound him to secrecy in order that nothing would be let out. I went back to quarters and called Cicero Kirkland of my company. Fate Harper of Co. "B" and———Watts (an Italian) of Co. "K" together and put them on to what I wanted to do, and that I had selected them to go with me. Yes, they were right in for it. I begun to give instructions as to each man's part to be played, and it was this: At twelve o'clock we were to start, pass through the Georgia line of pickets and form in single file, I in front followed by Kirkland, Harper and Watts in the order named. When we came near enough to be challenged, I would answer "Don't shoot, we are deserters." Each one was to carry an Enfield rifle, and conceal them as much as possible. When near enough, I was to seize his bridle reins and they were to spring at the same time and present their guns, and I demanding him in a low tone to surrender. All this was my instructions and thoroughly understood, and at the appointed time we started. Passing the Georgia pickets we formed in single file toward the Yankee. The large growth for fifty yards in his front had been cut down and a small growth of bushes had sprung up to about waist high. The moon shone brightly, and we advanced slowly. His position was on a little rise in the ground, and our line of advance was up a small incline. I could see him sitting on his horse between me and the sky beyond. We approached within ten steps of him before he commanded us to halt. He said "Halt there and surrender." I replied "Don't shoot" and just at that moment Watts from the rear stormed out "Surrender yourself," when whiz! went by a bullet from the Yankees carbine. He lay down on his horse, turned and fled across the old field to where his reserves was. Each one of us fired at him as he ran off but missed. We fired several shots into where the reserve was and must have caused some commotion in their camp from the noise and the sounding of trumpets that we heard. They must have thought the whole of Longstreet's Corps was right on to them, judging from the loud orders that were being given. After staying there as long as we wanted to, we returned to camp from whence we came, and retired for the night. I was utterly whipped out by the performance of Watts, as what he did destroyed all chance of success. The effort that we made to capture that Yankee had a good effect. It stopped so much desertion, as it made them afraid of being fired on. The month of March came in, and it being the "blowing" month the roads soon become so that active operations would soon commence. We could begin to hear of conflicts between Lee's and Grant's forces over at Petersburg, but seldom anything encouraging to us as Grant, with his great strength could keep extending his line to Lee's right, causing him to scatter his forces in the trenches in order to get troops to send to the right. There was nothing encouraging to us and the chance of our success was slim. As the firm weather of the middle of March came on history tells us that Grant had completed his preparations for a move all along the line, with such numbers as would compel us to abandon our position, and evacuate Richmond. It was a gloomy time with us, the end of the struggle would soon end, but who would live to see it? The last days of March the Yankees became very acitve in our front by sharpshooting all the time, which was indicative that something would soon happen that would startle the world. On the first of April Grant succeeded in turning Lee's right, and the next day breaking his line at Petersburg. We could hear the cannonading that was going on in front of Petersburg all day the first, and we were not surprised when we were called on to get up, take with us what we could carry on our backs and be ready to march at a moment's notice. About three o'clock we were ordered into line and moved off towards Richmond without making any noise. We moved out about a mile and halted, and there waited until the other three brigades of our division could be brought up, and put in the marching coulmn. This being done, the order to march was given, when we bid farewell to our last winter quarters on the Darbytown road, ten miles East of Richmond. Our march was brisk at times, especially when we began to draw near to Richmond. We arrived about sunrise and the part of the city that we went through was perfectly quiet, and those we saw were not alarmed in the least. Our line of march was in the extreme Southern part of the city, near the James, and the people down there did not know that at that time, arrangements were being made for its abandonment. Neither did we know it. We marched to the depot where there was a long train of flat cars waiting to carry us over to Petersburg. We hurried aboard without observing any form, seated ourselves and was ready to ride. Toot! toot! was sounded by the engineer, and the train began to move slowly across the James. I have no doubt that the move we were then making suggested to the mind of our drummer boy, Pat Brannon, this line of his renowned poem when he said, "Farewell dear

Richmond on the James, etc.," and sure enough it has proved to be a lasting farewell to many. The train was heavily loaded, and naturally run slow. About half way we met a train from Petersburg switched to one side, loaded with Yankee prisoners. Our train slowed up and stopped opposite them when a free for all discussion commenced between them and our boys. They said, "Boys, we are sorry for you, you don't know what you are running into. We have taken Petersburg and have your army nearly surrounded; the war will be over in two weeks," and they were glad that they were out of it. They could not make some of the boys believe this, and they told them that the first corps was still alive and that it never had been whipped, and the tide would turn as soon as our division could reach Petersburg, to this they laughed and said, "They had men lying back in the rear drilling that hardly knew the war was going on." I have been reliably informed since the war that this was true. I only acted as a silent listener, but took what they said seriously. I saw a fellow with a good pair of shoes on that I wanted. I called his attention and proposed to swap. He bluffed me at the start by telling me that he wanted to wear a good pair home, and that mine was too sorry for that. I then told him that I would give him five dollars in addition; to this he replied that my money was no good. The Yankee had more sense that I thought he had and I let him alone. We moved off, and left the train still standing on the track and I don't know until this day what went with them Yankee prisoners. We moved on, and nearing Petersburg we heard the cannons booming and the rattle of small arms. It was in the middle of the P. M. that we arrived and getting off the cars in the edge of the city we were sent hurriedly to the Western part of the city, where the Yankees had never bothered before. Line of battle was formed. Captain Waddell, with his battallion of sharpshooters and my company on his right deployed as skirmishers to cover the brigade. The Yankee skirmishers about three hundred yards distant opened fire on us at once. We ran down a hill, crossing a branch toward them, and was soon under cover, when we began to ascend the hill on the other side, creeping up cautiously so that we could see them, being near, the firing become spirited until the Yanks retired a short distance, when they reinforced and come again, extending farther to their left and overlaping my right. This day was Sunday the 2nd day of April, and will ever be remembered by all my old company that was there in that skirmish so long as life lasts, as being the last engagement, and losing H. F. Satcher, one of our best young men, so near the close of the war. He was shot through the head and died instantly. Captain Waddell, with his battallion of brigade sharpshooters, had flanked to the left, and I moving to the right we become separated, and fought independently of each other. My right rested on one of the main roads that went into the city from the West. The Yankees kept extending to their left and I had to keep in their front to keep from being captured. I kept on this way until my right come to the canal along side of the Appomattox river. I could go no farther, neither could the Yankees. My company kept up a regular fire on them all the while, keeping them back. Fortunately no one of my company was hit but Satcher, but they came near getting me, shooting a hole through my hat, and through my pants near my knee. The brigade had lay down in line where we left them, and had not moved. We had no supports, and was occupying an isolated position without orders and dark coming on. I knew to remain there till morning, it meant for me and my whole company to be captured. So soon as dark hid us from the view of the Yankees, I quietly, without making any noise, assembled my company and went back to my regiment. They were moving off, and I hurried to take my place in line. The fact was, we would have been left and sacrificed if I had not withdrew. We moved without making any noise back to the edge of the city and crossed Appomattox on a pontoon bridge. Then it was that we bid farewell to Petersburg and struck out on a road leading Northwest. None of us knew where we were going. We marched all night without sleeping a wink. A whole lot of sugar was issued to us while standing in the road, and as well as I remember now, it was the last ration of any kind issued to us by our government. During the night we could see flashes and hear the sound of something like unto large cannon in the direction of Richmond. The next day we were informed that Richmond had been evacuated and the flashes and sounds we heard the night before was caused by the blowing up of the powder magazines. We moved on all day, tired and sleepy, with but little to eat. As well as I remember it was on the 5th that we arrived at Amelia Court House, where it was understood that a long train of wagons from Richmond with an abundant supply of rations were in waiting for the army, but to our surprise they were not there. It is a matter of truthful history that there General Lee intended to ration his troops, but his order had been disobeyed. I had not seen General Lee in four or five months before that morning. On reaching the little village we were halted and allowed an hour's rest, and nearly all of us fell asleep. It was there I saw General Lee on an old traveler, surrounded by a few of his staff. He looked very serious, as if he were brooding over the disappointment that we had met in getting no rations. I heard him call "William, come here," and another General approached him, and after a few moment's conversation, and pointing with his finger to the left of our line of march, "William" rode off and I was told that that was General Lee's son, W. H. F. Lee, who commanded a brigade of cavalry in Fitzhue Lee's Division. Some of the boys went foraging around among the women of the place and got a little something to eat, and divided around with others, but it was mighty scant, for that country had been stripped. We moved on and in the evening we heard firing in our rear. The Yankees advanced cavalry had overtook our rear, and a small fight occurred, but we moved on undisturbed until late in the night when we halted and marched a few steps out of the road and was ordered to rest on our arms. We were nearly exhausted and rest at that time was a blessing to us; beside being exhausted and worn out our stomachs began to pinch for something to eat. The boys were just hungry enough to have whipped two or three lines of battle had there been any prospect of capturing a well filled haversack which was usually the case. It was said that an empty stomach made a soldier doubly fierce, any way, our boys was willing to run the risk if an opportunity had been offered. We rested until morning, and moved on. We still were in the dark as to our destination, but camp rumors were always afloat, and rumor had it that we were on our way to form a combination with Johnston's army, when we would combine and whip Sherman, and then about face and whip Grant. Such were the rumors on the march. Late in the evening we heard the sound of cannon and small arms on our right, to our left, and in our rear, which indicated that the Yankees were in hot pursuit, and was attacking the troops that were marching along different roads parallel with us, but they let us alone.

On the march that day we were under strict orders to march in line, no straggling allowed as it was expected that we would be attacked. We pased by a large tobacco barn, and men from other commands, mostly stragglers, were in there helping themselves. I told the boys to stay in ranks and I would go in and try to get some for them. I went in and there it was in abundance in the hank, packed in hogsheads ready for shipment. I run my sword under a tier of it about two inches thick and prized it up, running my sword through the center, I threw it across my shoulder and moved in quick time until I overtook the company, when it was distributed among all that wanted it. It was fine natural leaf and good to smoke around the camp fires. I don't remember how far we would go in a day, but some days not very far as we would have to wait on our wagon train that was preceeding us, as we could not afford to let them get in the rear for fear of capture. Late in the evening of the 7th we arrived at a little village called Farmville, situated on the Appomattox river. Before we arrived we heard firing on our right, caused by the Yankees trying to capture what was known to us as the high railroad bridge across the Appomattox on the railroad from Lynchburg to Richmond, but they failed. As we marched through the town a distribution of meat was going on, by throwing it promiscuously into the crowd. I ran out to where it was going on and entered the scramble for a piece. They were small home made bacon sides, and would sail like a piece of pine bark. As they would come over I would try and stick my sword through them, and after several attempts I finally succeeded, and had to hug it in my arms to keep some fellow from taking it away from me. It was small, but I divided with the men. We were hurried across the wagon bridge that spanned the river, and ascended a long hill. The sun was about one hour high. We were halted on the hill and our regiment was ordered back across the river and through the town, halting on the outer skirts on the same road that we had just come in on. We were not formed in line, and no one knew for what purpose we were sent back. We only remained a few minutes when we were ordered to retrace our steps and recross the river. Just before we reached the bridge we were ordered to double-quick, and when we arrived at the bridge they were making ready to set it on fire. We marched up the hill and rejoined our brigade, but by this time the sun was setting and a terrible fire of small arms had broke loose up the river from where we were, accompanied by a terrible huzahing. All eyes were turned in that direction, and to our astonishment our cavalry was in full retreat and the Yankee cavalry in pursuit. Our fellows run right into the river and made their escape. The river was shallow, with low banks, and a crossing was easy. Two or three pieces of our cannon was brought to bear and with a few well directed shots of shell put a stop to further pursuit for the night, but they took possession of the town. On this hill I saw several of our brigade wagons cut down and papers of the brigade scattered on the ground, there were some of our regimental papers lying around loose. I looked upon them with suspicion but said nothing. When dark came, we were marched off in the direction of the high bridge to our right, and coming to some troops in line we quietly took their place, when they were marched off to the rear. It proved to be the 6th Alabama and Co. "B" (the Henry Greys) of that regiment was from my town in which I had schoolmates and kin-folks, but I could not get the chance to speak to them. Both the bridges had been burned, which put a check on the Yankee's advance until morning. We remained in line until two or three o'clock the next morning, when we were roused up and quietly fell into line and moved back up to the road, and pursued our journey. We had not marched over a mile when we turned off to the left and went marching through fields and woods. It was very dark and I noticed that occasionally we would pass a man standing still, and I learned the next day they were guides placed there for us to march out of a snare that we were in, however, we marched on without being molested. As the day was breaking we came to a large white house surrounded by numerous outhouses, and a beautiful oak grove. We passed right through and came across some artilleryment burying two twelve pound brass Napolean guns. Their horses had give out and rather than for them to fall into the hands of the Yankees they preferred to bury them. We passed on through fields, crossing numerous fences, ditches and gullies, and through thickets for several miles when about nine o'clock we came to a road. Marching down a long slant, we crossed a large branch with no bushes on its sides at all. There was a belt of woods in front, and the creek was about half way the clearing, some four hundred yards wide. We marched in this piece of woods and the whole brigade halted and stacked arms. It was reported that crackers would be issued to us there. I noticed a hill to our right that had four guns in position, pointing to the rear, as if they were expecting an attack. While waiting here I took four canteens from some of the boys and went back to the branch to fill them, and to bathe my face and hands. Several others came for the same purpose, and was scattered all along above and below me. I filled the canteens the first thing I did, and laid them on the bank with the straps all together. While down enjoying the bath, I heard a cavalry horn sound in the woods from our rear; I looked up and here came a scattering line of blue coats on horses. My God! this wont do for me, and I leaped up on the bank, snatched at the canteen straps, and with hat in the other hand I made a hasty retreat toward my command in the woods. Zip! zip! zip! came their bullets, Halt! halt! they yelled, but I had no notion to halt. The bullets would pass over, some would strike the ground at my sides, but I stooped low and kept moving. Others to my right and left were doing the same thing, while some clung to the side of the branch and would not run, preferred to be captured. Boom! boom! went our cannon on the hill and the Yanks fell back to the woods from whence they came. We fell in and moved off, without the crackers. Another false report. About eleven or twelve o'clock we heard firing in every direction except the front. Some cavalryman would pass occasionally and would give bad reports of what was going on. In the afternoon Sheridan's Cavalry had become extremely saucy and had assumed the boldness to charge right into a line of infantry and had been so successful until they had captured thousands of our men. It was understood by our commanding officers that at a certain place they would charge Fields' Division. We were organized. We had not become panic stricken, and were ready to give them a warm reception. Each regiment formed and marched in a square for several miles. The men loaded their guns and put on their bayonets and didn't care a whit if they did come. We passed over the threatened point without being disturbed, resumed our position in line, and move don. Late in the evening we heard the booming of cannon in our front. What could it mean? Was it possible that the Yankees had got in our front? Yes, they had established a strong line squarely in our front, and was disputing the further progress of our advance, led by Gen.

John B. Gordon's Corps. The firing seemed to be four or five miles in our front, and was very rapid at times, but we heard no small arms. We marched on slowly, the sun was nearly setting, and we all began to think that something was going to happen, and that tomorrow we would fight a battle. About sun-down we were marched out of the road to the left, ordered to stack arms and rest. We had some coffee, and the men began to make fires to boil as it was the first chance they had had since leaving winter quarters on the second. Captain Waddell, who had been marching in the rear in command of the brigade sharpshooters came in late in the night and reported that a large force were forming in his front and that he expected to be attacked early the next morning and said if they did we would hear something. We slept soundly and was up early making coffee, for that was about all we had to stay the stomach. We fell into line and marched back about two hundred yards, and formed line of battle to await an attack. I expected to hear Waddell's skirmishers every moment, as they were half mile to the front. Pulasky Kirkland, of my company, had a little meal that he had brought all the way from winter quarters, and he had it "made-up" and in a frying pan, trying to cook it on fires that had been made by some other troops who had just left there. We kept moving, sometimes to the right and then to the left, but only a short distance at the time. Pugh, as we always called him, remained with his frying pan and bread, all the time watching us in order that he would not be left too far. He stuck to his job, until he got it so it would stick together and picked up his pan and ran to where we were. There were more fires, and he would put his pan on and cook a little more, and in this way he got it done, broke it up, handed me a piece and put the balance in his haversack. It was amusing to see him running from fire to fire putting his pan on to cook. There was no such thing as throwing it away or leaving it for some one else to get. It was too precious to waste. I really did enjoy it. Nine o'clock came. No firing to be heard anywhere, what could it mean? Presently we saw General Lee pass through our lines going towards the Yankees, followed by two of his staff. A report came that Lee had surrendered. What! I didn't believe a word of it. After he passed we were marched back to our camping ground of the night before. Stacked arms and ordered to rest. The road was not far off, and hot riders were frequently passing to and fro, inquiries being made as to the report. By twelve o'clock the news was confirmed that General Lee had surrendered the Army of Northern Virginia to Gen. U. S. Grant, commander of the Army of the Potomac. Now what. What next. Here we are surrounded by one hundred and fifty thousand Yankees. What will they do with us, that was the topic of the conversation. Captain Waddell came in with his sharpshooters unarmed, he dismissed them to go to their several commands, (as they were made up by detail from each regiment.) Before leaving his position, a Yankee captain advanced under a flag of truce and told him Lee had surrendered, but as he had had no official notice he held his position and would have fired on the Yankees had they advanced, but it was not long before he was ordered in, but before leaving he assembled his men and had each man to break his gun against a tree. He was mad. That was Sunday evening, April 9th, 1865, and in the latter part of the evening the Yankees began to form a solid line around us, making escape impossible. The bands came up to the line and played for us to our heart's content. We talked freely to each other, as nothing had never happened. They divided their crackers with us as much as they could, for they were short themselves. They were proud that the war was over with us, and never cast a slur or reflection on our downfall nor gloried in their victory, but rather commended us for our bravery and courage under such adverse circumstances from the beginning. They treated us gentlemanly. We passed the night quietly, but I could not realize that it was a fact, that the war was ended, and I had been spared to live through. The next morning we were informed that we were going to be paroled and allowed to return to our homes. Glorious thought, but would I ever live to get there and how? that was the question. A thousand miles from home on foot, without money or anything to eat, and the prospect looked gloomy to me, but all these things I kept to myself. That evening General Lee pased down the road near our camp on old "Traveler" on his way to Richmond, his home. A score of us ran up to the road and bid him farewell. He acknowledged by pulling off his hat, and with tears trickling down his cheeks bowed his head. There my eyes beheld for the last time my beloved commander, the grandest man in every particular that America had ever produced. Not even his enemies

North has ever used any harsh criticisms, but rather extolled his virtue as being one of the greatest of Americans. On the morning of the 11th the Yankees issued to us a small ration of beef, the best they could do. I went up to where General Perry's horses were fed, and picked up a good quantity of scattered corn that they had dropped. I carried it to camp and washed it, put it into a pan and parched it brown. I broiled my beef on a stick until I got it brown and with that and my parched corn and coffee, I appeased my hunger. That evening Capt. James W. Stokes, who was captured on the 9th had been released and he happened to come to my camp in search of his command. He was a friend of mine, and commanded a company from Abbeville, Henry County, Alabama and belonged to the 60th Alabama. He looked very much depressed. I divided my rations with him, which he greatly appreciated. We have talked of the circumstance many times since the war ended, and he never did lose his gratitude toward me for that one act. It was a source of pleasure to me to hear him tell how he appreciated the parched corn and coffee, and I always felt glad that I divided my last morsel with him, but he has crossed over. On the morning of the 12th, our brigade formed and marched two miles to Appomattox Court House and stacked arms in front of a Yankee brigade standing at "parade rest" twenty steps away. They were as orderly as could be, not a jeer escaped their lips. No guying, in fact, nothing was said or done as I heard or saw while we were in prison to make us feel hacked. After we stacked arms we went back to camp, and received our paroles and that evening we set out on our long journey for home "sweet home." Our route lay across the states of N. C., S. C. and Georgia. The next day we got plenty to eat, and I felt happy that after so many hard fought battle I had escaped and was on my way home to mother. I marched at leisure and fared well on the way, except I was a little sick two or three days and did not go far neither day, but I made the trip without accident and arrived at home on the 7th of May. O! how happy I was, found all well, and mother looking for me. She had been told that I was spared and was on my way home. She was looking by day and listening at night for the sound of footsteps from her only soldier boy. I was not twenty-one till August. I have lived to see the sunny South reinstated and now in her granduer, occupy an envious place in the eyes of the world for chivalry and patriotism as American citizens. The "Tomahawk" has been buried, angry huzas and Rebel yells have ceased to be heard, and peace reigns in our Southland today. And now, kind reader, I bid you adieu. In the first part of this book I told you how I got in and now I will tell you how I got out. Here it is:

Appomattox Court House, Va.
April 10th, 1865.

The bearer, 1st Lieutenant W. A. McClendon of Company "G," 15th Regiment of Alabama Infantry, a paroled prisoner of the Army of Northern Virginia, has permission to go to his home, and there remain undisturbed.

A. A. LOWTHER,
Colonel Commanding 15th Alabama Regiment.

SONG "LONG AGO."

By J. M. CARMICHAEL, *Ozark, Ala.*

Air: *When You and I Were Young, "Maggie."*

Long ago we were boys in the ranks comrades,
    Our hearts light and happy as the day,
Cheeks were ruddy, eyes bright, locks dark, comrades,
    As we marched from our homes far away.

CHORUS.

But now we are aged and gray comrades,
    The trials of life are nearly done,
But to us life's as dear as it was comrades,
    When you and I were young.

Then we were young as the day dawning,
    And hopeful and sanguine and brave,
No fear and no cringing, no nor fawning,
    Brave men not afraid of the grave.
    CHORUS.

Long ago we were marching away comrades,
    Our flags to the breeze gaily flung,
Our bosoms were bare to the foe comrades,
    When you and I were young.
    CHORUS.

Long ago we were camping in storms comrades,
    Our courage and muscle tautly strung,
But no army could drive us away comrades,
    When you and I were young.
    CHORUS.

Long ago we were falling fast comrades,
    Our ranks daily much thinner grew,
Our courage the cause could not win comrades,
    When the men in the ranks were so few.
    CHORUS.

Staggering and bleeding alone comrades,
   Outnumbered three to one everywhere,
The world coldly watching our fate comrades,
   Not even a sigh or a tear.
     CHORUS.

As fall heroes struggling for homes comrades,
   So fell the soldiers in grey,
Their honor unsullied lives comrades,
   As the time when they marched far away.
     CHORUS.

We fell 'neath the numbers of the foe, comrades,
   We fell but are risen now again,
In falling we lost not our love comrades,
   For that which ennobles brave men.
     CHORUS.

Though we are aged and gray comrades,
   And the trials of life are nearly done,
To us life's as dear as it was comrades,
   When you and I were young.
     CHORUS.